Books by Richard O'Connor

Fiction

GUNS OF CHICKAMAUGA

COMPANY Q

OFFICERS AND LADIES

THE VANDAL

Nonfiction

THOMAS: ROCK OF CHICKAMAUGA

HOOD: CAVALIER GENERAL

SHERIDAN THE INEVITABLE

HIGH JINKS ON THE KLONDIKE

BAT MASTERSON

JOHNSTOWN: THE DAY THE DAM BROKE

HELL'S KITCHEN

WILD BILL HICKOK

PAT GARRETT

BLACK JACK PERSHING

GOULD'S MILLIONS

THE SCANDALOUS MR. BENNETT

COURTROOM WARRIOR: THE COMBATIVE CAREER
OF WILLIAM TRAVERS JEROME

JACK LONDON: A BIOGRAPHY

BRET HARTE: A BIOGRAPHY

Bret Harte

A Biography

Bret Harte

A Biography

BY

RICHARD O'CONNOR

with illustrations

Little, Brown and Company · Boston · Toronto

The author acknowledges with gratitude the permission granted
by Houghton Mifflin Company to quote from *The Letters of Bret
Harte*, edited by Geoffrey Harte and published in 1926.

*Published simultaneously in Canada
by Little, Brown & Company (Canada) Limited*

PRINTED IN THE UNITED STATES OF AMERICA

To Julie

Contents

List of Illustrations

I Argonaut

Prologue

"DO you know Bret Harte?" Henry James casually inquired of Mark Twain.

"Yes," replied Twain, less casually, "I know the son of a bitch."

The dialogue, overheard by Finley Peter Dunne at the Players one day in New York, must have shaken the august Mr. James from his stately brow to his handmade boot heels.[1] In England, men of letters did not discuss each other in such blunt terms. Furthermore Bret Harte's name, in England, was almost revered. Yet here in America, by the turn of the century, Harte was not only relegated to obscurity but was denounced in the strongest personal terms by the greatest living American writer. Little wonder that Mr. James valued the amenities, and the politer malice, of the literary life abroad.

The paradox of Harte's high reputation abroad and his rejection on his native soil dismayed him, of course, but it was only one of many contradictions in his life and work.

The man whose writings formed the matrix of that rudest and unruliest of myths, the saga of the Wild West, was a cultured and rather effete Easterner. He was a literary artist whose stories, as Van Wyck Brooks observed, were the "prototypes of all the 'Westerns' "[2] — the creator of a uniquely American art form, more honored elsewhere than on its native ground, which evolved into an industry fabricating in its century-long history a tremendous outpouring of dime novels, pulp magazines, motion pictures and television serials. The total revenue from this industry runs into the hundreds of millions of dollars, an endless bonanza which threatens to peter out in each generation but is revived with the onset of the next. Harte, the founder, almost the patent-holder of the basic story machinery of the industry, died leaving three hundred sixty pounds, six shillings and nine-pence.

One of the most rigid rules governing the Western in its post-Harte development was its sexlessness: the hero's devotion is bent toward his horse and the far horizon; the occasional heroines are simpering nonentities. Yet Harte was the first American writer of stature to insist on the "power of sex," as Henry Adams noted, in human conduct. His feminine characters, though many were coated with sentiment, often expressed themselves with a pungency not usually attributed to Victorian womanhood. Miss Mary, the genteel schoolmarm of "The Idyll of Red Gulch," for instance, writing to a friend in Boston: "I think I find the intoxicated portion of this community the least objectionable. I refer, my dear, to the men, of course. I do not know anything that could make the women tolerable."

The ironic contradictions of his life were all but endless. No writer's work is more American in content than Harte's, yet he expatriated himself for the last quarter-century of his life, and continued to write of the mining camps of the Sierra slopes while settled in a country house in Surrey. He placed the highest value on home, hearth and the pleasures of domesticity, but was never at home anywhere. In the foothill settlements of northern California, he was regarded as an impossible character, a dude, a snob, a fake gentleman. When he went East, the process was reversed. In the Boston of Emerson, Longfellow, Whittier and Holmes, he was a lively cu-

[4]

riosity at best — the man who delivered a Harvard Commencement address while wearing green gloves. In New York, despite his craving for respectability and all the other attributes of a gentleman, he gained the reputation of being a drunkard, a deserter of wife and family, a deadbeat. In the third of the worlds he uneasily inhabited, the London of Queen Victoria, he was a fascinating envoy from the Wild West who dined out for two decades on the strength of a legend he detested. Much as he was responsible for glorifying the American West, he regarded it as a crude and barbaric place to which, once he made his name there, he never returned. Yearning for esteem as he did, he was dogged by the enmity of Mark Twain and the scandalized whispers on two continents of his ambiguous relationship with his wife and his supposed relationships with other women. According to Twain, not always such a standard-bearer for conventional morality, "he was kept, at different times, by a couple of women . . . He lived in their houses, and in the house of one of them he died."

Twain had been his friend in the California days and admitted that he owed much of his success as a writer to what he had learned from Harte. Yet Twain would write of him, "He was bad, distinctly bad; he had no feelings and he had no conscience." He had liked Harte in their younger days but he "got over" it. "Bret Harte was one of the pleasantest men I have ever known. He was also one of the unpleasantest men I have ever known . . . He hasn't a sincere fiber in him. I think he was incapable of emotion, for I think he had nothing to feel with. I think his heart was merely a pump and had no other function." There was, in fact, no one Twain recalled with more bitterness in the literary world when he composed his fragmentary autobiography. The kindest thing he could find to say of Harte, in summation, was that "the

[5]

law of his nature was stronger than man's statutes and he had to obey it." [3]

Paradox not only threaded its way through every phase of his life, but it was the most remarkable element in his story-telling, in the creation of characters which became "some of our most venerable literary stereotypes." [4] From Dickens he learned the art of juxtaposing, of mingling humor and pathos, so that his characters have a built-in fascination from their first appearance. In one brief paragraph he scatters paradox over the assemblage in "The Luck of Roaring Camp" like a sprinkling of sequins:

Physically they exhibited no indication of their past lives and character. The greatest scamp had a Raphael face, with a profusion of blond hair; Oakhurst, a gambler, had the melancholy air and intellectual abstraction of a Hamlet; the coolest and most courageous man was scarcely over five feet in height, with a soft voice and an embarrassed, timid manner. The term "roughs" applied to them was a distinction rather than a definition. Perhaps in the minor details of fingers, toes, ears, etc., the camp may have been deficient, but these slight omissions did not detract from their aggregate force. The strongest man had but three fingers on his right hand; the best shot had but one eye.

The story cited above, along with "The Outcasts of Poker Flat," is about all of Harte that endures in the consciousness of his homeland — and they only because they are included in the required reading for secondary schools. The twenty volumes of the Riverside edition of his works gather a new layer of dust every year in the rearmost stacks of the public libraries. In recent years literary biographers and historians have raked over the tailings of American literature in a relentless search for neglected genius to be reclaimed and reevaluated. None has staked out a claim on Bret Harte. He

[6]

was, in the fashionable view, merely a storyteller; no symbolism, no "levels of meaning," no dark mysteries to be analyzed and exclaimed over. The last biography of him, George R. Stewart's *Bret Harte: Argonaut and Exile*, was published in 1931. His place in literary history has been defined as that of a minor talent who struck it rich for a short time, enjoyed a brief popularity, and then rightly faded from view.

Perhaps a fairer way of judging him would be to consider the gap which would appear in the American literary tradition if he had never lived and written, if he had not created a mining-camp world as artistically real as Yoknapatawpha County or Twain's Hannibal, Missouri. Where would the American legend be without Jack Hamlin and John Oakhurst, the chivalrous and gentlemanly gamblers; without Yuba Bill, the garrulous comedian on the stagecoach driver's box; without Colonel Culpepper Starbottle, the epitome of all bombastic Southern gentlemen; without the refined schoolmarms, the golden-hearted whores and madams, the rough-mannered but tenderhearted miners and gunmen he brought to the printed page? The loss would be greater than academic critics might be willing to grant — those cloistered gentlemen of whom Van Wyck Brooks wrote particularly in regard to Bret Harte:

Have there ever been such literary spoilsports as the formalist critics? I used to think that half the pleasure of being a Californian would be that one came from Bret Harte's country; for, with all his occasional crudity, Bret Harte invested with magic the Sierras, the bay of San Francisco and the Sacramento River. But could any such feeling survive, in the mind of a young Californian, the discipline of these academic fashionable critics? They would condition him to see only the ways in which Bret Harte fell short of the models they study, and all the magic he might have found in his story-telling countryman would have died in a

[7]

clatter of analysis and scientific prosing. How many literary windows these critics have closed! How much they have destroyed of the savour and flavour that literature has always imparted to society and life![5]

In a curious and unpredictable way, the vital force of a writer who has something imperishable to say — something that endures beyond the quibbling of tastemakers and literary fashion experts — bounces off distant walls like a far-ranging echo. It is of little historic consequence that Kipling said he owed "many things" to the storyteller's art he learned from reading Harte, or that H. L. Mencken believed he was entitled to "a sort of immortality," or that the even tougher critic Ambrose Bierce granted him a place "very close to the head of American authors" if only for that brief period when Harte "illuminated everything he touched."

It is of greater consequence in human affairs that Harte was translated into Russian, among many other languages, and that one of his Russian admirers was, quite unaccountably, Joseph Stalin. Ordinarily the least suggestible and romantic of men, Stalin decided in 1927, after reading Harte's stories of the California gold rush, to set up a gold trust and reopen the Siberian mines.[6] Ten years later the Siberian gold mines were producing $183,000,000 annually, and since then the Soviet Union has been enabled to survive numerous setbacks, including a recent crisis in farm production, by the continuous river of gold flowing from Siberia. Few writers in history have produced an impact to equal that.

ONE

An Eleven-Year-Old Poet

O N the afternoon of March 26, 1854, the storm-battered paddlewheel steamer *Brother Jonathan* churned its way through the Golden Gate and disembarked its passengers at the Jackson Street wharf in San Francisco. Among them was Francis Brett Harte, then several months short of his eighteenth birthday, and his sister Margaret, who was two years younger.

Alerted by the new telegraph system, hundreds of San Franciscans had gathered around the wharf as soon as word of the *Brother Jonathan*'s arrival spread. The steamer was days overdue, having been struck by gales and heavy seas on the voyage up the coast from Nicaragua, and had been feared lost at sea. Thus young Harte's life in California, the beginning of the seventeen years he spent there, started out with a sense of drama. The crowd gathered at the wharf was one of the largest in the city's brief history, and its cheers as the weary and shaken passengers came down the gangplank may in retrospect have seemed to be an omen to the pale young man from New York City.

Young Harte — Frank, as he was then known — must have seemed a delicate specimen in that crowd of robust men and assertive women, most of them Forty-niners or close enough to it to claim the distinction. He was slender, of medium height (about five feet eight), with black curly hair and the brave beginnings of a mustache on his upper lip. His face was slightly pocked by the attack of smallpox suffered almost two years earlier. His pallor bespoke a bookish childhood, a lifelong aversion to any unseemly amount of physical activity.

The youth seemed, in fact, much too delicate to survive for long in his new environment. Only a half-dozen years before gold had been discovered near Sutter's Fort; only the year before that the Donner Party had succumbed to privation and cannibalism in a snowbound pass high in the Sierra. Only a year before the *Brother Jonathan* landed, Joaquin Murietta supposedly had been captured and beheaded by state rangers, with the "Head of Joaquin" preserved in a jar of alcohol and proudly displayed to newcomers.

It was a wicked and turbulent place, San Francisco in 1854, swarming with ex-convicts from Australia, miners from Mexico and Chile, shady characters and reckless adventurers from the eastern United States, renegades and outlaws from all over. Chinese immigrants, despised, tenacious and industrious, were arriving at the rate of ten thousand yearly. You could be shot in the street without anyone finding it remarkable, you could be lynched without trial, you could be robbed, rolled, gulled, shanghaied if you let your guard down for a moment. You could spatter mud on a man's boots — particularly if he were a hotheaded Southerner — and be challenged to a duel. Criminals, in the period before the formation of the Second Vigilance Committee, were running wild and making San Francisco the most lawless town on the American continent. Vice was equally rampant and unabashed, one establishment frankly styling itself Ye Olde Whore Shoppe, and the pitfalls for impressionable youth were everywhere at hand. The young men who had come to

California with bright visions of striking it rich in a few months often ended up suddenly dead, disgraced or debauched. "They forget the admonitions of their mothers and sisters, given them at parting," as the editor of the *Alta California* of San Francisco recorded. "They forget the purity of their early youth, the hopes of their riper manhood. They sink lower and lower, until they become thieves, robbers and desperadoes." [7]

A frightening prospect. His first glimpses of San Francisco must have borne out that warning for young Harte. The crowds on the wharf and the street behind it were noisy, disorderly. The batwings of the saloons fluttered incessantly as men strutted in for their shots of red-eye and staggered out or were propelled by the boot of a bartender. Many of the women were painted and conspicuously lacking in virtue or shame. The city had been hastily constructed and had not yet attained even that approximation of style which Harte later sardonically termed Union Pacific Renaissance. Completed just the year before he arrived, the Montgomery Block, with its four stories and its hundred rooms, was the most impressive building on view. Later the stronghold of artists, writers and musicians, it was now given over to trade and journalism, the largest commercial structure on the Pacific Coast. It had been known as Halleck's Folly — the chief promoter being Henry W. Halleck, a former army officer, ten years hence to become chief of staff of the Union armies — until all the offices were rented and Halleck's faith in San Francisco's future was justified. [8] The Montgomery Block, however, was one of the few tangible evidences that the city on the Bay was not totally immersed in drinking, gambling, whoring and engaging in crime and violence. It must have been fairly frightening to the seventeen-year-old youth who had been reared in poverty that was never less than genteel.

Francis Brett Harte — the name was originally spelled without the *e*, which his father added — was born in Albany, New York, on August 25, 1836. His family called him Frank. Later he always signed himself Bret — dropping a *t* as his father had added an *e* to the surname — and he will be henceforth referred to by that name to simplify matters. His father, Henry, had taught at the Albany Female Academy and now operated a private school in his home at 15 Columbia Street. His mother, the former Elizabeth Rebecca Ostrander, came of an upstate farming family of English and Dutch ancestry. At the time of Bret's birth there were two older children, Eliza, born in 1831, and Henry, born almost two years before Bret. The fourth child, Margaret, was born two years after Bret.

On his father's side of the house, there was both a shadow of mystery and secrecy and a brighter gleam of Colonial aristocracy. The shadow came from Bret's unacknowledged but legitimate paternal grandfather, Bernard Hart, an English Jew who migrated to America in the 1770's. Shortly after the Revolutionary War Bernard Hart moved to New York City from Canada and soon attained social and financial prominence, along with considerable wealth. His one slipup, as a practitioner of the Jewish faith, was to fall in love with, and worse yet marry, a Gentile woman, in 1799. She was Catherine Brett, whose ancestors had settled the Hudson Valley and stemmed from the Colonial ascendency (several of whom had been governors of Connecticut) and whose mother had married an English naval officer. The marriage was kept secret and was dissolved shortly after the birth of their son in 1800. A short time later Bernard Hart married a woman of his own faith and raised a new family kept unaware of the son of his mésalliance.[9]

Henry Harte, however, was not kept in ignorance of his

father's identity, nor were his descendants. He was bitterly conscious of the fact that his half brothers and sisters were being reared in luxury while his mother was hard put to send him to Union College. Perhaps he added that *e* on the end of his surname less for its touch of elegance than to differentiate himself from his father's side of the house. Whatever he felt about his father's disavowal, and the presumably religious reasons for it, apparently was transmitted to his own children. It must have been difficult to explain to them why they could never know their paternal grandfather. Bret Harte himself may have developed an ambivalent attitude toward Jews from the family experience. None of his stories contained Jewish characters. One of his few recorded observations on people of that faith was a scalding bit of verse titled "That Ebrew Jew," the opening stanza of which read:

> *There once was a tradesman renowned as a screw*
> *Who sold pins and needles and calicoes too,*
> *Till he built up a fortune — the which as it grew*
> *Just ruined small traders the whole city through —*
> *   Yet one thing he knew,*
> *   Between me and you,*
> *   There was a distinction*
> *   'Twixt Christian and Jew.*[10]

A year after Bret was born came the panic of '37, and his father's private school evidently failed from lack of pupils whose fathers could still afford the tuition. Henry Harte became a wandering schoolmaster, a gentle and scholarly man ill-equipped to support himself, his wife and four children. He moved from job to job, his family from city to city — Hudson, New Brunswick, Philadelphia, Providence, Boston, Lowell. The Hartes existed on a bare subsistence level. And there were certain religious differences in a home seemingly haunted by matters of faith: his father was converted to Catholicism, while his mother was a Low Church Episcopalian. Bret was brought up an Episcopalian, but it didn't take. With a Jewish grandfather ashamed of his first-born, a Catholic father and a Protestant mother, he had good reason to believe that religion, especially when unaccompanied by tolerance, brought little solace to humanity. He would always remember reading a Sunday school tract relating a supposed conversation between a "converted heathen" and a missionary, and how he rejoiced in the barbarian's "tuft of plumes, his martial plumes, his oiled and painted skin." Bret was quite certain, he recalled, that during the alleged conversation between the heathen and the missionary the former's eyes were "resting on the calves of that missionary's legs with anthropophagous lust and longing."

One amenity the Harte home possessed in all its travels was a small but excellent library. At six Bret began reading Shakespeare. A year later he was engrossed by Dickens's *The Old Curiosity Shop*. In rapid succession he read his way through Defoe, Fielding, Smollett, Goldsmith, Cervantes, Washington Irving and the elder Dumas's *The Count of Monte Cristo* which, years later, he still regarded as his favorite novel of all time. Dumas's novel, he later wrote, bore out in every way his belief that "the primary function of the novel is to interest the reader in its *story* — in the progress of some well-developed plot to a well-defined climax, which may either be expected or unexpected by him. . . . The average novel reader is still a child in the desires of the imagination; he wants to know what 'happened' and to what end." [11]

It was just as well that his inclinations were solitary and literary even at an extraordinarily early age, because his childhood was dogged by ill-health. He was a weak and sickly child, apparently suffered from the rickets, and had to be sheltered from the rough antics of other children.

The only adventure of his boyhood he would recall in later years was running away from home one summer while the family was staying in New York City with a maternal aunt. It was the subject of one of his earliest published stories.[12] He was somewhere between six and nine years old when he was "subjected to an act of grievous injustice" and decided to strike out on his own. He carried with him two cents in cash, a knife, a roll of twine, a button, two pieces of colored glass, a piece of Bolivar cake, two fishhooks, the top of a gold pencil, and a brass runner from the leg of a chair which he regarded with "a strong faith in its utility." He set out for the waterfront with the vague ambition of sailing off to "the island where Captain Cook was killed." The streets of New York, it soon became obvious, teemed with adventure and mischance on this first essay at expatriation, his first exploration of the world beyond his family circle. A stray dog shared his piece of cake, then deserted him. An Irish boy two or three years older separated him from all the possessions in his pockets. He fancied he was Dick Whittington and listened for a similar message from the bells of lower Manhattan: St. John's seemed to be sounding the alarm "Ran-a-way, ran-a-way!" and Trinity's tower seemed to be responding, "Send-him-back, send-him-back." Either Bow Bells were more sympathetic to runaway boys or his early reading had misled him.

He stood outside a theater on the Bowery, and a young man invited him to attend the performance of *King John* as his guest. It was the first time Bret had ever seen a play, and it impressed him — particularly a scene in which a character was branded with hot irons — as no other theatrical performance he saw in later years. He slipped away from his host a few blocks from the theater, wandered the streets until nightfall and was found by friends of his aunt. He returned home "a hero and the envy of my brother who used to bully me . . ."

In 1845, when Bret was nine years old, his father died and left the family penniless. In later years his son would remember his "labor and struggle and thwarted literary ambition. . . . he was true to his training and inspiration, for he would not give up a vocation which enabled him to cultivate the literary graces, even though by so doing he could have earned a little more money. . . . I had rather have my family cherish the memory of their grandfather Harte than the traditions associated with five governors of Connecticut." [13]

Family pride must have suffered, though, when Henry Hart's death made it necessary for the widow and her four children to live off the handouts of her family and worse yet approach Bernard Hart, at eighty-one the secretary of the New York Stock Exchange and patriarch of his acknowledged family in Brooklyn, for a temporary subsidy. Bret's grandfather came through in the crisis, apparently with the proviso that his charity would be kept secret.

Elizabeth Harte and her children settled down in New York and struggled to maintain their self-respect. They were conscious of a necessity to maintain the standards of gentle birth and lineage. In the process, undoubtedly, Bret acquired those slightly haughty traits which afterward caused people less conscious of the demands of breeding to call him a snob; they were a defense against the shabbiness of his boyhood and the suspicion that people would look down on him unless he looked down on them first.

Bret continued his schooling until he was thirteen. He had acquired a smattering of Latin, chemistry, natural philoso-

[16]

phy; during a convalescence a year later he studied Greek on his own. His reading in English, however, was what continued to nourish his mind: every Dickens novel as soon as it was published, Fenimore Cooper, Captain Marryat, *Pilgrim's Progress*, the *Arabian Nights, Gulliver's Travels*.

At eleven he had made his own debut in print, with a poem titled "Autumn Musings," which the *Sunday Morning Atlas* published. With justified trepidation, he showed the poem to other members of the family and was ridiculed for the juvenile sentiments expressed in verse. "I sometimes wonder," he said later, "that I ever wrote another line of verse." He left no doubt that he was deeply hurt by the experience, apparently because his mother joined in the ridicule. He and his mother were never particularly close, possibly because of her subsequent remarriage and also her disapproval of the woman Bret married. In none of his work was there any warm appreciation for motherhood, though he could wax sentimental enough about whores and madams.

On leaving school at thirteen, Bret went to work in a lawyer's office for a year, then in a counting house. Meanwhile his older brother had run off to join the army during the war against Mexico, had been wounded, and finally wound up in San Francisco with the first wave of gold-rushers. Bret had little to do with him, either, in later years, but was on closer terms with his sisters Eliza and Margaret, each of whom he used as a refuge when times grew difficult.

The family was breaking up, and would never be entirely reunited again. In 1851 Eliza married F. F. Knaufft and established a home at 16 Fifth Avenue. About the same time Colonel Andrew Williams — it was a courtesy title well suited to his florid style — began courting Bret's mother. Williams had attended Union College with her late husband. Late in 1853 Mrs. Harte and Colonel Williams announced their engagement, and a short time later she journeyed to California and married him on her arrival in San Francisco. Bret and Margaret were left behind in Eliza's care until Margaret's school term ended early in February. Then they were to join their mother and stepfather, who promised to be at least a good provider. Bret evidently had no great enthusiasm for the journey; his nature was sedentary and he could find all the adventure he wanted on the streets of New York or between the covers of his books. Certainly he had no ambition to wrench a fortune out of the California foothills, nor did anything so crude as a gold rush stir his imagination unbearably.

The violent mishaps of the journey — New York to Nicaragua, across to the Pacific coast of that country, then up to San Francisco on another vessel — must have confirmed his view that adventure was meant for the brainless and reckless.

Bret and Margaret left New York on February 20, 1854, aboard the steamer *Star of the West*. A storm off Cape Hatteras battered the ship, but she arrived safely at the fever port of Greytown on the Nicaragua coast. There the passengers were transferred to sternwheelers for the 120-mile journey up the San Juan River through a jungle noisy with monkeys and parrots and the occasional roaring yawn of an alligator. On reaching Lake Nicaragua they changed to a lake steamer for Virgin Bay, followed by a twelve-mile journey over forested mountains on mule wagons and donkeyback. Finally they reached the Pacific port of San Juan del Sur, where they lived in a shanty-like hotel and dined off beans and hardtack until the sidewheeler *Brother Jonathan* arrived to take them to San Francisco.

So far the passage had been smooth enough, if not particularly comfortable, for Bret and his fifteen-year-old sister. Life aboard the *Brother Jonathan* was much more perilous.

[18]

They left San Juan del Sur the night of March 8 and ran into roaring gales in the Gulf of Tehuantepec. On March 10 the engines failed them and had to be repaired while the *Brother Jonathan* tossed in the rough waters with her anchor down.

The *Brother Jonathan* somehow made it to the harbor below the cliffs of Acapulco. She and her eleven hundred passengers had to lie in the Mexican port for two days while further repairs were made to the boiler.

Meanwhile, from the town above the harbor, came occasional bursts of gunfire. A rebel named Alvarez, "The Panther of the South," was fortifying Acapulco and preparing for a siege against the government's forces. It was a question whether the *Brother Jonathan* would be able to lift anchor before the local revolution flamed out over the water.

The steamer finally managed to cook up enough steam to continue the coastal passage. It was well away from Acapulco when a steam line broke and the whole ship was flooded with clouds of the hot vapor. The passengers flew into a panic and almost capsized the old boat, which a few voyages later sank with the loss of two hundred lives. Once more the damage was repaired ad lib. Only one paddlewheel was turning over, however, and the rest of the voyage up the coast was continued at a crawl. It took eighteen days, in fact, to complete the journey from San Juan del Sur to San Francisco. No doubt Bret and his fellow passengers felt they deserved the wharfside welcome they received.[14]

Bret and Margaret caught a ferry for the trip across the bay to Oakland, where Colonel Williams had established a home for his new family. Oakland had been founded four years before and regarded itself as the queen city of the East Bay region. In 1854 it was a huddle of one story wooden buildings and small redwood houses: the main street, Broadway, was only a block long. Then and always it struggled for existence in the mighty shadow of the city across the Bay.

The youth had come West without any great expectations so was not greatly disappointed by the backwater in which he found himself. He worked in Sanford's Pharmacy for a time that summer and apparently brooded over means of escaping. Not that he found his new stepfather hard to get along with. Colonel Williams was a good-natured, rather windy and pompous gentleman, just smart enough to prosper in business and politics. The following year he was elected to the city council and in 1857 to the mayor's office. His pomposity may have been irksome at times, but the good colonel probably served as chief model for one of his stepson's most picturesque characters, the bombastic Colonel Starbottle, whom the late W. C. Fields could have played to perfection.

Undoubtedly the youth had a certain concealed resentment of Andrew Williams as his father's successor. The two men may have been friends, but they were direct opposites in character and personality. The elder Harte was a man of quiet intelligence and bookish wisdom, destined for stark failure in the competitive bustle of mid-century America; his stepfather a blustery, back-slapping go-getter — and therefore a success. It must have secretly irked Bret that his mother could choose someone like Williams for a husband; from his prejudiced viewpoint it must have been almost an insult to his father's memory. To a woman, undoubtedly her choice was more understandable.

What drove him from the colonel's home, however, was the dullness of Oakland rather than a distaste for his mother's new husband. Some hint of his feelings toward Oakland were contained in a humorous sketch he wrote ("Ruins of San Francisco") in the following decade when an earthquake jarred San Francisco but not Oakland. He quoted a fictional

[20]

German geologist named Schwappelfurt as saying that "there are some things the earth cannot swallow" — meaning Oakland.

Some time late in 1854 he left Oakland for six years of drifting through northern California as a schoolteacher, miner, printer and perhaps a few other things. They were the years in which he gathered the impressions, the sights and sounds and smells of a frontier slowly being civilized, of mining camps becoming ghost towns, of mountain crossroads becoming towns, that lasted him for a literary career of more than forty years.

TWO

Wanderer in the Foothills

TO the rough, red-shirted men who first saw Bret Harte venturing into the Mother Lode country, he must have been just about the most outlandish specimen they had glimpsed in many a season. That country saw weird characters, some of them barely civilized, from many nations. None was so hilarious a spectacle to them as the species termed "Eastern dude." And that term, purely opprobrious, fitted Bret to the last scornful syllable. His faint scribble of a mustache was handicap enough, especially when heightened by his delicate manner, his precise speech, his pale brow, and dark, disdainful eyes. But this wandervogel from New York City — the worst place to be from, in a Westerner's view — also carried a morocco dressing case and was daintily shod in patent-leather shoes. He was dressed for a stroll down Fifth Avenue, perhaps, but not for venturing into the Sierra foothills.

In addition, he wore a secondhand revolver that "insisted on working around and dangling, embarrassing and unromantic, right in front," as he later recalled.

Yet this foothill country into which he ventured, the "southern mines district," which probably knew his presence for not much more than a year, is now designated "Bret Harte country." Along Highway 49 the chambers of commerce bait their traps for tourists with his name, while those who opened the country, sought their fortunes in it, labored for years in the pocket mines, fought and sweat and died on its slopes and high valleys are entirely forgotten. The pen is mightier than the miner's pick. For on brief acquaintance, and with only the haziest idea of its true geography, Bret established a claim on it more durable than the most diligent and venturesome prospector's.*

He left no record of his travels in the southern mines area, except for the autobiographical sketch "How I Went to the Mines" and traces of personal experience. The year 1855 is still a matter of conjecture, gossip and rumor as far as he was concerned. No archives, and only one rather garbled memoir,[1] survive to tell the tale. The gold-rush period, which lasted less than ten years, until the surviving Forty-niners stampeded over the Sierra to the Comstock Lode, is hazy and ephemeral, and Harte himself is a no less insubstantial figure in it — so far as the records are concerned — than the first ghost town to slide into a gully.

From all the evidence, he taught school in LaGrange, a fairly large settlement on the Tuolumne River, with Red Mountain towering to the northeast, as his first occupation in the foothills. He taught in the school there for several months until it was forced to close, apparently for lack of pupils. More importantly it served as the scene of several of his better-known stories, "M'liss: An Idyll of Red Mountain," "Cressy," and "The Tale of Three Truants." In both "M'liss" and "Cressy," the central figure is a young schoolmaster with whom an adolescent girl pupil falls in love.

---

* Oddly enough, the second of California's literary legends, Jack London, spent almost the same amount of time in the Klondike, which was epitomized in his work as the California gold rush was in Harte's. London, however, was not Harte's direct literary descendant. He was influenced by Kipling, who acknowledged Harte as one of his preceptors.

In "M'liss," the town of LaGrange is disguised as Smith's Pocket, and to the cosmopolitan eye of the young New Yorker apparently it had little to recommend it but its splendidly bucolic setting. As he described the place in "M'liss" it could barely be distinguished from the rugged scenery which enveloped it:

Just where the Sierra Nevada begins to subside in gentle undulations, and the rivers grow less rapid and yellow, on the side of a great red mountain stands Smith's Pocket. Seen from the red road at sunset, in the red light and the red dust, its white houses look like the outcroppings of quartz on the mountainside. The red stage, topped with red-shirted passengers, is lost to view half a dozen times in the tortuous descent, turning up unexpectedly in out-of-the-way places, and vanishing altogether within a hundred yards of the town. It is probably owing to this sudden twist in the road that the advent of a stranger at Smith's Pocket is usually attended with a peculiar circumstance. Dismounting from the vehicle at the stage office the too-confident traveler is apt to walk straight out of town under the impression that it lies in quite another direction.

Regarding himself as something of a fashion plate even at eighteen, the young schoolmaster noted that the "greater portion of the population to whom the Sabbath, with a change of linen, brought merely the necessity of cleanliness without the luxury of adornment" was outraged when anyone dared to dress more elegantly than the dismal norm. In "M'liss" he hinted frequently at his contempt for most of the citizenry, his young pupils excepted, especially the girls. One or two of the girls bothered him, if "M'liss" is autobiographical to any extent, in a way that can get young schoolteachers in trouble. He described one girl as having "round curves and plump outlines" which "afforded an extensive pinching surface." [2]

Apparently, however, he resisted such temptations and drifted out of LaGrange without the ritual presentation of a coat of tar and feathers. He struck out on foot for Robinson's Ferry[3] on the Stanislaus River, forty miles due north of LaGrange. It was May and the weather was fine. He had decided to look up an acquaintance who was supposed to be mining on the Stanislaus. His confidence gradually evaporated as he slogged up and down the mountain road. He had only two dollars in his pockets, having spent most of his salary on boiled shirts and other apparel. The exact meaning of the term tenderfoot was also brought home to him. His patent leather shoes pinched and blistered so that he finally had to walk along barefoot. His first night out in the open he forgot to camp near water. On the evening of the second day, disheveled and footsore and demoralized, he finally reached the settlement on the Stanislaus. To brace himself for further encounters, he limped into the nearest barroom. A moment after the bartender slid his shot of whiskey over to him a gunfight broke out between two other patrons. The shots went wild, one of them smashing Bret's glass before he had a chance to down the whiskey. With a coolness that threatened to make him a legend in Robinson's Ferry, Bret eyed the shattered glass and demanded that the barkeep pour him another drink; this before the wisps of gunsmoke had dissipated. All of this, it should be added, was according to his own account.[4]

Later that evening he found the cabin in which his acquaintance was supposed to have been staying, but the latter had already moved on. Those present, taking inventory of his road-worn condition, invited him to take one of the bunks lining the cabin walls. Next morning the several young men in the camp voted to take him in as a partner. A tenderfoot was supposed to be good luck. He would help them work the claim. That first morning he found "color" (gold dust) in the first pan of gravel he scooped up, and a short time later found a nugget that weighed in at twelve dollars. "Then we worked the claim daily, dutifully and regularly for three weeks," he wrote. "We sometimes got 'the color,' we sometimes didn't, but we nearly always got enough for our daily grub. We laughed, joked, told stories, 'spouted poetry,' and enjoyed ourselves as in a perpetual picnic." [5]

Judging from writings other than "How I Went to the Mines," he apparently moved on with his partners to other claims along the Stanislaus. He may have ventured as far north as Angel's Camp and as far south as Table Mountain, again judging from the countryside he described in his stories.[6] After that he disappeared from view until December of 1855. Whatever he did between the time he worked the claims along the Stanislaus, from May to August at most, until he limped into the Gillis brothers' cabin at Jackass Hill, he didn't find many more twelve-dollar nuggets. He didn't even have stage fare back to San Francisco, and he had found the Sierra frontier, as he later wrote, "hard, ugly, unwashed, vulgar and lawless." [7]

But not unkind, so far as the Gillis brothers' hospitality was concerned. The Gillises — Jim, Bill and Steve — mined a claim on Jackass Hill which Mark Twain later visited for three months of loafing and tall-tale-telling. There were certain discrepancies in the accounts later given by the Gillis brothers. One said Harte showed up on Jackass Hill "one hot afternoon." [8] Another said it was "a stormy night in December." [9] Undoubtedly the month was December.

As usual Bret's feet, still shod in cracked patent leather, were bothering him. He was thinly clad and soaked to the skin from the winter rain. Bill Gillis recalled that he men-

tioned the fact he was on his way from Westpoint, in Calaveras County, to San Francisco, where he hoped to find
work on a newspaper.

Bret was immediately sized up as a "dude" and found
wanting — this was the inevitable reaction — but he was
offered the hospitality of the Gillis cabin.

He stayed overnight and part of the next day until the
stage came along. Jim Gillis, according to his brother Bill's
account, took pity on the youth's condition and sent him on
his way in better shape than when he arrived on Jackass Hill.

"Bret," Jim Gillis said, "it's going to be a cold ride to
Sonora this morning, so I will lend you my overcoat. You
can leave it with the clerk at the stage office."

Bret accepted the coat, then remarked on the fact that he
was almost broke and would probably have to "foot it" from
Sonora to San Francisco.

"How much have you got?" Jim Gillis asked.

Bret removed all the money he had in his pockets and
showed it to his host. The total came to four half-dollars,
two quarters and a three-cent piece: two dollars and fifty-
three cents. All the time he was in the foothills, in "the new
Golconda," he could never seem to acquire a cash balance of
more than a few dollars. But he was beginning to learn that
the Lord — or one of his creatures — would provide. It was
more blessed, if less respectable, to be a debtor than a creditor. In time it was an attitude which would sustain him
through many vicissitudes, many charges that he was careless
about borrowing and casual about repaying.

Jim Gillis, disliking him but still touched by his plight and
holding to the hospitable code of the foothills, handed Bret a
twenty-dollar gold piece.[10]

By Steve Gillis's account, Jim also gave Bret a letter to
Steve, then working as a printer on a San Francisco periodi-

cal. Steve claimed that he got Bret a job but "he was a poor printer, never drawing down over $10 a week." This, however, was pure moonshine. Bret didn't take up the printer's trade until more than a year later.[11]

There was a rather shabby sequel to the overnight stay at the Gillis cabin. Some years later, after Bret had obtained a well-paid job at the United States Mint in San Francisco, Jim Gillis saw him on the street, said hello and was royally snubbed. Jim followed Bret to the Mint, stalked into his office and demanded the twenty dollars he had loaned him on Jackass Hill. With "a lofty air," Bret inquired how much he owed Jim and made out a check for the amount demanded.[12]

After his year in the foothills, Bret returned to his stepfather's home in Oakland for an extended stay. He told his family that he intended to become a writer, and settled down in a room in the new house his stepfather had built at Fifth and Clay Streets. It must have been rather lonely for him, since his sister Margaret, the only member of his family he was close to, had married B. H. Wyman, a purser on a coastal steamer, and had gone to live in Union, a town on Humboldt Bay north of San Francisco.

The summer of 1856 he worked in Sanford's Pharmacy again, bought a set of Dickens and read his way through him again. Early in the fall he became a tutor to the four sons of Abner Bryan, a cattle rancher in the Sycamore Valley about twenty miles from Oakland. The ranch lay at the foot of Mount Diablo, and his spare-time roaming of the countryside probably provided the material for a later story ("A Legend of Monte del Diablo").

When he wrote his sister Margaret on October 8, 1856, he was seemingly content with his tutorial post, his ruggedly beautiful surroundings and the Bryan family. The ranch, he informed Margaret, was "as wild as the God of nature made it." His four pupils were "tractable and docile. . . . George has religion; Wise is a mighty hunter; Tom, mischievous and rides a colt as wild as himself; Jonathan, a natural mathematician." If there was one flaw in life on the Bryan ranch it was perhaps the elder Bryan's evangelistic brand of religion — and Bret always responded with distaste to the overly religious. Much against his will, no doubt, he was persuaded to attend a revival meeting in the nearby Tassajara Valley. Thirty years later, in "An Apostle of the Tules," he recalled the occasion with a vivid distaste. The ranting of the evangelist, the moaning, over-emotional response of his listeners, and the unattractive way the farm girls dressed all repelled him and convinced him that the frontier brand of homemade religion was an unhealthy thing. The "God of nature" was much more compelling to his poetic soul, serene and everlasting compared to the mouthings and frothings of obsessed rural St. Paul's.

Bret left his job as tutor on the Bryan ranch late in 1856 or early in 1857. His next job, apparently, was a brief period as a Wells Fargo guard on stages carrying currency, bullion or other valuables. Experts on the Harte legend have found it hard to believe that the lackadaisical young man, literary minded, lacking in any real enthusiasm for danger, more concerned with foppish dress than flexing his muscles of his trigger finger, could ever have occupied such a perilous post.[13] Banditti, after all, roamed the hills and frequented the stage routes, and Joaquin Murietta & Co. had been active only a few years before. There seems little doubt, however, that Bret did "ride shotgun" — actually he must have carried a revolver — for a short time, perhaps no more than a month or two. In a diary he kept briefly he wrote, on December 31, 1857, reviewing the events of the past year, that "for a brief delightful hour" he had been employed by Wells Fargo to guard its treasure in transit. He did not mention what stage routes he rode, but in 1894 told an interviewer: "My predecessor in the position had been shot through the arm, and my successor was killed. I held the post for some months . . ." [14]

"Delightful" or not he soon left his post on the box of a stagecoach, but the experience was sufficient to gather the impressions which later formed the notable fictional character of Yuba Bill, stage driver. Bill himself may have been an amalgam of several drivers Harte rode with on lonely mountain roads, with the omnipresent fear that a masked band of ruffians at any moment would confront him with the classic demand to stand and deliver. The fact that in retrospect he considered the experience delightful suggests that he was never called upon to protect Wells Fargo's moneybags with life and limb.

In the spring of 1857 his first verses since his poetic essay as an eleven-year-old began appearing in the *Golden Era* of San Francisco, sentimental items titled "The Valentine," "Lines Written in a Prayerbook," "Love and Physic." From then on, he never lost sight of his aim of becoming a writer.

Eventually he approached his literary ambition through the medium of frontier journalism, which, considering the high mortality rate of country editors in duels and drinking bouts, was a more hazardous occupation than riding shotgun for Wells Fargo through bandit country.

The story Mark Twain told of Bret's first dip into journalism was, if nothing else, highly colorful. His source for the account, Twain related in his autobiography, was Harte himself. The only conclusion to be drawn from it is that either Twain could not resist a tall tale, whether of his own or Harte's concoction, or Harte did not mind adding picaresque trimmings to the often drab reality of his youth. Either conclusion is warrantable.

As Twain told it, Bret assumed the post of editor of a weekly newspaper in Yreka which was operated by two printers. One of his duties was reading proof before the paper went to press. Not long after he began his editorship a galley proof was placed on his desk late one afternoon. One of the stories on it was the obituary of a Mrs. Thompson. At the end of the half-column eulogy, there was the usual polite presumption: "Our loss is her eternal gain."

Just above it was the line, "Even in Yreka her chastity was conspicuous." It was a typographical error, of course. "Chastity" had been mistakenly substituted for "charity." Bret caught the typo and, following standard practice, underlined the word "chastity" and placed a question mark on the margin of the proof. This meant that the printer, on getting the proof back, was supposed to refer to the copy from which the type was set and make the necessary correction. Somehow it didn't work out that way.

The paper went to press that night, and next morning editor Harte glanced through the product of his labors. When he came to the Thompson obituary, he knew that his stay in Yreka would be soon terminated, voluntarily or otherwise.

The sentence that was supposed to be corrected now read: "Even in Yreka her *chastity* was conspicuous (?)."

Bret, the way Twain told it, "levied on a mule that was not being watched and cantered out of town, knowing well that in a very little while there was going to be a visit from the widower, with his gun." [15]

The story is too good to pass by, merely because it didn't happen, but the truth of Bret's first journalistic experience was almost as colorful as — and a lot more creditable than — the Twain version.

Nor was it quite true, as his friend Charles Warren Stoddard wrote, that Bret "sat in the seat of the scornful — a village editor." [16] Actually Bret started out as an apprentice, or
printer's devil, on the *Northern Californian*, published in
Union, Humboldt County.[17] He journeyed to Union early in
the summer of 1857 to join his sister Margaret, whose husband was frequently away from home.

Charles A. Murdock, a young man of his own age with
whom he soon became friendly, recalled that his first glimpse
was of Bret digging postholes and building a fence on his
sister's property "with results somewhat unsatisfactory." It
was the only time anyone remembered him being engaged in
manual labor. Meeting him later, young Murdock was
amused by his languid, somewhat superior manner. Bret, he
said, was "inclined to be sarcastic in a good-natured way"
and apparently considered himself both a gentleman and a
dilettante. It was a rare, even a courageous attitude to assume
in a tough little frontier town of five hundred population.
To play the dandy, the "dude," in such circumstances was
more dangerous than roaring into a barrelhouse slapping
leather and issuing challenges to a shootout.

He was slender, and well dressed, carried himself with
grace and distinction and cultivated his mustache in the
sweepingly elegant Dundreary style largely affected by men
of foppish inclination. At times, Murdock observed, his barbs
could draw blood in polite society as his aloof figure attracted jeers from the roughnecks loafing around the plaza.
Perhaps because there were so few well-mannered young
men available he was invited to the best homes, including
that of Alex Brizard, the local nabob, who owned a chain of
trading posts in Humboldt and Trinity counties.

Another home where he was made welcome was that of a
New England woman who had married an Englishman, well-

off through his mercantile endeavors but still possessing his Cockney accent. Bret liked to tease her about her husband's habit of dropping his *h*'s. One night at their dinner table he spoke admiringly of "Kathleen Mavourneen," and with a malicious smile added: "What are the words? I can never remember them."

His host fell into the trap and began reciting, "The 'orn of the 'unter is 'eard on the 'ill."

At which, Murdock observed, Bret's "merry eyes fairly danced" and their hostess's "snapped and swore." [18]

Union in that day was a new settlement with few refinements such as the New England lady offered. Located at the northern end of Humboldt Bay, it served as a trading center and transshipment point for the pack trains which carried supplies to the Trinity River mining camps. Packers and drovers brawled in the saloons of its main thoroughfare, which was further enlivened occasionally by the appearance of a miner who had struck it rich on the Trinity River and announced his intention of getting the populace and himself roaring drunk. Indians, displaced by the advent of what passed for civilization in those parts, hung around the entrances of the saloons hopeful of a handout or a dose of the white man's firewater.

In the fall of 1857 he took another tutor's post, this time with the family of a Captain Liscom at twenty-five dollars a month. His charges were two teen-aged boys whom he instructed in the usual subjects plus, oddly enough, "journalism," a calling in which his practical experience consisted of selling several poems to the *Golden Era*.

It was an easy life, suited to his currently low-pressure temperament. In the mornings he taught the two Liscom boys, in the afternoon he went duck hunting in the nearby marshes with indifferent results, and frequently in the evenings he dipped into the rudimentary social life of the town. Once he attended a dance, "tried to dance and couldn't — very much annoyed, came home incontinentally — went to bed and spent a restless night," as he confided to the diary he had just started keeping. At one of the parties he met a girl named Lizzie Bull, the daughter of the local hotel owner, and fell incontinentally — to use a favorite word of his at the time — in love with her. As with most literary types, it was mostly an affair of the pen, of yearning verse and moody sighs. He wrote a poem to her, changing her unromantic given name to Elise, the last stanza of which read:

> *And thus some heart tossed on the stream*
> *Of time — impelled by passion's breeze,*
> *And folly's breath — may find a dream*
> *Of Hope — upon this breast — Elise!* [19]

"Folly's breath" apparently was not long upon him, however, and by New Year's he was lamenting in his diary that "the simplest pleasures fail to please me."

On that same day, he inscribed his determination to "consecrate" himself to literature. He was twenty-one years old now, but was finding it difficult to settle down and earn a living. The local opportunities were not very promising. He left his tutor's post with the Liscom family and its twenty-five-dollar monthly salary; for two weeks he filled in as a pharmacist; a short time later he started up a private school for children of the few families around Union who could afford to pay tuition, but it was as short-lived as any of his ventures from gold-mining to guarding stagecoaches. He wasn't a wastrel, never allowed himself to be seen in the riotous saloons on the main street, although he would take a drink or two with friends and had begun smoking. It was just that none of the local opportunities aroused much hope or ambition in him.

His sister worried that he was becoming an idler, a common concern of the families of embryonic writers. In his memoirs published sixty-odd years later, Murdock, one of his few friends in Union, recalled that Bret was "willing to do anything, but with very little ability to help himself. He was simply untrained for doing anything that needed doing in that community." To his fellow citizens, Murdock added, Bret "seemed clever rather than forcible, and presented a pathetic figure as of one who had gained no foothold on success." Nor was he likely to win many friends among people who might help. Except for Murdock and a few others who suspected his lofty attitude might be a defense against hidden feelings of inferiority, most of the townspeople considered him a high-nosed snob who deserved to come a cropper. Somewhat more admiringly, Leon Chevret, the proprietor of the Hotel Français, was quoted by Murdock as saying Bret had a "Napoleonic nose" — it was indeed one of those thin, curved noses often associated with conquest — but M. Chevret also observed that "his debts trouble him very little." [20] A lifelong pattern already was set in the young man; his linen would be immaculate, his clothing fashionable, no matter how his credit rating might suffer.

Early in the spring of 1858 there was a bad Indian scare in the Humboldt Bay region. The tribesmen living around the settlements on the bay were peaceful Diggers, content to scrounge for a living and spend what they made in Union's general stores, but back from the coast, in the hills, there were Indians less willing to reconcile themselves to the encroachments of civilization. That summer they raided the smaller settlements of northern California and burned out a number of farms and ranches. Union itself had no reason to fear greatly; there was an army post on Humboldt Bay, and the men of the town had organized themselves into militia companies. On September 26 the rumor sped down from the hills that dissident tribesmen had attacked a Digger village not far from Union and were headed for the town itself in full cry. The women and children of Union were herded into the only brick building in town while their menfolk girded for a frontal assault. It never came, and soon thereafter the threat of a widespread uprising died down.

Presumably Bret was pressed into service with the militia, but there is no record of any martial exploits he might have undertaken. Scouting parties and punitive expeditions were launched into the surrounding territory and he may well have accompanied some of them. At least one of his early biographers was informed (by Harte himself) that he had spent almost a year defending the California frontier against the Indians.[21] At best, however, he must have spent no more than a few days marching into the foothills with his comrades. Murdock, oddly enough, does not mention anything at all of Bret's service with the militia. It seems unlikely, given his pacifistic character, that he did any more civilian-soldiering than was required under proclamation of martial law. In any case, the state of emergency lasted only from the spring of 1858 until late in the fall, when the onset of winter discouraged the Indians from further expression of their resentments. As he was to make plain — much too plain for their taste — to his fellow citizens of Union during a subsequent incident involving the Indians, he had no stomach for harassing the aborigines simply because they belonged to another race and another way of life. He may have expanded a bit on his militia experience in later years, but his real attitude toward punitive expeditions was one of violent distaste.

At the end of 1858 Bret had spent two years in Union,

during which he occupied himself desultorily in posthole-digging, tutoring, pill-rolling, and poetry-writing. Aside from an occasional contribution to the *Golden Era*'s poetry columns, he had little to show for his endeavors after twenty-two years on earth. He was finally set on the path of manhood and gainful employment when Colonel S. G. Whipple and Major A. H. Murdock, the father of his friend Charles A. Murdock, decided to establish the *Northern Californian*, a weekly newspaper, to offset the clamorous boosterism of the *Humboldt Times*, which was published at the county seat of Eureka eight miles to the south.

The colonel and the major needed an apprentice to assist the journeyman printer in setting type, pulling proofs, helping with the job printing, and sweeping out the place. The job paid sixteen dollars a month for a seventy-two-hour week. Obviously it was no place for a young poet with his head in the clouds, an elegant youth who prided himself on his style of dress and speech. Yet Bret loved it. Perhaps he recognized that it was a practical start toward a professional career, perhaps he realized that it was time he got his feet on the ground. Even the mechanics of printing engrossed him. He was enough of a romantic to succumb to his first whiff of printer's ink.

The first issue of the *Northern Californian* came off the press on December 15, 1858. A few weeks later, in addition to helping the journeyman in the backshop, Bret was enlisted as an editorial assistant by Colonel Whipple, who edited the weekly. Bret went around town gathering "locals," one-paragraph items relating the comings and goings of the citizenry, covering meetings of the Lyceum, the fount of Union's intellectual life, and reporting on plans for construction of a wagon road to the Trinity River mining settlements, which would keep Union alive as a trading center. He quickly adapted himself to the demands of journalism, which are quite opposite to those of poetry, and the discipline — if not prolonged — had a salutary effect on his style. The work taught him economy, precision, accuracy, simplicity. The flowery phrase-making in which he had indulged himself had a lesser place in the prosaic columns of the *Northern Californian*. A brief experience of journalism can be the making of a writer, just as too much of it can permanently cripple the imagination.

Evidently Colonel Whipple was pleased with his work as both an apprentice printer and an apprentice reporter. Several months after the paper was founded Whipple had to leave for three weeks in San Francisco. Bret was placed in charge of the paper while he was gone, which Whipple acknowledged on his return. "Mr. Harte has frequently contributed to our columns," he added, "and is a graceful and easy writer." During the ensuing months Whipple referred to Bret as his "junior," or associate editor, and twice more left the *Northern Californian* in his care while making business trips.

During one absence of Colonel Whipple's, Bret advised the readership that he was anxiously awaiting his chief's return from San Francisco. About all that Whipple had left him with, Bret wrote, was "the one half of a broken pair of scissors, the Derringer . . . which won't imitate his example and go off, a challenge, two quarrels, a few letters written in an indignant female hand . . ." [22]

Obviously his elder was giving Bret a free hand, and obviously Bret was enjoying it. His account of a shooting at the bar of the Drummond House followed the traditions of frontier journalism in its mingling of humor with violence. The participants, an American and a Spaniard, had been drinking, he noted ("titely slight" was his playful way of putting it), and no one knew what caused the outburst of gun and knife play. He continued:

It appears that the Spaniard opened the ball, by sending one from a revolver at the American's head. Ajax's shield was nowhere in comparison with the head it struck; the ball raked all around the skull and then glanced off — considerably damaged.

The American retaliated — in the old fashion of indictments — with divers guns, bullets, knives, hands and feet, and considerable blood was spilled; but the injuries of either party are not serious. We are not aware of any arrests made, as neither party gave themselves up.[23]

Yet the demands of journalism had not entirely stamped out the romantic poet in Bret, and occasionally he was permitted to contribute a few scraps of verse to the page opposite editorial, including a poem titled "Why She Didn't Dance":

Tell me, brown-eyed maiden, O, gazelle-eyed houri,
Draped in gorgeous raiment, circumscribed in gingham,
Round thy neck a coral, and from each auricular
    Pendulous an earring.

To which the country maiden, in a dialect which later was to be an overpraised facet of the Harte style, replied:

I've jest sot and sot — till I'm nearly rooted,
Waiting for the fellers, dern their lazy picters,
Stranger, I'll trot with ye, ef you'll wait a minit,
    Till I've chawed my rawzum.[24]

For fourteen months as the bright young man of the *Northern Californian* Bret enjoyed himself to the utmost. At last he had made his mark in the community. The mark he left on it, as a result of the events of late February 1860, was more indelible than he could have foreseen.

Confident of the maturity and editorial judgment of his young assistant, Colonel Whipple left for another business trip to San Francisco in the last week of February. There were rumors drifting around that the citizenry of Eureka, whose rivalry with Union led to constant editorial feuding and skirmishing between their two weekly organs of opinion, were about to administer a severe lesson to the Indians living in their neighborhood. Whipple, however, did not believe that the possibility of an unofficial punitive expedition required that he put off his trip.

Perhaps Colonel Whipple did not realize that Bret's views on the Indian question — the question being whether to apply genocide or let them live in peace provided they "walked the white man's way" — ran counter to the general opinion. General Sheridan had not yet supplied the condign formulation that "the only good Indian is a dead Indian," usually attributed to him a decade later when he was supervising the campaigns against the Plains tribes, but it summed up the beliefs of most people on the western frontier. (Sheridan, the lord high executioner of the Indian race on this continent, was then commanding a company of dragoons on the Grande Ronde reservation across the line in Oregon. When a band of Chinooks refused to submit to his "practical supervision," they were encumbered with ball and chain and "made to work at the post until their rebellious spirit was broken.")[25]

A short time after the incident near Eureka, a public meeting in that community, somewhat defensively, with the smell of blood still in their nostrils, passed a resolution epitomizing not only their own but most settlers' views on the Indian question: "Resolved, that as it is the white man who pays and supports government, their lives and property should be the first to receive protection from that government." They were willing to concede only that the Indians should be protected, if they behaved themselves, because whites were "human beings of a superior race." And the way they could best be protected, the resolution added, was to place the Indians on reservations — that is, deprive them of their lands and place them in eternal quarantine.[26]

Ever since the summer of 1858 there had been incidents back in the hills, bushwhackings and barn-burnings and ambushes. In the isolated areas back of the coast, Indians and settlers shot at each other on sight. The tribesmen living on the rim of Humboldt Bay, however, had remained peaceful. More so, in fact, than their white neighbors. The whites around Eureka passed around rumors that the local Diggers, amiable as they appeared, were secretly communicating with their brethren in the hills and planning to join an uprising against all the whites in northern California. Guilt plus greed plus an overblown belief in the superior destiny of the Anglo-Saxon breed were brewing a dangerous situation in Eureka. Probably even those who gave violent expression to those feelings did not anticipate the horror of the coming Sabbath.

On Friday, February 24, the Indian tribe living on a spit of land a few miles from Eureka, out in the fogs of Humboldt Bay, began holding a three-day fiesta with much dancing, drinking and feasting. Thirty of their fellow tribesmen from the Mad River district had joined them for the celebration. Aside from getting drunk and sleeping where they fell, in a manner not too different from the Anglo-Saxons they emulated, the several hundred coastal Indians did nothing to annoy even the most censorious observer. Perhaps their shouts could be heard across the water in Eureka, but they were no worse than the sounds emanating from the row of saloons on the town's main street.

Nevertheless, on the cold foggy dawn of Sunday, February 26, a small band of Eurekans crept up on the Indian colony, which was sleeping off the effects of the climactic celebration on Saturday night. The few bucks present were rendered immobile by the dregs of the firewater they had consumed. Most of those around the campfires, it was later agreed by impartial observers, were women and children.

The whites from Eureka were armed with guns, knives and axes — and a murderous sense of righteousness. It was barely light when they attacked with all the fury of an SS detachment descending on a Polish ghetto. There was so little resistance that only a few shots were fired, mostly at the backs of Indians trying to escape the slaughter. For this kind of work, simple butchery, the knives and axes served best. Red-handed and blood-maddened, the whites rampaged through the colony and killed everything that showed a sign of life.

By the time they vanished into the fog the Indians of that rancheria knew the full meaning of pacification. Sixty — most of them women and children — were killed. The few who escaped the slaughter either had played dead or were sober and nimble enough to find cover in the surrounding brush. The Sunday sportsmen of Eureka had allowed only a few badly slashed and mutilated survivors to wander about wondering what kind of hell had descended upon them.

A correspondent of the San Francisco *Bulletin*, who arrived on the scene shortly after dawn revealed in all its glory the handiwork of Eureka's master race, described his experience in a manner not calculated to win him the friendship of his fellow northern Californians:

A short time after [the massacre], the writer was upon the ground with feet treading in human blood, horrified with the awful and sickening sights which met the eye wherever it turned. Here was a mother fatally wounded hugging the mutilated carcass of her dying infant to her bosom; there a poor child of two years old, with its ear and scalp torn from the side of its little head.

Here a father frantic with grief over the bloody corpses of his four little children and wife; there a brother and sister bitterly weeping, and trying to soothe with cold water the pallid face of a dying relative. There an aged female still living and sitting up, though covered with ghastly wounds, and dyed in her own blood; there a living infant by its dead mother desirous of drawing some nourishment from a source that had ceased to flow.

The wounded, dead, and dying were found all around, and in every lodge the skulls and frames of women and children cleft with axes and hatchets, and stabbed with knives, and the brains of an infant oozing from its broken head to the ground.[27]

Bret himself apparently did not visit the scene of the massacre. By the time the news reached Union, Eureka had already cleaned up the mess, buried the dead, patched up the survivors, and decided that with a little luck the news of the incident would not reach the outside world. A conspiracy of silence was ordained. The rough element of Eureka had carried out the bloody mission, but they only expressed in axe-blows what politer citizens had been mouthing for months. The Indians had needed a sharp lesson, it had been administered, perhaps with unnecessary force, and the proper thing was to forget about it.

The same attitude was prevalent among the solid citizens of Union, despite their rivalry with the Eurekans. Best not to rake up the live coals. Undoubtedly they expected that the editor pro tem of the *Northern Californian* would have the

[43]

decency to reflect this safe and sane approach. Harte, after all, was regarded as a fop, a fancy talker, an amateur wit and scribbler. He might not be very practical, but he knew when to keep his mouth shut and his pen under control.

They underestimated him and underrated his conscience and his sense of human responsibility. He watched as the mutilated bodies of the Mad River tribesmen were carried ashore from canoes by their kinsmen. He watched as the survivors disappeared into the hills with their dead. He listened as people who had seen the aftermath of the slaughter near Eureka described how the Indian village looked after the whites had stormed through it.

If his fellow townspeople expected him to suppress the story, they were dead wrong. Perhaps because of his own mixed ancestry, because of the tolerance and idealism of the home in which he had been reared, and of the wide range of reading he had done, Bret knew he had to tell what happened regardless of the consequences. Raw courage may not have been his outstanding characteristic, nor had he a sharp appetite for controversy, but he was determined to publish the story. His own attitude toward the Indians was in advance of his time. He had learned something of their ways, a bit of their language, and was sympathetic toward their plight. Later he would not romanticize them in his stories, but he always treated them fairly, as fellow human beings.

He must have agonized over his responsibilities to the management of the *Northern Californian*. Colonel Whipple, he knew, would not have favored an indignant approach to reciting the facts of the massacre, let alone editorializing over them. The previous September there had been an outbreak of ill feeling when a white man attempted to rape an Indian woman near Trinidad, stabbed her and was released without punishment after she recovered from her wound. The

[44]

Northern Californian then spoke out against mistreatment of the Indian, warning: "Thus does injustice beget injustice and crime beget crime." By early February, however, Colonel Whipple's attitude stiffened as reports came of bitterness among the Indians. In an editorial published on February 8, he suggested that the general commanding the army's Pacific division send troops to prevent an Indian outbreak in the hills behind Humboldt Bay. Bret knew that a forthright account of the massacre, in addition to his opposing himself to Colonel Whipple's views, could damage the *Northern Californian*'s advertising, circulation and job-printing business.

Apparently he did not consult with anyone over how he intended to handle the massacre. Union was shocked and outraged when the February 29 issue of the paper appeared.

Perhaps he set the type himself on the headline he had written over his story: INDISCRIMINATE MASSACRE OF INDIANS — WOMEN AND CHILDREN BUTCHERED.

"Little children and old women," he wrote,

were mercilessly stabbed and their skulls crushed with axes. When the bodies were landed at Union, a more shocking and revolting spectacle never was exhibited to the eyes of a Christian and civilized people. Old women, wrinkled and decrepit, lay weltering in blood, their brains dashed out and dabbled with their long gray hair. Infants scarcely a span long, with their faces cloven with hatchets and their bodies ghastly with wounds.

No resistance was made, it is said, to the butchers who did the work, but as they ran or huddled together for protection like sheep, they were struck down with hatchets.

The slaughter was performed by "parties unknown," he added, but he left no doubt where the responsibility lay — among the whole white community of Humboldt Bay and its easy talk of good Indians and belief that the aborigines were somehow less than human. He did not need to expand on the bitter irony of selling goods to the Indians six days of the week and on the seventh day, dedicated to the "Lord's work," slaughtering them while they slept. Commenting editorially, he admitted that it was not easy to deal with a subject race in their midst, especially one with grievances over its displacement, but killing was not the answer.

"We can conceive of no palliation for woman and child slaughter," he wrote in his editorial.

We can conceive of no wrong that a babe's blood can atone for. . . .

An "irrepressible conflict" is really here. Knowing this, was it policy to commence the work of extermination with the most peaceful? And what assistance can be expected from a Legislature already perplexed with doubts and suspicion, in the face of the bloody record we today publish?

The morning of February 29, when he held the ink-damp sheets of the paper in his hand, he must have realized that he was risking everything — perhaps including his life—to take such an unpopular stand. There was an angry murmur of voices in the plaza outside the *Northern Californian* office; presses had been wrecked and type fonts smashed for less effrontery than Bret had shown. Soon the grumbling swelled to an uproar of denunciation, and there was talk of calling in Judge Lynch to remedy the situation. Quite possibly Bret had to go into hiding until local passions cooled. His friend Murdock later recalled that Bret was "seriously threatened and in no little danger." [28]

According to legend, Bret was actually confronted by a mob brandishing a noose and had to be rescued by a detachment of troops from the nearby army garrison, then fled town under the cover of darkness.

Actually he left town of necessity but departed in dignity — and not before a final appeal to local consciences with an editorial, on March 7, reminding the townspeople that the Indians wanted to work and that the interracial trouble might die down if they were given a chance to support themselves. "Let us suggest that our farmers give them a trial."

He had to agree with Colonel Whipple that it wouldn't be possible for him to stay on. Slightly more than three weeks after the inflammatory issue of February 29 appeared, he boarded a coastal steamer for San Francisco. On March 28 Colonel Whipple informed his readers in a paragraph in the editorial columns that Mr. F. B. Harte had left Union several days before. "He is a warm-hearted, genial companion, and a gentleman in every sense of the word," Whipple wrote in what was undoubtedly a reluctant farewell. "We wish our friend the success to which his talents entitle him, and cordially commend him to the fraternity of the Big City."

As his steamer tossed in the coastal swell, Bret had every reason for self-congratulation. Whatever his fellow citizens thought of his conduct as a journalist, he knew that he had behaved like a man, and a brave one. Never in his life would he have better reason to feel proud of himself. His three years in Union at least had matured him to the point where he could fret over something more important than the impeccability of his linen. He had learned that all that matters is what a man thinks of himself. It was a lesson in *amour propre* that could carry him, in the scandalized view of his contemporaries, to the heights of permissibility.

THREE

A Lesson in Flag-Waving

H IS courage in standing alone against the mob mind of
Humboldt County must have produced a salutary effect either on his luck or his character. Soon he began hitting
his stride as a careerist of letters, politics and war propaganda. On March 27, 1860, he arrived in San Francisco
aboard the steamer *Columbia* with the undersheriff of Humboldt County, who had taken seven hundred dollars in
county funds as unofficial severance pay, among his fellow
passengers.

San Francisco must have looked pretty good to him after
three years on Humboldt Bay and amid the mist-covered
marshes and redwood forests of its back country. It was a
rather bleak and dismal coast, dark, dank and fog-ridden
much of the time. Its eerie landscape haunted his imagination for years afterward, almost at times with the intensity of
an Edgar Allan Poe, as when he wrote:

Where the Redwood spires together
Pierce the mists in stormy weather,
Where the willow's topmost feather
*   Waves the limpid water o'er;*
Where the long and sweeping surges
Sing their melancholy dirges,

There the river just emerges
On the sad Pacific's shore.[1]

Now, as he told an early biographer, "the great mass of primary impressions on my mind became sufficiently clarified for literary use."[2] He had spent six years in California in drift and occasional despair at his failure to gain a footing anywhere. He had taught school, mined for gold, worked for a country newspaper, wandered the southern mines and the northern foothills, and nothing visible or material had accrued to him. Yet on the day he landed in San Francisco he had acquired the raw materials of his literary career.

On leaving San Francisco three years before, he had written in a sketch for the *Golden Era* that he decided to leave the city because "I had grown wearied of an endless repetition of dirty streets, sand hills, bricks and mortar. The smiling but vacant serenity of the morning skies, the regular annoyance of afternoon gales and evening fogs, had become contemptuously familiar."[3]

The weather may have been the same on his return to the city, but San Francisco was growing up, down and sideways. Its population had risen to eighty thousand, new buildings had been constructed to rival the Montgomery Block, the more flagrant forms of vice had been confined to the Barbary Coast, and much of the populace had changed from red flannel shirts and gunbelts to silk hats and claw hammer coats. The city, as he said, was at least "half-tamed" by now, midway in transition from a hell-roaring frontier town to one of the great cities of the world. To a boy brought up in New York, of course, its transition would never seem as glorious as it did to others who were flocking down from the mining camps which even now were tumbling into ghost towns.

Bret's mother and stepfather still lived in Oakland, and his sister Margaret, her husband and child had preceded him to San Francisco by several months. Now twenty-three and no longer tied to the apron strings of a younger sister, he took lodgings over a restaurant in Commercial Street. Almost immediately after his arrival, he caught on with the *Golden Era*, to which he had been contributing off and on for the past few years. The only job open to him, however, was in the composing room. Once again he was a printer, but at least he had the privilege of submitting contributions in verse and prose directly to the management, and within a few weeks his sketches and stories began appearing in its columns.

Of his occupation at the type fonts, he wrote rather plaintively that a printer was

a mechanical curiosity, with brain and fingers — a thing that will set so many type in a day — a machine that will think and act, but still a machine — a being who undertakes the most systematic and monotonous drudgery, yet one the ingenuity of man has never supplanted mechanically . . .

A printer — yet for all his sometimes dissipated and reckless habits — a worker. At all times and hours, day and night; sitting up in a close, unhealthy office, when gay crowds are hurrying to the theatre — later still, when the street revelers are gone and the city sleeps — in the fresh air of the morning — in the broad and gushing sunlight — some printing machine is at the case, with its eternal unvarying *click! click!* [4]

The *Golden Era*, longest-lived of the Western literary weeklies, had been established in 1852 and was, as Charles Warren Stoddard said, "the cradle and grave of many a high hope — there was nothing to be compared with it that side of the Mississippi." [5] It looked more like a newspaper, with its six wide columns to the page, than a literary journal; unlike most periodicals of its type it was breezy, informal, original, venturesome, often pixyish, and carried more than a whiff of mining-camp journalism in the early sixties. It was not only read by but contributed to by miners, ranchers, boomers, prospectors and gamblers. Their contributions often were published above comments that would have discouraged less hardy souls. An imitator of Robert Burns was advised, "It is a pity you did not imbibe more Burns before you burst." Another correspondent was singed with the comment that "You must have used a crowbar instead of a pen, and liquefied asphaltum as a substitute for ink. Sacrificed!"

About the time Bret went to work in its composing room, the *Golden Era* changed hands and editorial policy. The new management decided to appeal to a more sophisticated and metropolitan readership in San Francisco, meanwhile hoping to hang onto its rural circulation. The new editor and co-owner with James Brooks was Joseph E. Lawrence, a smooth and persuasive New Yorker, who had come out in '49 and worked on various San Francisco dailies. Lawrence was an easy-going, amiable, persuasive man with a meerschaum always poking its way out of his bearded face. His ability to find and woo literary talent was remarkable, much of the persuasion being accomplished over a table at the Lick House where mixed drinks and unmixed flattery were dispensed to young beginners and visiting celebrities whom Lawrence wanted to contribute at the standard rate of one dollar a column (and they were wide columns, set in eight point type).

One of the new departments Lawrence dreamed up for the *Golden Era* — in addition to such standbys as *Gossip Abroad, Surface Diggings and Siftings, Farm, Garden and Household* and *Eastern Intelligence* — was a column of local comment variously headed *Table and Town Talk, Lucubra-*

tions and *The Bohemian Feuilleton.** This department was supposed to be sophisticated, sprightly and written with a sparkle that would attract the newly culture-conscious citizens of the Bay area. To get the required luster the astute Lawrence soon recruited such young and promising talents as Bret Harte, Prentice Mulford, Charles H. Webb, Ralph Keeler, Frances Fuller Victor, and several years later Charles Warren Stoddard.

Bret continued to set type in the *Golden Era*'s backshop while contributing stories and sketches, some of which (according to legend attested to by Mark Twain and Ina Coolbrith) he composed at the typecase without bothering to put the words on paper first. "The editor and proprietor, Joe Lawrence," Twain wrote, "never saw Harte's manuscripts, because there weren't any. Harte spun his literature out of his head while at work at the case, and set it up as he spun. The *Golden Era* was ostensibly and ostentatiously a literary paper, but its literature was pretty feeble and sloppy and only exhibited the literary forms, without really being literature." [6] Twain, it should be pointed out, didn't come to San Francisco until two or three years later and could only have been repeating hearsay. Others, such as Stoddard, who knew him better, said Harte's methods of composition were "fastidious to a degree," accompanied by much rewriting and revising. And Lawrence may have been an easygoing editor, but he wasn't so slipshod as to allow his journal to be stuffed with items ad-libbed at the typecase.

Harte's early contributions were self-consciously literary, self-indulgently preoccupied with "fine" writing and elaborate phrase-making, all common faults in a young writer which would be pared away — though perhaps not quite enough, by the sternest standards — as Bret learned his craft.

* The closest modern parallel is the *New Yorker*'s leadoff section.

His first story was "My Metamorphosis," [7] published only a few weeks after he caught on at the *Golden Era*. It was a humorous account of how a young man, "passionately fond of swimming," got caught taking a nude dip in a fountain and had to pose as a statue when a crowd suddenly appeared. Among them was the girl he loved. "But, Ada, my darling, how was it that your bright eyes alone detected in the marble statue a living imposture?" "Why, I never before saw a marble statue with a plain gold ring upon its little finger."

In short order "Boggs on a Horse," "Story of the Revolution," "A Child's Ghost Story," "Facts Concerning a Meerschaum," "My Other Self," "His Wife's Sister" and "A Case of Blasted Affections" made their appearance in the *Golden Era's* columns. In the latter, his alter ego Alexis Puffer figured as a young man who fell in love with a girl on the North Beach omnibus, a case of love at first sight terminated when he accidentally struck her in the face and her glass eye rolled out. "Puffer sank senseless in the straw. He was removed at the terminus." His stories, running only a few thousand words at most, were imitative and callow — Charles Dickens and Washington Irving, along with the California-nurtured humorist "John Phoenix" (George H. Derby, an unusually frolicsome army captain), were his models — but they showed vitality and variety.

No doubt it was one of the happiest, most carefree periods of his life. No blazing light on the literary scene as yet, he was at least being regularly published and was making enough money as typesetter and contributor to enjoy himself in his rather cautious way. His blood ran a little too thin, his temperament was too cautious to place him in any danger of drowning in the fleshpots or losing himself in unmeasured merriment. The thing he feared most was making a fool of himself; the impetuosity of an Alexis Puffer represented the daydreaming side of his nature, something to be avoided at all costs with his real and nonliterary self. He would take a drink or two with friends, but he had never been drunk — a curious failing in a young man of twenty-four. His attitude toward women was romantic and poetic; he was attracted only toward the virtuous, and the idea of seducing one from her virtue was unthinkable. The one vice that seemed to lure him was gambling. He liked to watch the action in the plentiful gambling joints, listen to the music of the roulette wheels, clicking chips, galloping dice. "Perhaps from my Puritan training," he said, "I experienced a more fearful joy in the gambling saloons." [8] But he didn't have the means to join the play, and thus was saved from becoming a Jack Hamlin or John Oakhurst himself. That two of his most famous fictional creations were gamblers undoubtedly was traceable to his own fascination with their occupation. He admired their dress, their manner, their cool recklessness, their aloofness — the last more than anything, perhaps. The gambler always stood alone. With his dark and slightly saturnine looks Bret could have passed for a gambler himself.

His life as a young bachelor was quiet, controlled and orderly. Every morning he breakfasted at a German restaurant on Westphalian ham, rolls and coffee. He put in a long day at the *Golden Era*. In the evenings he wrote, wandered the city or attended the opera and theater on press passes, which allowed him to squire a young lady without wrecking his budget. Sundays he often followed the local custom of drinking lager in one of the outlying beer gardens. Mostly, in his spare time, he explored San Francisco and soaked up the impressions which were transmuted, sometimes cloaked in fiction, sometimes as unadorned observation, into sketches for the *Golden Era*'s *Table and Town Talk*. (These contributions were variously signed as Bret, F.B.H., or one of his pseudonyms, J. Keyser, Jefferson Brick, Alexis Puffer.) The early sketches reflected what was to be the warp and woof of his work, a sympathy for the outcast and the underdog, a tender understanding of children and animals, a strong talent for local color which was to make him one of the first and foremost of "regional" writers. He defended the Chinese immigrants, that pig-tailed and dog-trotting horde with its sinister Oriental ways, its singsong girls, opium pipes and irksome diligence, at a time when "John Chinaman" was the most unpopular creature under the Western stars; a dozen years hence the fieriest political agitator in the city's history would be advocating, in all seriousness, that Chinatown be leveled by dropping sticks of dynamite from balloons. He told of a dog who died fighting progress in the form of streetcars.[9] Ranging the city and its outskirts from the Twin Peaks to the Embarcadero, he was particularly fascinated by the Mission Dolores, near which duels often were fought. One day he saw a man's body in a little hollow behind the mission, the loser in an affair of honor.[10] The corpse, perhaps, added a touch to the gloomy-fated Oakhurst and Hamlin as those gentlemen-gamblers were slowly taking shape in his creative mind. The mission itself he described without trying to conceal its decay: "its ragged senility contrasting with the smart spring sunshine, its two gouty pillars with the plaster dropping away like tattered bandages, its rayless windows, its crumbling entrances, and the leper spots on its whitewashed wall eating through the dark adobe."

At the same time he was working on a long story originally published under the title "The Work on Red Mountain," later more famous as "M'liss," under which title it was dramatized and became a standard repertory and stock item for many years, as well as forming the basis of three silent films, one of them starring Mary Pickford. In "M'liss," for the first time he made use of his experiences in the mining camps of the foothills, particularly those as a schoolteacher at LaGrange. His heroine, Melissa Smith, was the daughter of a drunkard, for whom Smith's Pocket was named, and who thought he had struck an outcropping of the Mother Lode but saw his envisioned fortune vanish as the "lead" turned out to be a mere isolated "pocket."

His observations on mining-camp society had an almost sociological exactitude, and he achieved a Dickensian mixture of pathos and humor which contemporary readers found ir-resistible. He even got away with portraying the local evan-gelist, Reverend McSnagley, as "that unskillful pilot," and his prating of "Christewanity" with a hostile realism. The story was published by the *Golden Era* in two installments, on De-cember 9 and 16, 1860; it created something of a regional stir, and became nationally celebrated — of the most popular tales of the Civil War generation — when republished several years later.

By then Bret had gained not only a growing local reputa-tion but something else he needed, or thought he needed — a patroness, one with more than a little of the lioness about her.

Jessie Benton Frémont, daughter of Senator Thomas Hart Benton and wife of General John Charles Frémont, was one of those female dreadnoughts — delicate and feminine though they usually are — who have created more than their share of havoc in American history.

Mrs. Frémont at thirty-seven, though worn by "care and sorrow and childbirth pain," as she wrote in the family Bible, was a woman of some beauty and greater force. Spirited hardly begins to describe the woman who made something of the brave but vainglorious Frémont. She had married the

[56]

young army officer at the age of seventeen, enabled him to become the Great Pathfinder of Western exploration, steeled him with her courage and tenacity and intelligence when he was court-martialed for bungling a revolution in California, helped him campaign for the Presidency in 1856 when he was nominated as the new Republican party's first candidate for that office. After that unsuccessful campaign the Frémonts had returned to California and their vast foothill estate in Mariposa County.

In addition to the Mariposa estate, the Frémonts maintained a house at Black Point out near the Presidio where they could escape the summer heat of the foothills. The restless Jessie practically commuted by wagon road and river steamer between their country home and town house, usually taking her eighteen-year-old daughter Elizabeth and other children with her.

One day on the steamer bound for San Francisco she picked up a copy of the *Golden Era*, read one of Bret Harte's sketches and was impressed sufficiently to summon him to her home at Black Point. Literary as well as political, charming as well as intelligent, kindly (at least toward struggling young artists) as well as maturely beautiful, she must have enchanted the young man. She was the first great lady he had ever met, and perhaps from her he learned an appreciation of great ladies that was to be notable.

At first Bret approached the Frémont circle with an awed hesitation. "I had to insist this very shy young man should come to see me," she wrote in her memoir, *Souvenirs of My Time*, "but soon he settled into a regular visit . . . and for more than a year dined with us that day, bringing his manuscripts, astonished by the effect of some, at times huffed by less flattering opinion on others, but growing rapidly into larger perceptions as he saw much of various people to

whom I made him known." (Bret was conscious of the fact
that he appeared timorous in such glittering company, but
insisted [in "My Other Self," published in the *Golden Era*,
September 30, 1860] that there was a bolder Bret existing
inside the bashful shell. "My acquaintances, generally, look
upon me as a mild dyspeptic, governed . . . by bodily sym-
pathies; and a rather quiet, ladylike young man. Just so. But I
have another self they know nothing about — a brilliant
healthy fellow, with huge lungs; a little given to romance
and enthusiasm, who requires all my care and attention to
keep him out of mischief.")

Soon he was appearing for dinner every Sunday night at
the Frémont home, was meeting the Frémonts' circle of
friends and collaborators and stepping into a world of fashion and intellect where, he had long been convinced, he belonged as from birthright. Good food, intelligent conversation and not least of all the friendly interest in his literary
career of Mrs. Frémont and her family and friends warmed
and sustained him. It was a striking example of what would
later be called upward mobility that a young printer whose
writing thus far was a sideline could be calling at the Frémont home and treated as an equal. But Jessie Frémont, of
course, had a shrewd eye for promising talent. Herself the
author of several books, she was the first to spot in Bret
Harte the makings of a major writer. She read his work before it was submitted for publication, discussed and praised
and criticized it. His use of English certainly improved on
acquaintance with Mrs. Frémont. She gave him confidence,
an incalculable asset in a young writer struggling to find himself, as well as less tangible gifts that contributed to polishing
him both socially and professionally. She taught him the
value of self-criticism.

Inevitably the Frémonts and their friends drew him into

what concerned them much more than the struggles of the beginning writer. They formed the hard core of determination that, in the civil war they foresaw, California would side with the Union. That fall, of course, Abraham Lincoln was running for President; Kansas was the scene of a bloody guerrilla conflict between the Free Soil and pro-slavery factions, and rumors of war and secession reached even the remotest state in the Union. As ardent Abolitionists the Frémonts and their associates were not at all dismayed by the probable cost of the coming conflict.

One of the leading members of the Frémont circle was the Reverend Thomas Starr King, a Bostonian with great oratorical power who had taken over the pulpit of the First Unitarian Church earlier in 1860. He was to take up the Unionist banner when the Frémonts, the following year, went East and the general, whose genius was more political than military, assumed command of the Western theater of operations against the Confederacy.

Another familiar in the Frémont home was Senator Edward D. Baker, also a superb orator and personal friend of Abraham Lincoln. As senator from Oregon, he campaigned throughout the Pacific states for the Union cause, and contributed greatly to Lincoln's carrying California by a narrow margin despite the fact that there were many Southerners in the state as flamingly devoted to the cause of Secession as the Frémonts and their friends were to the Union.

In all the as yet united States there were no more fanatic and eloquent apostles of Unionism and Abolition than the Frémonts, Reverend King and Senator Baker. No doubt it was under the impact of their arguments and discussions around the Frémont dinner table that Bret, anything but a political animal, was enlisted in their crusade.

This transplanted fervor probably was responsible for the

one emotional, uncharacteristically hammy and florid gesture of Bret's public life. On October 26, 1860, a great mass meeting at the Metropolitan Theater was held, with 4000 inside the structure and another 8000 thronging the streets outside. The principal speaker was Senator Baker, who was in top form.

We are a city set on a hill. Our light cannot be hid. As for me, I dare not, I will not be false to freedom. Where the feet of my youth were planted, there, by freedom, my feet shall stand . . . I have seen her bound to the stake; I have seen them give her ashes to the winds. But when they turned to exult, I have seen her again meet them face to face, resplendent in shining steel, brandishing in her right hand a flaming sword, red with insufferable light. I take courage. People gather round her. The genius of America will at last lead her sons to freedom.[11]

With a sweeping gesture, Senator Baker then pretended to draw his own sword from its scabbard.

At that moment Bret Harte, undoubtedly coached by Jessie Frémont, jumped up on the platform waving the Stars and Stripes. For fifteen minutes the audience cheered, with those outside taking up the refrain. It was the most dramatic moment in California politics since the days of the Bear Republic. Always diffident before an audience, Bret must have needed a lot of prodding to make that gesture; it conflicted in every respect with the character in which he had cloaked himself since early youth, the poised, sardonic, aloof figure who played it cool and was always self-contained.

His Union patriotism, however, did not dwindle as war approached and the steamer *Star of the West* — the same ship which had taken Bret and his sister from New York to Nicaragua — was fired upon as she attempted to bring supplies to the forts in Charleston Harbor. Three months later war broke out, but among those who rushed to the colors was *not* the young flag-waver who had so stirred the assemblage at the Metropolitan Theater. Bret opted out, and continued to do so even after his friend Senator Baker was killed in one of the first skirmishes of the Civil War. He was young, had no family responsibilities and was among the most ardent of the Unionist-Republican-Abolitionist faction. Later he would not object when addressed, far from San Francisco, as "Colonel" nor would he deny reports that he had won his colonelcy at the head of a regiment in the Army of the Potomac. At the time when it counted, however, he had no yearning for the uniform, no enthusiasm for flinging himself into the conflict which he and his friends had welcomed in such glowing terms. All in all, it would be easy enough to overlook his decision against joining the ranks of the righteous if only he hadn't jumped on that stage waving the flag with so much élan. A writer can always claim the privilege of standing outside great events, of nonparticipation on grounds of artistic objectivity, but not one who is so forceful in urging others into the fight.

A few weeks after the war started, Bret changed jobs and stopped writing for the *Golden Era*. Apparently he had had a row with someone connected with the management of the periodical, and he did not resume contributing to it for almost a year.[12] Instead he obtained employment, probably through the influence of the Frémont circle, as a clerk in the surveyor general's office. His pay was one hundred dollars a month, a considerable improvement over what the *Golden Era* paid him as typesetter and contributor.

He often attended meetings at which Thomas Starr King rallied the citizenry to support the war effort, collected hundreds of thousands of dollars for the Sanitary Commission (a woefully inefficient forerunner of the Red Cross) and fulmi-

nated against the remaining pockets of Confederate sentiment in the state. By this time the Reverend King had attracted much of the animus which Southerners formerly had
felt for the Frémonts. King, wrote the Southern-minded editor of a Sonora newspaper, was a "fair representative of the
rabid, fanatical, godless school of Boston political preachers.
Their cry now is nigger, nigger, blood, blood! The peace
doctrine of the meek and lowly Jesus, who taught peace on
earth, is scouted as treasonable by those fantastical mounte-
banks of the clerical school."

In his chosen noncombatant role Bret was pressed into
service as a poet-propagandist and his verse was read at patriotic rallies throughout the state. Although torrents of mili-
tant verse were composed, uttered and printed during the
war years, Bret's became the best known and most honored
by repetition. Which is not to say it had any intrinsic merit
beyond raising a drumbeat pulse in all good Unionists and
infuriating all good Confederates. The poems' titles included
"A Volunteer Stocking," "Banks and the Slave Girl," "The
Battle Autumn," "Semmes," "A Cavalry Song," "Of One
Who Fell in Battle," "The Hero of Sugar Pine," "St. Valentine in Camp," "The Vendue of Jefferson Davis," "In Me-
moriam" and "The Wrath of McDawdle," a denunciation of
General George B. McClellan, whom Harte and other war-
hawks considered dilatory in his campaigns against Rich-
mond.[13]

When Reverend King died of diphtheria in 1864, an event
marked by the tolling of minute-guns in Union Square and
heavier artillery in the defenses of Alcatraz Island, Bret supplied verse for the occasion titled "Relieving Guard":

> *"A star? There's nothing strange in that."*
> *"No, nothing; but, above the thicket*

Somehow it seemed to me that God
Somewhere had just relieved a picket."

Across the continent the armies of the North contended
with varying success against those of the South; the men of
Bret's generation fought and died for what they believed in,
or were told they did; the war seesawed along the Potomac,
down the Western rivers, around the Southern coasts, with
the Union often acutely in peril, but Bret continued to express his militancy in verse about lone sentries, watch fires
above dark rivers, dastardly Confederates and heroic Unionists, and youth falling in battle.

Something worse than risking his life on the battle line had
happened to the poet laureate of the California propagan-
dists. He had fallen in love with the wrong woman.

Wrong, that is, for a struggling writer. She was eminently
respectable, indelibly middle-class, immutably virtuous. All
she needed to be happy was an attentive husband with a
steady and substantial income, an ambition which disquali-
fied her for the role of a writer's wife, along with the fact
that she was self-centered, demanding and inclined to domi-
neer. Writers bound for success really need two wives, in
succession, of course: the first a subservient creature who
will take care of him while he is clawing out a foothold on
recognition and fortune, who will build up his anemic ego,
type his manuscripts, and act as a lightning rod for his frus-
trations; the second everything her predecessor is not, to
grace and enhance his days of success. The two are rarely
found in combination, which may account for the matrimonial confusion marking the lives of many successful writers.

Bret had been infatuated, to judge from his poetry, three
or four times since coming to California. None of the pre-

vious attachments, however, had been earthbound enough to be called a love affair. When he finally fell in love with an attainable object, it was under the prosaic auspices of Reverend Thomas Starr King.

The young woman was Anna Griswold, the daughter of Daniel and Mary Griswold of New York City. A contralto, she sang in the choir of the First Unitarian Church along with her sister and brother-in-law, Mr. and Mrs. Leach, with whom she was living in San Francisco. Thirty years old when she met Bret, she must have despaired of getting married. It was then the custom for spinsters to put the show on the road and visit their married relatives in the hope of attracting suitors in fresh locales.

Undoubtedly they were introduced by Reverend King, who regarded them both as his protégés, Miss Griswold having a voice which her friends insisted was almost of concert caliber. She was a tall, dark-haired woman not overwhelmingly attractive, judging from her photographs, with a heavy-lidded gaze, a wide mouth and a (deceptively) receding chin. Not at all disheartened by the dimness of her matrimonial prospects, she held herself in an esteem which some people must have found mysterious.

Little is known of their courtship, except that it must have been rapid and that it was marked by dissension among their family and friends. Bret's mother objected to Anna on the grounds that she was five years older and of an unsuitable temperament. Anna's friends — but presumably not her sister and brother-in-law — argued that she came of a distinguished Colonial family and had a magnificent voice, that she would be demeaning herself by marrying a clerk in the surveyor general's office.[14]

Perhaps the romance was only spurred along by the opposition of family and friends, because on August 11, 1862, the two slipped away to San Rafael and were married by the Reverend Harry Gilbert.

Just two weeks short of his twenty-sixth birthday Bret settled down with his bride in a house, badly in need of repair, at 542 Sutter Street. Needing to supplement his income, he made his peace with the *Golden Era* and again contributed verse, sketches and stories. Some of them reflected his new condition, one piece telling of the difficulty of growing anything but hollyhocks in his small garden, another recounting the minor stresses of living in a rather rough neighborhood. In a subsequent sketch, "Fixing Up an Old House," he related with a doleful humor the misadventures of a young husband embarking on do-it-yourself home repair. There was an inkling of Anna's slightly contemptuous attitude toward his literary labors — which still brought in only a dollar for a column of closely set type — in her suggestion that Bret do the paperhanging himself. "You might do it yourself after office hours instead of writing," he quoted her as saying, "and you'd save money by it." [15]

Bret thus found himself entangled in domestic chores for which he was ill-equipped. "I would like to forget the singular propensity which that paper displayed to entwine itself lovingly in damp curves around my legs, and how I vainly endeavored to evade its chaste and cold embrace as I was putting it on." Neighborhood children came in off the street and helped remove the old paper, "scattering it far and wide through the streets." Finally he was forced to call in a paperhanger to take over the job. Bret then applied himself to painting the interior of the house, but that too turned out to be a botch. When "the whole woodwork took to weeping" from his poorly mixed applications, he again had to call in a professional to take over. The doors and windows also needed repair, so he engaged a carpenter who spent the morning in "an animated and desultory conversation in which he delivered an account of his past life and history." This craftsman required not only an audience but Bret's assistance in "handing him nails when required and bringing him tools out of his chest."

Perhaps it was the vexations of being a householder, the first faint disillusionment of being a husband whose main function was to be a "provider" — a function quite remote from the poetic fancies of his youth — that caused him to recount the adventures of Melons, a young vagabond, for the *Golden Era*. There was more than a touch of wistfulness to his tales of a street waif unencumbered by home, wife and creditors.

FOUR

"Filling the Void"

"I was engaged in filling a void
in the literature of the Pacific
Coast."
—Bret Harte, 1862

MIDWAY through the Civil War the artistic ferment
which has now bubbled and boiled in San Francisco
for a century, with results sometimes indifferent and more
often brilliant, began seething in earnest. The "misty city,"
as Bret called it, was acquiring new outlets for its creative
energy; it was the literary capital of all the vast territories
west of the Great Plains, and it was comfortably distant from
Vicksburg, Gettysburg and Chattanooga, where the Union
fought for its life. San Francisco was thriving on the stream
of silver flowing from the Comstock Lode, on the war-
inflated prices it was receiving for cattle-raising and fruit-
growing. In this busy and comparatively happy place an
amazing group of writers sprang up and flourished; none of
them, however, achieving a more startling growth than Bret
Harte.

The roster of those who lighted up the literary scene for
varying periods of time, some for weeks and some for years
and one or two until the end of their lives, read like a Who's
Who of the celebrated and notorious of the sixties. The fact

that many of them, like Bret, were of an age that rendered them capable of military service suggests that writers with some claim to being established were more attuned to cannonades in print than on the battlefield. Joaquin Miller, later renowned as "the sweet singer of the Sierras," kept a list of people he met in Joe Lawrence's office at the *Golden Era* during this period. It included Mark Twain, Prentice Mulford, Charles Warren Stoddard, Adah Isaacs Menken and her husband Robert H. Newell (the humorist "Orpheus C. Kerr"), Fitzhugh Ludlow, Albert Bierstadt, Bret Harte, and Artemus Ward, who was reputed to be President Lincoln's favorite humorist.[1] Ada Clare, the "Queen of Bohemia," also bustled into town and caused a great flutter among the literature-conscious. Sir Richard Burton, the great traveler, translator, author and adventurer, spent a couple of weeks roaming the city on his way home from Utah, where he had gathered material for his book about the Mormons.

Bret was friendly with most of them, and influenced many of them as the leading local example of how to make literature out of the materials closest at hand.

His fortunes took an upturn in the spring of 1863 at a time when his wife was expecting their first child, a son to be named Griswold, and complaining that the lot of an author's wife was an unhappy one. Anna Harte spoke bitterly to friends of "the hardships of poverty which she had to undergo." Bret's salary at the surveyor general's office, slightly augmented by earnings from his contributions to the *Golden Era*, wasn't enough to maintain a household in the middle-class style to which Anna had been accustomed, and the author-starving-in-a-garret tradition had no romantic appeal whatever to her. Bret must be a provider first, a scribbler second. Fortunately for his peace of mind a sinecure, which paid one hundred eighty dollars a month and entailed few responsibilities, was found in the superintendent's office at the local branch of the United States Mint.

The way Mark Twain told it, Robert B. Swain, the superintendent of the Mint, like Jessie Frémont, was attracted to Bret by his writings in the *Golden Era* and found them

a new and fresh and spirited note that rose above that orchestra's mumbling confusion . . . It seemed to Mr. Swain a shame that Harte should be wasting himself in such a place and on such a pittance so he took him away, made him his private secretary on a good salary, with little or nothing to do, and told him to follow his own bent and develop his talent. Harte was willing and the development began.[2]

Actually Bret got the job through the fond patronage of Thomas Starr King, whose parishioner Swain was at the First Unitarian Church. It probably didn't hurt that Bret was a Republican and a vigorous propagandist for the war effort. All good things seemed to flow from that fount of Unitarianism: he had found his wife in its choir loft, state-wide publicity as a poet through its pastor, and a cushy job through one of his fellow parishioners. Yet when Reverend King died, he drifted away from the congregation and readopted his former attitude that religion was so much excess baggage to the man of sensibility and intellect.

Bret now had a firm base from which to operate, none of his fellow writers was more secure financially, and these facts undoubtedly aided him in getting his career under way. He was now able to do much of his writing at the Mint, and at the government's expense, instead of working for newspapers or turning out hack work as most of his colleagues were forced to do. If he had married the wrong woman, he had at least cultivated the right people and assumed the proper attitudes to assist his career.

With his feet so firmly planted on the ground, he still insisted that he was a citizen of La Boheme. The name of the column which he frequently filled with his observations of metropolitan life was titled *The Bohemian Feuilleton*, and the name to which he gave his collected essays and sketches of the period was *The Bohemian Papers*. This, of course, was sheer romanticizing. He was a husband and father who came home for dinner every evening, a thoroughly domesticated man who preferred the seclusion of his study and the coziness of his hearth to the wildest revels and headiest talk of his more feckless associates. Not for him the feuds and hoaxes, the boozing and wenching, nor the nineteenth-century Bohemian tradition of "making taverns into rendezvous of arts, and of dying drunk and delirious in the gutter, an attic, or the back room of a saloon," as Albert Parry has written.[3] If he descended into a species of Bohemianism later in life, it was more a matter of circumstance than of temperament.

Charles H. Webb, a fellow paragrapher on the *Golden Era*, took a certain restrained but malicious delight in pointing up the paradox of Harte's imposture. No doubt it was a reflection of a certain bitchiness among Bret's colleagues over his holding down a government sinecure, over his sponsorship by the rudimentary Establishment of the city. Bret, Webb wrote, "occupies a high responsible and lucrative position in the Mint," adding as a stinging afterthought, "with very little to do." Webb also remarked in an earlier paragraph that all of the *Golden Era*'s regular contributors were respectable and sober-minded citizens with the exception of one "Bret," whose drinking and loose living was a matter of concern to them all — meaning just the opposite.[4]

Despite these barbs, Webb became Bret's closest associate and most intimate friend during the middle part of the decade. A redhaired and free-swinging bachelor, Webb was the

genuine article, an envoy from the center of Bohemian life in
America. In temperament and proclivities he was Bret's direct opposite, which may have been a leading factor in their
friendship. As a youth he had shipped out on a whaler after
reading *Moby Dick* and spent four years in the South Seas
and the Arctic; during one voyage he had met a fellow crew-
man of Melville's who had rescued him from imprisonment
in the valley of Typee. Returning to New York he had become a contributor to the *Saturday Press* and *Vanity Fair*
and joined the literary Bohemians who hung out in Pfaff's
cellar tavern on Broadway near Bleecker Street. Pfaff's was
the seedbed of Bohemianism in America; a century later it
had moved only a few blocks away. After his immersion in
the wild talk and iced lager at Pfaff's, Webb had sallied forth
as a war correspondent, but his baptism of fire during the
rout at First Manassas was also his farewell to arms. A year
after joining the stampede from Manassas Creek, in which,
he confessed, he had the springiest heels of all who ran before
the loping Confederates, he migrated to San Francisco and
soon became its free-lance master of revels. He had a breezy,
hit-and-run style that makes his humor seem more modern
today than the wordier and more labored efforts of his contemporaries: he avoided their elaborate cuteness, their reli-
ance on dialect; and Bret could and probably did learn something from his economic use of the language. In his *Golden
Era* column *Things*, which has been called "the best column
to appear in that journal in the sixties," [5] his wit crackled
over everything in sight that needed taking down a peg. Sam
Brannan, the leading moneygrubber in the city, was "a thing
of booty and a bore forever." He advised the Episcopal
bishop of San Francisco, regarding Adah Menken's bare-
backed entrance in *Mazeppa*, clad in tights and little else, that
"her line is not a clothesline, Bishop."

[71]

Another new friend of Bret's, also redhaired and crackling with wit and energy, was Samuel Clemens, a wandering journalist from Missouri who had just started signing his stuff as Mark Twain. He too had opted out as far as the war was concerned. Joining a Confederate militia company, he had almost drowned while fording a river and injured himself falling out of a hayloft while on maneuvers. Utterly discouraged, he resigned from military life and headed for the Nevada mines. In Virginia City he had joined the staff of the *Territorial Enterprise*. Now, in San Francisco, he was a reporter for the *Call*. The newspaper's editorial offices were on the floor above those occupied by the Mint, where Bret worked. The two young men spent hours talking, mostly in Bret's office. Twain was a year older but junior to Bret in writing experience. If either was the mentor, it was Bret, whom Twain admired and looked up to. At first acquaintance he was, Twain wrote later, "bright, cheerful, easy-laughing." Twain's style of dress befitted his marginal existence as an underpaid legman for the *Call* while Bret, as he later recalled, was something of a fashion plate. Bret's clothes "always had a single smart little accent, effectively located, and that accent would have distinguished Harte from any of the other ultrafashionables." Usually it was his necktie, "a flash of flame under his chin; or it was indigo blue and as hot and vivid as if one of those splendid and luminous Brazilian butterflies had lighted there." The way Bret carried himself struck Twain, who slouched in the standard Western manner, as offensively aristocratic. "His carriage was easy and graceful, his gait was of the mincing sort but was the right gait for him, for an unaffected one would not have harmonized with the rest of the man and his clothes." [6]

Twain returned to Virginia City shortly, but later became a sort of protégé and pupil of Bret's when the latter edited the *Californian* and the *Overland Monthly*. Genius is always self-discovered, but Bret certainly was one of the first to recognize that Twain, once the rough edges were buffed down, was destined for something better than journalism. Later Twain would explode with rage at the mere mention of Harte's name, but Bret had nothing but admiration for him, so far as his written comment shows, as the greatest living American writer.

The visit of Artemus Ward to San Francisco on a lecture tour in the fall of 1863 may well have turned Bret's attention to putting more humor into his own work. Perhaps because they helped to relieve the gloom of the war years, the most popular writers in America were Ward and other humorists such as Orpheus C. Kerr and Petroleum V. Nasby.

A Down East Yankee, Ward was at the height of his popularity when he appeared in San Francisco. *Artemus Ward: His Book* was the literary hit of 1862. On the night of November 13, Platt's Hall was crammed with his admirers, Bret Harte among them. So was his friend Webb, who wrote of Ward's droll if meandering performance that it was the epitome of showmanship, reminiscent of the talk "in which a clever man, two-thirds tight, indulges when he sits down with a friend or two to finish the business."

Bret was obviously there to learn something, as his article in the *Golden Era* indicated. His review of the Ward lecture, or performance, was as coolly objective as a surgical operation. The mainspring of Ward's humor, as he analyzed it, was uninhibited exaggeration and "perfect lawlessness"; it belonged to "the country of boundless prairies, limitless rivers and stupendous cataracts"; it was the indigenous American humor, "the essence of that fun which overlies the surface of our national life, which is met in the stage, rail-car, canal and flat boat, which bursts out over camp-fires and around bar-room stoves." [7] Probably his analysis of Artemus Ward led Bret to tap a more natural source of humor in his future writings, an echo of the robust joking and boasting he had heard in the mining camps, than had appeared thus far. "Within a few years," wrote Franklin Walker in *San Francisco's Literary Frontier*, "Harte was to draw from the raucous life of the mining camp a vitality which had been absent from his early work. Certainly Artemus Ward helped to show him the right direction."

Ten years later, having achieved an even greater fame himself, Bret was more critical of Ward, though he still conceded that Ward was the "perfect flower" on the "dry stalk of our national life." In his lecture on "American Humor," Bret said he felt that "there is a want of purpose in him. He never leads and is always on a line of popular sentiment or satire. . . . He contributes no single figure to American literature but his own character of showman, and it is very doubtful if even that figure, respectable as it is, bears any real resemblance to any known American type." Twain, he added, "stood alone as the most original humorist that America has yet produced." If he found a fault in American humor, it was the fact that it insisted on "a little too much fun. Laughter makes us doubly serious afterward, and we do not want to be humorists always, turning up like a prizefighter at each round still smiling . . . Perhaps our true humorist is yet to come: when he does he will show that a nation which laughs so easily has still a great capacity for deep feeling . . ." [8]

Another visitor who made an impact on the San Francisco literary world that autumn was Adah Isaacs Menken, the actress-poet, who swept into town at the height of her theatrical fame with her fourth husband, Robert H. Newell, better known as Orpheus C. Kerr, under which name he wrote a series of satiric sketches on wartime Washington.

With her plump figure and glossy black hair, she made a striking appearance as Mazeppa in pink tights and a wispy loincloth which gave the impression of nudity under the flickering kerosene footlights. No one had created such a theatrical sensation since Lola Montez toured the mining camps. One newspaper warned that "no pure youth could witness her performance and come away untainted." Part poetess, part adventuress, and always the exhibitionist, she created an even greater stir among San Francisco's literary-minded. In addition to her publicity as "the most perfectly developed woman in the world," she claimed to have translated the *Iliad* before she was twelve, and in her own poems, collected in a volume titled *Infelicia,* she portrayed herself as a "daughter of the stars" who draped her "white bosom with crimson roses" — an uncorseted image that caused contemporary pulses to race. After shucking off her fourth husband, she was supposed to have inspired Swinburne's *Dolores* and also had hectic affairs with Dumas *père* and Dumas *fils.* Naturally she starred in many columns of smitten prose in the city's literary periodicals. Charles Warren Stoddard declared that her figure was "as appealing as a line in a Persian love song," though that virginal youth knew even less of anatomy that he did of Middle Eastern poetry. Webb commented that she was "a thing of beauty and a boy forever," presumably referring to her equestrian skill. Twain showed her some of his writings for criticism, but after the Menken company had moved on he wrote in the *Call* that *Mazeppa* was a disaster, dramatically speaking, aside from the display of Adah's figure; "worse than a Chinese tragedy, wooden shoes, gongs, and all the rest.

[75]

Bret Harte, however, was apparently immune to her fascinations, physical and literary, and seemed to foresee the day when, burned out by her emotions, she would die alone and in poverty. In *Crusade of the Excelsior* he based the character of Mrs. Hurlstone on Adah Menken. A raddled figure of many marriages and still given to hysterics, Mrs. Hurlstone had "such a figure in tights," but her poetry was pure slush on the theme of liberating women "from — er — I may say certain domestic shackles."

Nor was he much impressed by the appearance of another actress-poet, Ada Clare, a blue-eyed blonde who'd queened it over the boys in the back room at Pfaff's. She also wrote passionately about passion, and to prove she was in earnest produced an illegitimate son while living it up in the Latin Quarter of Paris. Ada Clare and Son, as she billed herself, came to San Francisco to appear in, and as, fittingly enough, *Camille*, and at the same time to write for the *Golden Era*, which proclaimed her "the fairest and most accomplished lady ever associated with American journalism." [9] Like the brunette Adah's, however, the blonde Ada's stock in trade was not talent but a public delight in shocking Mother Grundy. The critics drummed her Camille off the stage, and the previously smitten editors of the *Golden Era* decided her effusions, in prose and verse, were lacking in appeal to their readership. She soon found the atmosphere "malarious" in more ways than one.

On the subject of talent, Bret could rarely be fooled, and certainly publicity, such as that which preceded Adah and Ada, could not sway him. His critical and editorial faculties, while as yet untested, were part of a slowly and painfully acquired professionalism. While his colleagues were buzzing around the likes of brunette Adah and blonde Ada, he was stealing away from home and office to spend long hours in the Mercantile Library. In the fall of that year the *Atlantic Monthly*, the first Eastern periodical to look upon his work and find it good, accepted "The Legend of Monte Del Diablo" for publication in its October 1863 issue. Already, it was apparent, he was looking to the East for approval and perhaps dreaming of the day when he could go back in triumph. Laid against the twin peaks of the mountain which overlooked the valley ranch where he had once worked as a tutor, and reflecting his romantic interest in the more spacious days of Spanish rule, the story was an Irvingesque tale of the struggle between a Jesuit missionary and the Devil. It brought him kindly attention, but no more.

Late that same year Bret and his friend Charles H. Webb began making plans for establishing a literary weekly of their own. The *Golden Era* would continue publication for several years, even after Joe Lawrence sold out his interest in 1866 and retired, but it was losing readership and prestige. It was something of a hodge-podge, publishing what were then known as "sensation" novels of low caliber, the musings of lady writers with more gentility than talent and the outpouring of doggerel from the mining camps — which produced more poetic dross than golden ore — along with the flashes of brilliance from people like Harte, Webb, Prentice Mulford and a few others. It may also have foundered through trying to hold on to its outland audience as well as appealing to the more sophisticated readers in San Francisco. Even Mark Twain complained it wasn't "high-toned" enough at a time when he himself stood badly in need of burnishing. An ex-editor of the *Golden Era*, no feminist, insisted afterward that it was the ladies who were principally responsible for the periodical's decline. "Yes, they killed it — they literally killed it, with their namby-pamby school-girl trash." [10]

Webb, as "Inigo" in his *Golden Era* column, began sending up rockets heralding the journalistic birth in November, using the indulgent *Era* as a platform from which to summon financial backers and contributors. Only partly in jest, Webb announced that Harte would supply the literary excellence, he (Webb) would take the credit for it, and Frances Fuller Victor, another contributor to the *Golden Era*, would come up with the money. It would be called, Webb said, *Inigo's Christian Weekly Watchman* or possibly *Bret's Hebdomadal Social Guardian*.

On May 28, 1864, the first issue of Webb's and Harte's weekly appeared for the first time. The *Californian*, proclaiming itself "the best journal on the Pacific Coast, and the equal of any on the continent," was the name it bore on the logotype. Webb's name appeared on the masthead as editor and proprietor, with Bret to spell him whenever he felt like taking time off. Bret's contributions, a sketch and a poem, the former "Neighborhoods I Have Moved From," the latter "The Ballad of the Emeu," covered two of the three double columns on the first page. In subsequent issues Harte himself, along with Mark Twain, Charles Warren Stoddard and Ina Coolbrith, were the chief contributors.* The *Californian* published for two years under the Webb-Harte management, and two years after that under different ownership, but it never quite attained the excellence it proclaimed.

Twain apparently had been brought into the fold by Bret who, as his sponsor, nominated himself as editor-in-charge-of-Mark-Twain. Twain was engaged to contribute an article a week at a salary of fifty dollars a month (he was still working as a reporter on the *Call*). His first sketch in the *Californian* was "A Notable Conundrum." Over that and subsequent contributions he labored for hours with Bret in the latter's office in the Mint. Twain's crude vitality and unfet-

* Henry George and Ambrose Bierce later joined the roll of contributors.

tered exuberance needed taming down, and Bret was just the coolly objective man to do it. Each man in a way complemented the other, at that stage of their careers, though their only attempt at collaboration — years later — ended disastrously. Bret had more polish than substance at that time; he also had a literary background possessed by few through constant reading since early boyhood. Twain, on the other hand, had been schooled only in frontier journalism. The precise use of the language was a tool strange to his grip. He was crammed with experience, but lacked the means to make literary use of it.

Later Twain, much as he came to detest his mentor, was still generous enough to credit Bret with shaping him and giving aim as well as force to his expression. "Bret Harte," he wrote, "trimmed and trained and schooled me patiently until he changed me from an awkward utterer of coarse grotesquenesses to a writer of paragraphs and chapters that have found a certain favour in the eyes of some of the very decentest people in the land." [11]

And there were others, then and later, to testify that Bret was at his best as an editor and teacher. A certain waspish hauteur, more cultivated than real, initially the defense mechanism of a "dude" who refused to change his ways in the horny-handed West, was absent when Bret sat down in his office and went over manuscripts line by line, word by word, with other contributors to the *Californian*. He actually edited the periodical during two extended periods when Webb took leave, but all during his connection with the *Californian* he acted as a sort of ex-officio editor for some of the younger and brighter talent.

Among these embryonic talents was Charles Warren Stoddard, seven years younger than Harte and a native New Yorker. He had come to San Francisco as a child and began writing poetry for the *Golden Era* as "Pip Pepperpod." The elfin pseudonym suited him. He was a shy, frail, angelically handsome youth, his work all jeweled images, with a yearning for the exotic that placed him in the Lafcadio Hearn category. Later the islands of the Pacific lured him and inspired some of his more notable prose, for as he wrote Walt Whitman in 1870, "I know there is but one hope for me. I must get in amongst people who are not afraid of their instincts and who scorn hypocrisy. I am numbed with the frigid manners of the Christians; barbarism has given me the fullest joy of life and I long to return to it and be satisfied."

Stoddard, who was so shy he dropped his poems in a contributor's box outside the Clay Street offices of the *Golden Era*, met Harte shortly before the latter began planning publication of the *Californian* with Webb. It was a social occasion and Bret was surrounded by admirers. Stoddard approached Bret, a lordly and elegant figure in his eyes, with an autograph album of which he was very proud. He asked Bret for his autograph. Bret, who wanted even his signature to be seen only in the best places, "looked upon the idea with polite scorn," Stoddard recalled, until he saw that Thomas Starr King had autographed the first page. Assured that he was in good company, Bret then not only wrote his name but a stanza of poetry in the young man's book.[12]

Like Twain, Stoddard was also a quasi-protégé of Bret's, and the former worked long and hard over his manuscripts. Under his tutelage Stoddard turned from verse to prose. "To his advice and encouragement," Stoddard forty years later wrote, "I feel that I owe all that is best in my literary efforts." Harte, he recalled, could be very stern when he faltered, and once told him: "In 'Jason's Quest' you have made a mistake of subject. It is by no means suited to your best thought, and you are quite as much at sea in your mythology

as Jason was. You can do, have done and must do better."
Harte was, he said, seldom that impatient with him.[13]

Another young writer who moved into the Harte orbit
then — she was twenty-three years old to Stoddard's twenty-
one and Harte's twenty-eight — was the attractive, intelligent and graceful Ina Coolbrith. She alone of the young
luminaries of the sixties was to stay in San Francisco and endure as a sort of beacon light on Russian Hill; during the
eighty-seven years of her life she spanned most of the city's
artistic development, was Bierce's protégé as well as Harte's,
and in turn was the first to give a boost to young Jack London. As a still bright-eyed octogenarian in the 1920's she
would recall at meetings of the California Literary Society:

I was remembering yesterday what handsome men lived in San
Francisco in the old days. It was hard to tell whether Frank Harte
or Charlie Stoddard was the better-looking, and Joaquin Miller
was quite striking with his curly brown hair. Mark Twain had
an interesting face, but he was not as handsome as he was later.
What a glorious time I used to have matching limericks with
Frank — that's what we always called Bret Harte — or joshing
with Mark Twain, who was just a lanky, red-headed journalist
when he was working for the *Call* . . . we were never afraid of
life in those days, you know. . . .[14]

Tall, slender as a willow, with dark hair and large candid
gray eyes, she became a sort of sister-confessor and platonic
sweetheart of the group that formed with Bret Harte as its
nucleus. Unlike the verse of most poetesses of her day, Ina's
was cool and austere and dignified; she had learned through
bitter emotional experience to distrust the wilder passions. A
descendant of Joseph Smith, the founder of the Mormon
Church, she had crossed the Sierra in her infancy with the

first wagon train. Her widowed mother, determined to erase memories of the persecution of the Mormons, took Ina to Los Angeles. At seventeen she contracted a disastrous marriage with one Robert Carsley that ended in the divorce court after three hectic years. Then she came up to San Francisco, stayed there for the rest of her life, and as one literary historian wrote "wielded an influence on western letters that went far beyond her own writings." Not the least of her contributions in that line was made, twenty-odd years after she first met Bret Harte, when she was head librarian at the Oakland Public Library and a ten-year-old starveling named Jack London attracted her attention by his precocious appetite for reading. She steered him to the novels of Flaubert, Tolstoy, Melville and Dostoievsky, encouraged his ambitions to become a writer and was credited by him in after years with having made possible his meteoric career.[15]

As Twain later wrote, the *Californian* "circulated among the highest class of the community" and for a time it looked as though the periodical might succeed in its professed ambitions to equal or surpass the *Atlantic Monthly* and other Eastern magazines and to bring a new urbanity to the Western literary world. Webb, however, was an erratic fellow when it came to editorial responsibilities, more a witty paragrapher and bon vivant than a discoverer of talent (Twain, Stoddard and Coolbrith being Harte's finds) or a diligent administrator. Perhaps if his absences had been more frequent and prolonged the *Californian* would have fared better.

Bret wisely clung to his sinecure at the mint while producing as much copy as possible for the weekly. He still concentrated on light verse, satires and parodies, sketches on metropolitan life — his more carefully wrought short stories were still a few years in the offing. In "The Petroleum Fiend" he made fun of the first oil discoveries, and in "The Devil and the Broker" delivered a light-hearted cautionary against speculating in wildcat mining promotions. The back pages of the *Californian*, despite its avowed intent of seeking out originality, were usually stuffed with serialized novels, often translated from the French, and generally of indifferent quality. Most issues, too, were padded out with material reprinted from other journals. The *Californian*, almost from the first, tended to slip into the catchall, grab-bag style which would prove fatal both to it and the *Golden Era*. It was not, however, so foolishly hospitable to the gushier sort of women writers.

During this period one catches only an occasional glimpse of Bret's domestic life as retailed by his contemporaries. His growing attachment to Ina Coolbrith — undoubtedly platonic though it was — indicated that his wife Anna did not entirely satisfy whatever he needed from the other sex. Nobody, in that discreet day, ever suggested that his eye wandered for more than a flickering instant. Soon enough, though, he was spending long hours at Ina Coolbrith's flat on Russian Hill — usually with Stoddard or someone else also present — drinking tea, gossiping, even helping Ina with such chores as shelling peas.

His second son, Francis King Harte, was born in 1865, and there is no doubt whatever that, in those days, he was a fond and indulgent father. His oldest son soon was calling him "Bret." [16] He loved to play with his two sons, according to his partner Webb's recollection; one of his favorite games with Griswold was to lie on the floor, flat on his back, and toss the boy in the air with his feet, "turning the little fellow over like a butter-ball, and making him throw all sorts of somersets [somersaults] and handsprings. A summary stop was put to the amusement when Mrs. Bret entered the room, and, from the rapidity with which the curtain fell on the performance, I've an idea that she does not wish to see her children made a circus of." [17]

Few envied Bret in his role as a husband. In the published recollections of his male friends, she is rarely, and then only glancingly, mentioned. The women who knew the Hartes were more outspoken in their dislike of Anna, largely on grounds that she did not appreciate the fact that her husband was a man of artistic rank and should be treated accordingly. Ina Coolbrith's rather chilly appraisal of Mrs. Harte was that she had a nice voice but wasn't very attractive. One of Bret's female associates wrote that "Mrs. Harte never seemed a lovable woman to me. There was a morose, stubborn expression on her face which invited neither cordiality nor sympathy; and when she put her foot down her husband had to 'toe the mark.' More than once did she interfere with arrangements he was trying to make, and prevent him from writing what he had pledged himself to write." [18]

Among their friends it was well known that, lordly as Bret's demeanor could be outside the home, inside it he lived in Anna's shadow. He was anything but the Victorian papa whose wife and children tiptoed around him. The autocrat of the breakfast table was Mrs. Harte. He was, in short, a henpecked husband who increasingly sought refuge from domestic tyranny at his office, in the Mercantile Library or Miss Coolbrith's cozy flat overlooking the Bay; it would be years before he managed to find more efficacious means of escape.

The war had ended, the Union was preserved, and Bret had paid eloquent tribute to the slain Lincoln.

No other public man seems to me to have impressed his originality so strongly upon the people as did Abraham Lincoln. His person and peculiar characteristics were the familiar and common property of the Nation. In his character and physique the broad elements of a Western civilization and topography seem to have been roughly thrown together. . . . Even as the martyrdom of this great and good man brought him down to the level of the humblest soldier who died upon the battlefield for his country, so the common sympathy of our loss has drawn us all closer together . . .

For Bret, however, the end of the year 1865 brought no sudden stillness as at Appomattox. He was embattled with the most dangerous, when aroused, species of mankind — poets who have been overlooked, ignored or found wanting.

It all started innocently enough. A bookseller with publishing ambitions, Anton Roman, suggested earlier in the year that Bret edit an anthology of California verse. There was, God knows, plenty of it to be harvested and gleaned: more poetry than gold had been washed out of the foothill diggings; every camp had its contentious and recitative bards; every periodical was crammed with their offerings.

Roman, who came down from the hills with a hundred ounces of gold dust and invested it in a stock of books, had acquired a large collection of verse clipped from various newspapers and magazines by Mary Tingley, a young Oakland woman. He proposed that Miss Tingley's collection be used as the basis of the anthology, with other poetry to be selected and added by Harte. "We settled to our work with fatuous self-complacency," wrote Bret thirty years later, "and no suspicion of the trouble in store for us, or the storm that was presently to hurtle around our devoted heads. I winnowed the poems, and he [Roman] exploited a preliminary announcement to an eager and waiting press, and we moved together unwittingly to our doom." [19] Titled *Out-*

croppings, Being Selections of California Verse, it was sent to press for the Christmas trade. Bret's name appeared neither on the title page nor under the preface, which he wrote, acknowledging that much of the poetry had been collected by Miss Tingley and apologizing to poets whose work had not been included. It did not pretend to be definitive, nor to include all of the best that had been produced in the mining country. Its title suggested its contents: *Outcroppings*.

What cropped out, immediately on publication, was the bitterest controversy since the Bear Republic's flag was hoisted. "A beautiful bird known as the California Canary," wrote Bret sardonically, and much later, when he could afford to be sardonic, "appeared to have been shot at and winged by every poet from Portland to San Diego." [20] Almost as though anticipating controversy, Bret at the last moment contributed an anonymous review of the volume to the *Californian* in which he slyly complained that none of his own work had been included in the book, said the identity of the anthologist was unknown to all, and suggested that publication of *Outcroppings* was "premature." In the same issue, his friend Webb, as "Inigo," with even more acute forebodings about the reception of the book, announced that he was thankful that *he* hadn't edited it.[21] Their last-minute apprehensions were justified in full measure.

With more than a touch of hyperbole, the San Francisco *News Letter* told what happened when *Outcroppings* made its appearance on Anton Roman's shelves. The headline on its story of December 9 read:

A COMMOTION ON PARNASSUS

Mr. Frank Bret Harte's long-promised and much talked of book of the California poets has at last arrived in this city. Within two hours after it was known to be in town, a mob of poets, consisting of 1100 persons of various ages and colors, and of both sexes, besieged Roman's bookstore, all eager to ascertain whether they had been immortalized by Harte.

Mr. Bell, the poet of the *Elevator*, was the first who succeeded in securing a copy. But on issuing from the store, with his prize, seventeen *Flag*-poets, including eleven males and six females (four of the former being gentlemen of color) pounced upon the unfortunate . . . and captured the volume.

Meantime, an *Alta* poet, having discovered that he was left out in the cold, rushed down to Meiggs Wharf to drown himself, but upon observing the disagreeable temperature of the water, changed his mind, and concluded to abuse the heartless Harte in the newspapers instead.

On Tuesday the book arrived in San Francisco; on Thursday the news had been circulated throughout the State, and the "country poets" were in a fearful state of excitement. Yesterday it was rumored that a delegation of three or four hundred of these were coming down on the Sacramento boat, in a "fine phrensy," and swearing dire vengeance against Harte. That gentleman, by the advice of his friends, immediately repaired to the Station House, to be locked up for protection.

It may be doubted that Bret had to seek sanctuary with the police, but the editorial uprising that followed must have made it seem, for a time, a wise precaution. What particularly irked his critics was the fact that he left out the work of such temporary luminaries as Frank Soule, Joe Goodman, John R. Ridge, John Swett and others of the mining-camp school, and included that of such lilyhanded opportunists as his friends and collaborators on the *Californian*. Webb, the guzzling New Yorker, whose closest acquaintance with the mines was to lose his shirt speculating in wildcat stocks. Emily Lawson and Ina Coolbrith — *women!* And Charlie Stoddard, that willowy lad of unearthly beauty. The published

[87]

comments suggested that Bret's sole aim was to glorify his friends and denigrate, by exclusion, the crude rhymes, hasty doggerel and concealed pornography produced in the gold camps.*

The reviews ranged from the scurrilous to the calefactory. "Trash . . . most intolerable snobbery," said the *Territorial Enterprise* of Virginia City, several of those staff members were stung by exclusion from *Outcroppings*. The Gold Hill *Daily News* denounced it as "an insult to California . . . hogwash ladled out by some lop-eared Eastern apprentice." Another gold-country editor claimed that Bret had "strayed away from his parents and guardians while he was too fresh. He will not keep without a little salt." The *American Flag* declared it was "a Bohemian advertising medium for Webb, Harte & Co. As a collection of California poetry it is beneath contempt."

Even Charles H. Webb, though honored by inclusion in the volume, had his bit of fun with Bret in his column in the *Californian*. "I notice that the editor put none of his own compositions in the volume . . . making a feint of modesty. May we not say to him, 'feint, Harte, never won fair lady'?" Mark Twain, on the other hand, came to Bret's defense in the same periodical and denounced the critics, including his friends and former colleagues on the *Territorial Enterprise,* as "water-and-milk and thunder-and-earthquake poets."

Bret tried to laugh it off with an announcement that a second anthology would be published under the title *Tailings: Being Rejections of California Verse.* "We understand that 1280 copies are already spoken for — by a singular coin-

---

* Some of the verse he considered, Harte wrote later, contained "certain veiled libels and indecencies such as mark the 'first' publications on blank walls and fences of the average youth." Not unexpectedly, he also found much plagiarism in the work he examined, and some even included acrostics plugging certain patent medicines.[22]

cidence being the exact number of rejected poets." [23] He also comforted himself by observing that the heated controversy, in and out of print, caused a rush of buyers such as is rarely attracted by a slender volume of verse.

By Christmas the first and only printing was just about sold out, and after that it subsided into obscurity — where it belonged. Another volume brought out the following year, *Poetry of the Pacific*, only proved there wasn't enough worthwhile verse written between 1849 and 1864 to justify such a venture in the first place. A tempest in a chamberpot, the controversy over *Outcroppings* proved at least that literary life in California must be in a state of vigorous health to provoke it.

FIVE

The Golden Gate Trinity

BETWEEN the explosive publication of *Outcroppings* and his editorship of the new *Overland Monthly* in 1868, Bret Harte brilliantly demonstrated that it was possible to serve two or even three masters. He was promoted to a position in the United States Mint which paid him two hundred seventy dollars a month salary, a lordly compensation in those days; he continued his votive offerings to literature, and he made of journalism a substantial avocation. It was Harte the journalist who was in the ascendancy during those several years, rather than the poet and minnesinger of what he later called "an era replete with a certain heroic Greek poetry." San Francisco journalism was in a constant state of flux, with new periodicals springing up and others fading out of existence as they lost their vogue, and Bret proved himself an adept at leaping from one sinking venture to another rising one.

When the *Californian* showed signs of faltering. Bret began casting around for more suitable outlets. For some time before he stopped contributing to it in the summer of 1866, the high hopes for the *Californian* as the beacon light of Pacific Coast culture had been fading. His friend Webb was no genius at business administration, lost his money both in keeping the weekly afloat and in disastrous mining-stock speculation, and finally had to hand over control of the *Cal-ifornian*. By the summer of 1866 Webb was on his way back to New York and Bret was winding up his own association with the weekly.

Some years later Webb looked back on the experience with a rueful and sardonic eye. His contributors, it seemed to Webb, got a lot more out of the periodical than its pro-prietor.

"I was — and am — rather proud of that paper," he wrote in his memoir.

It represented considerable of my money and a good deal of my time, for all of which I had nothing to show. To the *Californian* under my management, many who have since received wide-spread reputations contributed, and it was called considerable of a paper, to be published so far away from Boston. True, the con-tributors never received much pay for their work, and no flatter-ing inducement of more was ever held out to them; but, on the other hand, they did not have to pay anything for the privilege of expressing themselves weekly, and this was a blessed immunity which never fell to my lot while owning the paper.

Bret's satiric jousting with the super-California mentality, which once threatened to rival the collective ego of Texas, appeared in the *Californian* at this time. It was occasioned by the discovery of what was termed, with considerable lo-cal pride, "the Pliocene skull." California boosters immedi-ately seized upon the discovery as evidence that aboriginal Californians had been around a lot longer than anyone else, even Bostonians.

"Doubtless," Bret predicted in the *Californian*, "the soci-ety of pioneers will claim the skull as a member."

The skull was found by a miner two hundred fifty feet down a shaft in Calaveras County. It came into the possession of a Dr. Jones, who passed it along to members of the state geological survey, which called it to the attention of Professor J. D. Whitney, whose reputation as a savant was almost as towering as the mountain peak named in his honor. Professor Whitney visited the mine shaft and rather hastily concluded, to the general delight, that the skull was that of a human being who died before the lava flowed over northern California. "This," Bret sardonically noted, "would make it antedate the mastodon, the pachyderms, and, indeed, most of the paleotheres:" The discovery — coming as it did seven years after publication of Darwin's *Origin of the Species* — hammered another nail in the coffin of organized religion, as Bret saw it. Dr. Jones, on examining the skull, was quoted as saying, "This knocks hell out of Moses!" Obviously Bret was convinced that the skull had been planted by the hoaxers who were rampant in the foothills and who spent more time in confounding the sober-minded than in honest effort.

Professor Whitney, however, insisted on reading a paper on the subject before the more or less learned California Academy of Natural Sciences, which had been far from hoax-proof in the past. He solemnly outlined the possibility that the skull changed all previous conceptions of mankind's history on earth. Two weeks after that lecture, Bret laughed the skull into obscurity with his verses "To the Pliocene Skull," in which he identified it as belonging to that western Everyman, "Joe Bowers of Pike," whose "crust was busted falling down a shaft in Calaveras County" and who posthumously begged those who were pawing over his noggin to "send the pieces home to old Missouri." San Francisco rocked with laughter, but there were many who thought that Bret was verging on the sacrilegious in poking fun at everything not-quite-native sons were inclined to hold dear.

After that parting fusillade in verse and prose, he contributed to a variety of journals. He was appointed Western correspondent for the Boston *Christian Register*, a Unitarian organ, and the Springfield *Republican*, then one of the most prestige-laden newspapers on the continent, under the crusty editorship of Samuel Bowles. He also contributed to various San Francisco newspapers. In 1867, the following year, he was further heartened by the publication of the first two books in which his work was collected. The prose volume, *Condensed Novels and Other Papers*, was published by Carleton in the fall of 1867. A collection of original verse, *The Lost Galleon and Other Tales*, was brought out a few weeks later by Towne & Bacon. Both the critical reception and the sales records indicated a polite interest in "F. Bret Harte," as he then signed himself. *Condensed Novels* sold out its first (and only) printing almost immediately, but the royalty return to Bret, at ten cents a copy, was less than a month's pay from his administrative job at the mint.

In addition to some of the "Bohemian Papers" and several other sketches and stories, *Condensed Novels* consisted of the fifteen parodies of well-known contemporary novels which had appeared in *Golden Era* and the *Californian*. The works he "condensed" were those of Dickens, Marryat, Charlotte Brontë, Dumas, Wilkie Collins, Bulwer, Hugo, Cooper and T. S. Arthur (*Ten Nights in a Barroom*). Since, like most Western writers, he kept one hopeful eye fixed on Boston for signs of approval, he must have been pleased with the *Atlantic Monthly*'s description of the parodies as "charming." Actually Bret's takeoffs indicated mastery of a minor but difficult literary form; he had the rare ability of dissecting an author's style without undue cruelty or ridicule, of conveying his essentials in the space of a few pages.

As for *The Lost Galleon*, its collection of verse published in various periodicals — all of it Bret's — was received with less of the fury which had greeted *Outcroppings*. One reviewer charged that the only worthwhile pieces were those Bret had plagiarized from his betters, and other commentators must have irked him by dwelling at length on the beauty of the binding and printing job the publishers did on the volume, but at least there were no suggestions that the author be tarred and feathered.

During 1867 Bret also contributed to the San Francisco *News Letter*, a free-swinging satirical weekly which allowed him to conduct further onslaughts on the California boosterism then growingly prevalent. It was less than a score of years since the Forty-niners had landed, yet already they were being canonized, glamorized and bowdlerized. There was no finer accolade than to be designated an "oldtimer," an "Argonaut," a "pioneer." Bret thought it a shoddy legend, not only false but falsely sentimental. The Forty-niners, he maintained, were not a company of heroes and saints but "blanked fools who landed here when the water came up to Montgomery Street." And in his correspondence to the *Christian Register* he declared, "The less said about the motives of some of our pioneers the better; very many were more concerned with getting away from where they were, than in going to any particular place." What impressed Bret Harte most about those early-comers to the foothills was their crudity, brutality and sheer oafishness. Nor could he see anything glamorous about the Western outlaw, the good-badman, who was already becoming a staple in popular fiction of the pre-Buntline era. He created his own frontier badman in "Sylvester Jayhawk" after reading *The Life and Confessions of James Gilbert Jenkins, the Murderer of Eighteen Men*, published just after the purported author was hanged for his careless attitude toward human life.

"Sylvester Jayhawk," as the first of a series to be entitled

Popular Biographies: Self-Made Men of Our Day, was a parody of the outlaw glorification which was soon to become a sizable industry under the deft hands of Ned Buntline, Prentiss Ingraham and other pseudonymous practitioners. Sylvester ran away from his Kansas home after killing a Negro slave out of boyish high spirits. "With no other property than a knife and a pistol, he early faced the cold world and began his career." A parting present from his mother was a deck of cards, which some people may have thought a curious gesture, but "who can fathom the mysterious logic of a mother's heart?" Sylvester began exercising his talent for homicide in California. "The removal of several employes of the Overland Mail Company along the line, the quiet absorption of valuable mail-matter, the permanent withdrawal of stock from different stations alone marked his progress." Later he moved to Virginia City and ran up his score to twenty-nine fatalities. As he explained to his biographer, "I had killed twenty-nine men up to the fall of 1860; I wanted to finish the year with an even number. So I killed a man keerlessly and without forethought." Thus, said his biographer, "a brilliant future was destroyed in a moment of unguarded enthusiasm." It was a lesson to be pondered by all who followed in Sylvester's footsteps. "Mr. Jayhawk, though he never married, left a large family to mourn his loss." [1]

It was not until a year or two later that Bret came to the realization that by viewing and recapturing the gold-rushers, including the hapless Sylvester Jayhawks, in a more mellow afterglow he might enthrall a sizable national and international readership, which cared less about abrasive reality than a good story with mostly lovable characters. Sentiment, he would realize, has always paid more grocer's bills than satire.

In his contributions to the *News Letter* Bret was allowed

to lampoon everything in striking distance, even that violent pride of origin which characterized the numerous Irish in northern California. He described the celebration of St. Patrick's Day in Slumgullion Center at which the Irish boasted of their love of liberty and freedom just after beating up a Negro and chasing several Chinese out of town. He also paraphrased the Fenian slogan to read, "Ireland for the Irish, America for the Naturalized, and Hell for Niggers and Chinese."

And his satirical whip flicked at the equally sacred topics of the California climate and the widely advertised, "health-giving" waters of the northern California spas. The waters, he wrote, were given their unique flavor by a mixture of broken soda-water bottles, poisoned gophers and rusting mule shoes, and added, "The patients who most profit by the water are those of enfeebled intellect." Those who boasted that California's climate approximated the Elysian ideal could only have been discomfited by an ode whose final paragraph read:

> *Then fly with me, love, ere the summer's begun,*
> *And the mercury mounts to one hundred and one;*
> *Ere the grass now so green shall be withered and sere,*
> *In the spring that obtains but one month of the year.*[2]

No greater literary gap could have existed, in fact, than that between his satirical verse and prose in the *News Letter* and earlier in the *Californian*, which lashed at everything the Forty-niners and the California boosters valued, and the sentimental, romantic approach of his short stories a year later.

His change of approach came about largely through the

establishment of the *Overland Monthly*, which was to attain a national standing through his skill as an editor and through the rocket-like success of the stories he contributed to it. Anton Roman, the bookseller who had published *Outcroppings*, decided to publish the new magazine early in 1868, just about the time the *Californian* was expiring.[3] A shrewd and energetic man, Roman evidently realized that a new and more popular approach to magazine publishing was needed; that the needling and joshing attitude of the San Francisco weeklies was too negative to capture a large audience, and that a more positive editorial stance, glorifying the California past and enthusing over its future, would attract both readers and advertisers. As he stated in his prospectus, the *Overland Monthly* would offer a sympathetic examination of manners and aspirations in the Golden West. It was the businesslike Roman who grasped the fact that "near the end of its frontier days, the West, having passed from naïveté to satire, reached the stage in which its early days became romantic," as Professor Franklin Walker has written.[4] By offering a readership a periodical that could become nationally a sort of West Coast counterpart of the *Atlantic Monthly*, Roman would be credited with concocting the strategy of the *Overland Monthly*'s success while Bret Harte was responsible for the issue-to-issue tactics.

Initially neither Roman nor Harte was eager to resume the publishing-editing association which had been marked by the uproar over *Outcroppings*. The intermediary between them was Charles Warren Stoddard. As Roman later recalled, "My only objection to Harte at that time was that he would be likely to lean too much to the purely literary articles, while what I was aiming at was a magazine that would help the material development of the Coast." Stoddard, however, persuaded him that Harte was the only man capable of editing a magazine that might reach beyond the Rockies for attention.

Now Roman had to convince Harte that he was the man for the job. Bret wasn't at all sure that the *Overland* could succeed where so many other periodicals had failed after a few years. He also suspected that he might be called upon to contribute much of the editorial matter since there was no great number of local writers who could supply the quality of poetry and prose both he and Roman believed essential. But the thing that seemed to trouble him most was the proposed magazine's financial prospects.

On the latter point Roman was able to reassure him immediately, showing him pledges of advertising support totaling nine hundred dollars a month and guaranteeing that the magazine would have a minimum circulation of three thousand copies. Finally Bret said he would accept Roman's offer on condition that he have complete editorial control, that no contributions be signed, and that two assistant editors be attached to the staff, Noah Brooks of the *Alta* and W. C. Bartlett of the *Bulletin*, both of them experienced journalists who would relieve him of the more tedious editorial chores.

The bargain struck, Roman and Harte decided to bring out their first issue in July. That gave them April, May and June to make preparations for the event. Much of that time — which Bret took off from his sinecure at the mint, a post to which he clung until the summer of the following year — the two men spent, together with both their families, in San Jose and in a remote camp in the Santa Cruz Mountains. They formulated their plans for the first issues, and even more importantly Roman argued Harte around to his way of thinking on the subject of the social history of the gold rush. The pioneers, Roman insisted, must be idealized, must be made more palatable than the unwashed, uncouth, intemperate ruffians and illiterates the literary sophisticates had been caricaturing.

The classic fruition of Roman's arguments, though undoubtedly they were motivated principally by the publisher's determination to produce a magazine which would attract advertising and circulation in a profitable volume, was Bret's first great short story, "The Luck of Roaring Camp." Bret outlined it while the Hartes and the Romans were camping in the mountains, read parts of it aloud over the campfire, and kept polishing away at it until it was ready for the magazine's second issue. He labored over it with a lapidary insistence on perfection because the story actually was supposed to lead off the first issue, but he wouldn't let it out of his hands until he was certain it couldn't be improved.

The appearance of the first issue on July 1 in its drab brown cover created no great stir in either San Francisco or the hinterland. Among its offerings were articles titled "Art Beginnings on the Pacific" and "By Rail Through France," other travel sketches of Mexico and Hawaii, a sprinkling of poetry, a number of book reviews and a back-of-the-book section containing editorial comment and titled *Etc*. Its contents could have been lifted out of any number of Eastern magazines; the kindliest critic could have said no more of it than that it was a fair imitation of the *Atlantic Monthly*. The most striking feature of the first issue, in fact, was the grizzly bear, one paw planted between railroad tracks, which snarled at readers from its title page. (The completion of the first transcontinental railroad, with the Central Pacific and the Union Pacific finally linking up May 10, 1869, was expected to bring immigrants by the hundreds of thousands to the Pacific states.) Originally, according to Mark Twain, only the bear, California's sacred emblem ever since the days of the

Bear Republic, had appeared on the title drawing. Somehow that menacing beast didn't present the proper image, and worse yet he was meaningless. At various editorial conferences it was argued that the bear ought to be dropped or replaced. "But presently," according to Twain, "Harte took a pencil and drew those two simple lines under his feet and behold he was a magnificent success! — the ancient symbol of California savagery snarling at the approaching type of high and progressive Civilization, the first Overland locomotive!" Never one to lavish praise on Bret Harte, Twain declared it "the prettiest fancy and the neatest that ever shot through Harte's brain." [5]

Actually, of course, the "prettiest fancy" of Bret's creative mind showed up in the *Overland*'s Volume I, Number 2, when the populace of Roaring Camp paraded across the magazine's pages. The moment proofsheets of "The Luck of Roaring Camp" were struck it became involved in controversy. Now considered almost too tame for inclusion on high school reading lists, it seemed daringly realistic in the summer of 1868. After all, the "Luck" of the title was the illegitimate son of a camp follower named Cherokee Sal, who died in childbirth. The characters were profane and ruffianly. The only thing that could have made it palatable to the mid-Victorian reader was that its theme was, biblically enough, "A little child shall lead them"; that a bunch of loose-living characters in a remote mining camp were regenerated, and were rewarded by prosperity, through the communal decision to rear the child born in their midst in more proper surroundings. The story would have been unbearably bathetic except for Bret's skill at blending in humor with pathos in the proportions formulated by Dickens — one part humor to two parts pathos — and found to be exactly to the public's taste in the latter decades of the nineteenth century.

Moralistic as was its theme, "The Luck of Roaring Camp" caused a commotion in the editorial offices of the *Overland* on the Plaza. First a proofreader named Sarah B. Cooper revolted. Miss Cooper announced that her sense of decency would not allow her to be responsible for certifying the galleys. She was shocked at the idea of a soiled dove such as Cherokee Sal appearing in the pages of a respectable journal, and according to Charles Warren Stoddard was "revolted at the unaccustomed combination of mental force, virility and originality." The controversy spread to the business and editorial offices, where other staff members professed themselves also shocked by the repeated answering of Kentuck, tenderly bemused by the fact that the baby bit his finger— "The d——d little cuss!"

Bret's reaction to the brouhaha was anger and indignation at the challenge to his editorial authority. According to Stoddard, he considered that his good taste and judgment had been "impeached," and threatened to resign if "The Luck of Roaring Camp" didn't appear in the August issue. He was not at all swayed by the opinion of his valued assistant Noah Brooks that the story might dissuade people from migrating to California.[6]

Publisher Roman, who had encouraged Bret to write the story and considered it a masterpiece, naturally sided with Bret — and thus the first and only mutiny against his authority was quelled. The incident, however, was not soon forgotten by its centerpiece. If the majority opinion in the offices of the *Overland Monthly* had prevailed, "The Luck of Roaring Camp" might not have been published; the *Overland* itself probably would not have caught on, and Bret's career might never have ascended from the level of a polite dabbler in letters, a man who wrote graceful bits and pieces. Certainly he did not forget Miss Sarah Cooper's protest against soiling her hands on its galleys. One of his co-workers, Josephine Clifford, recalled in later years that "kind, amiable and yielding as he could be, there was a singular tenacity of purpose in him when it came to a matter of any dislike he had once taken." This dislike, she said, was extended in full measure to Miss Cooper when she gave up proofreading for writing.

The lady was active in church and Sunday school circles, and she later prepared a number of papers on "Childhood," "Womanhood," "Motherhood," and kindred topics, and about once a month she would offer her manuscript to the editor of the *Overland* . . . Bret Harte always went through the same routine. The lady would hand him her manuscript; he would look at the title, return it with a polite bow, and say: "I will not trouble you to leave the manuscript; I am not publishing a Sunday school paper; I am publishing the *Overland Monthly*.[7]

The initial reception of "The Luck of Roaring Camp" — a trailblazer both in the development of the short story and in promoting the "regional" writing which subsequently added so much indigenous color and variety to American literature — was highly dubious. California did not immediately take it to its bosom but generally was repelled. Many California readers, Noah Brooks noted, "frantically excommunicated it, and anathematized it as the offspring of evil." With a few exceptions, the local press denounced it as dangerous to public morality. "Christians were cautioned against pollution by its contact; practical business men were gravely urged to condemn and frown upon this picture of California society that was not conducive to Eastern immigration," as Bret himself recorded.

It took weeks for the steamer to convey copies of the August *Overland* to the Eastern cities, the verdict of which, undoubtedly, Bret awaited with much more hope and trepidation than that of his local contemporaries, from whom he had learned to expect little in the way of praise. The verdict was overwhelming; "The Luck of Roaring Camp" was a brilliant success in the East, and the enthusiasm with which it was received in New York and Boston, Bret said, "half frightened its author." Bret was acclaimed as a new Dickens; his story was picked up and reprinted countless times. Not the least of the tributes came from the Boston publishers, Fields, Osgood & Co., who put out the *Atlantic Monthly*. The firm's letter was addressed to the "Author of 'The Luck of Roaring Camp,'" since the story was unsigned like all other contributions to the *Overland*. Fields, Osgood & Co. wanted him to turn out a similar story for the *Atlantic Monthly* as soon as possible.

Thereupon California saw the light, reread the story and rejoiced that literary genius had been discovered in its midst.

Seldom has one story, running a few thousand words, created such a sensation, made such a reputation for its author and lifted him from regional obscurity to national fame. In that story and the seven others which followed it into the columns of the *Overland Monthly* Bret Harte created a fictional world, robustly peopled and vividly described, as new and shining as the silver cartwheels which came out of the United States Mint. In a day when writers spread themselves at enormously self-indulgent length, Bret told his story with an economy and precision that were almost breathtaking. Briefly and vividly he created a believable world of mining camps perched in the foothills in which, beneath red flannel shirts and long underwear, there were men of good heart, and sinners could paradoxically become saint-like, and whores, undone by a sudden acquaintance with virtue and charity, could blush beneath their painted cheeks. Even Californians afflicted with the most virulent boosterism could see that, viewed through the eyes of outlanders, Bret's mining-camp world might, for all its surface rashness, seem glamorous and attractive: it was the birth of Western legend, which would grow but never essentially change from the stereotype Bret Harte presented to posterity.

Nor, having found his successful formula, would Bret ever advance in any significant way from the writer he was in 1868, when he was thirty-two years old. He had the capacity but somehow lacked the initiative for change, for growth and experiment. If he had died one year after the publication of "The Luck of Roaring Camp," his reputation would have been as secure as it was with his death thirty-four years later. He became the prisoner of his own success. The reasons for that lack of venturesomeness perhaps could be found in the listless passivity of his youth, in his fatalistic acceptance of an unhappy marriage and the humiliations of being publicly domineered by his wife. Somehow he suffered from low blood pressure of the psyche. There is no reason to doubt that he was "half frightened" by the prospect of fame, with all the demands it could make upon him; he hated the mob and the marketplaces it frequented. The mild, the tepid, the cozy had the greatest of attractions for him. He would have liked his recognition in small, regular doses. Instead it struck him like a thunderclap, and he never knew quite what to make of it.

So predictability became the safest as well as the easiest course. The warp of sentiment interwoven with the woof of humor. He did it so neatly and gracefully, as when he described the contributions made by the miners of Roaring Camp to the welfare fund collected for the little bastard born in their midst:

A silver tobacco box; a doubloon; a Navy revolver, silver mounted; a gold specimen; a very beautifully embroidered lady's handkerchief (from Oakhurst the gambler) a diamond breastpin; a diamond ring (suggested by the pin, with the remark that he "saw that pin and went two diamonds better"); a slung shot; a Bible (contributor not detected); a golden spur; a silver teaspoon (the initials, I regret to say, were not the giver's); a pair of surgeon's shears; a lancet; a Bank of England note for £5; and about $200 in loose gold and silver coin.

Even as he worked away at this profitable vein, following up the success of "The Luck of Roaring Camp" with "The Outcasts of Poker Flat" and "Tennessee's Partner," he did not allow himself to slip into the hack writer's quick and easy methods. Publishers could clamor for the product of his pen but he would turn it over only when he was satisfied that it was the best work he was capable of doing. If he wrote within a tight framework, it was all the more necessary to make his miniatures accurate to the meticulous detail, even though he had to ask Noah Brooks to help him figure out how the snowbound "Outcasts of Poker Flat" could live on a half-sack of flour and six pounds of bacon.* Brooks said that Bret was the most "fastidious" and "laborious" writer he had ever known.[8]

Once when he was raking Charles Warren Stoddard over the coals for a slipshod manuscript the latter had submitted, Stoddard tried to distract him by remarking that he had just met a man who claimed he had wept over something Harte wrote.

"He had a right to," Bret snapped. "I wept when I wrote it!"[9]

* Apparently Bret was unwilling to trust Brooks's estimate, because in the final draft of "Outcasts" he did not state exactly how much flour and bacon they had, except that there was "an extra mule loaded with provisions."

In the fall of 1868 began the two most fruitful and prosperous years of Bret's life. He was one of the town's celebrities. Elegantly dressed, he was pointed out wherever he
went. Visiting Easterners were as eager for a glimpse of him
as of the Golden Gate or the notorious depravities of the
Barbary Coast. To his great annoyance people even asked for
his autograph. When the California theater, built by the
flamboyant banker William C. Ralston, opened on the night
of January 16, 1869, Bret was naturally called upon to grace
the occasion. The boxes were thronged with the beauty and
chivalry of the booming city. The famous actors Lawrence
Barrett and John McCullough acted as hosts, but Bret was
the star of the evening as he appeared on stage to read a six-
stanza poem he had written for the occasion.

Famous he undoubtedly was, but popularity was something else. Beloved and adored in his small circle of friends,
he was a bit too aloof, fastidious and disdainful to attract a
nimbus of well-wishers. Many resented his ostentation as he
strode down Montgomery Street in a bulky coat with an
astrakhan collar suitable for a Russian impresario. Others
couldn't help but resent it that a fellow who had been a mere
printer a few years ago should now be swanking it. Some
claimed that after the success of "The Luck of Roaring
Camp" he had fallen into the habit of "cutting" acquaintances of lesser importance. Yet when Thomas D. Beasley met
him at the height of his fame Bret, he wrote, seemed "singularly modest and utterly devoid of any form of affectation.
To be well dressed in a period when little attention was paid
to clothes by San Franciscans might . . . in some men have
suggested an assumption of superiority; but with Mr. Harte
to dress well was simply a natural instinct." [10]

The envy of many of his fellow writers was also evident.
The fact that he held down the sinecure at the mint even

while earning a fairly good salary as editor of the *Overland* and additional amounts as a writer, meanwhile nobbling whatever other plums fell his way, did not endear him to the members of a notoriously ill-paid profession. Nor was he always at his gentlest and most tactful in rejecting their manuscripts. Walt Whitman's "Passage to India" was rejected with what was described as a "very curt" letter. Joaquin Miller, "the Sweet Singer of the Sierras," also learned that Bret could be harsh with poetic sensibilities.

Miller was easily the most picturesque figure who ever stomped through the San Francisco literary world. His sense of showmanship was nothing less than gorgeous, his whole life a production which unfortunately antedated Cinemascope and stereophonic sound. The generally successful image he projected with bottomless energy in San Francisco and later in the drawing rooms of Pre-Raphaelite London was that of a frontiersman (he dressed in buckskins, boots and a bearskin flung cape-like around his shoulders) who had through native genius become a poet.

Singularly unimpressed by the vaudeville act, not to mention the chromatic splendors of his verse, was Bret Harte. Their eventual feud was one of the livelier topics of literary gossip, predestined by their clashing personalities and their rival claims to being the true spokesman for the California of the glorious past. Undoubtedly it was first sparked when Miller sent Harte a copy of his privately printed volume of poems, *Joaquin et al.*, and also submitted two poems for publication in the *Overland Monthly*. Naturally, he hoped Harte would review the volume in his magazine.

Harte's reply was later characterized by Miller as "a savage little letter," which turned down the poems he submitted and suggested it would be better if *Joaquin et al.* weren't subjected to public criticism.

[107]

Actually the letter included constructive and sensible criticism which Miller might well have taken to heart. Miller's choice of subjects in his poetry, Bret wrote, seemed to "foster and develop a certain theatrical tendency and feverish exaltation, which would be better under restraint . . . I see nothing in you worse than faults of excess, which you can easily check by selecting less emotional themes for your muse . . . The best thing in 'Peccavi' is the quietest — the very felicitous and natural lie at its close. The rest is ecstasy . . ." As for *Joaquin et al.*, Bret suggested, "Let this informal and well-meaning attempt at criticism take the place of a notice in the 'O.M.' " [11]

Miller not only considered the letter tactless and brutal but insisted, in further correspondence, that he wanted Bret to review his volume of poetry. The review appeared in the *Etc.* department at the back of the *Overland Monthly*, had a few kind words for Miller's natural talent for verse, but also observed that he was given to florid dramatics, "and at such times his neck is generally clothed with thunder, and the glory of his nostrils is terrible." The phrase described so exactly Miller's purplish passions when in the throes of composition that the poet never quite lived it down and even in old age, when he had set himself up as the white-bearded patriarch of Pacific letters, he would sputter with rage at the mention of his critic's name.

Nonliterary sensibilities were also abraided by Bret in his role of editor of the *Overland*. The monthly had been founded by his friend Roman with the pledge that it would promote the development of San Francisco and its hinterland. Yet Bret often insisted on being a knocker rather than a booster. In the *Etc.* department he would refer to contemporary architecture as "Union Pacific Renaissance." He attacked that growingly influential and nostalgic organization the Society of California Pioneers; what was really needed, he said, was a Society for the Suppression of Local Pride. He also published an article by J. W. Watkins, one of the *News Letter's* more effective gadflies, in which San Francisco was arraigned in the bluntest terms. Watkins insisted that the city was badly constructed, its foggy climate less than salubrious, its attitude far from progressive, liberal or tolerant, its citizenry — this may have been the unkindest cut to a people already priding themselves on their cosmopolitanism — smugly provincial. He noted that capital invested in the city often paid little or nothing in return, and indicated that San Francisco's chief claim to municipal fame was that its citizens went mad or killed themselves more frequently than those of other cities.

Certainly the publication of "The Outcasts of Poker Flat" in the *Overland Monthly's* January 1869 issue was not calculated to improve the raffish image projected in Bret's earlier story, even though it increased the *Overland's* prestige as a literary organ and its author's reputation as a master of the short story. The outcasts driven from Poker Flat included Jack Hamlin, a part-Indian gambler; The Duchess, a young whore; Mother Shipton, an old whore, and Uncle Billy, "a suspected sluice-robber and confirmed drunkard." Was that sordid company supposed to represent a microcosm of the California frontier? Did it really help boost California very much that, in the end, the gambler and the two prostitutes sacrificed themselves to give two innocents who had stumbled into the snowbound camp a chance for survival?

The businessmen upon whom the *Overland's* publisher must depend for advertising contracts could not have been greatly comforted by Bret Harte's personal success, which was so resounding that in homes across the nation people read his stories aloud and that its echo swiftly reached England, where a dying Charles Dickens went to the trouble of sending for copies of the *Overland* which contained "The Luck of Roaring Camp" and "The Outcasts of Poker Flat."

A friend said that he had rarely seen Dickens so "honestly moved" by another man's work. Dickens, in fact, was so impressed that he wrote Bret inviting him to stay with him if and when he came to England. By the time Bret received the letter, however, news had come of Dickens's death.*

By that time Bret Harte was the youngish doyen of the city's literary Establishment. The two persons closest to him were Ina Coolbrith and Charles Warren Stoddard. Together they regarded the *Overland Monthly*, though they owned not a share of its stock, as their own personal mouthpiece, a matter of growing resentment to publisher Roman. The only three keys to the editorial offices on Clay Street were kept in their possession.

So cozy and exclusive was the partnership, so we-happy-few the attitude they presented toward outsiders, that they were mockingly canonized by other writers as "The Golden Gate Trinity."

They spent long afternoons lounging, joking, gossiping, making up limericks, drinking tea in Bret's office or Miss Coolbrith's flat on Russian Hill. Occasionally an outsider would be permitted to join the mutual admiration society, Mark Twain if he happened to be passing through town, assistant editors Brooks and Bartlett, Clarence King, Prentice Mulford or Josephine Clifford, who was Bret's protégé and confidante at the office. In later years Ina said her feelings toward Harte and Stoddard were sisterly and platonic, but

---

* Of which Bret wrote in an *Overland* editorial in the July 1870 issue: "Of his humanity it is pleasant now to think. He was an optimist, without the disadvantage also of being a philosopher . . . in his tender and human pictures of classes on whom the world hitherto had bestowed but scant sentiment, was he truly great. He brought the poor nearer our hearts."

she would add that if she had ever thought of marrying again it would have been someone like Bret, witty, amiable and handsome, with a touch of distinction now that streaks of gray were beginning to appear at his temples.

Ten years after his death she would write the most moving of tributes, two stanzas of which were:

> *The magic of his wizard pen*
> *Still holds the world in thrall;*
> *From lordly laurels won of men*
> *No leaf may fade or fall . . .*

> *The great Sierras piercing blue*
> *Of sky with snowy crest,*
> *He knew and loved them best they knew,*
> *They* know, *and love him best . . .*

Bret himself was probably never closer to anyone in the literary world than the other two members of the "Trinity." Ina's Brontësque verse was adjudged the best appearing in the *Overland*, and the frail, dreamy-eyed Stoddard's "Chumming with a Savage," based on his Hawaiian travels, created almost as great a sensation as Bret's short stories. After the publication of that piece, Bret told Stoddard, "Now you have struck it. Keep on this vein and presently you will have enough to fill a volume and you can call it South Sea Bubbles!" In their company he could be himself — and it was a charming, graceful, companionable self that few other persons more than glimpsed.

His office and Miss Coolbrith's flat continued to serve as refuges from domestic tyranny. He was fearfully faithful to Anna, he was a devoted father, but his home, from available testimony, was not a happy one. The Hartes were living across the Bay in San Rafael because Anna's parents had moved there and she liked the suburban atmosphere, inconvenient though it was for Bret. His home life was not serene, according to Josephine Clifford, who helped out around the *Overland* office after the magazine began publishing her realistic sketches of the life of an army officer's wife at frontier outposts, and who occasionally consoled Bret on his domestic tribulations along with Hattie Dolson, who had succeeded to the position of proofreader.

"Miss Dolson," Josephine Clifford wrote years later,

was a very capable woman with rather advanced ideas, in whose judgment Harte placed unreserved confidence, though she was only from New York, not from Boston. Not only did she give advice on matters pertaining to the magazine, but she advised him, one day, not to allow himself to be guided, ruled over and dictated to by his wife . . .

One day in the Clay Street office . . . Miss Dolson told him, bluntly and plainly, that it was absurd in him to give up to his wife in everything, to the detriment of his own interests and against his own better judgment. His answer was:

"I don't care about making points; when it comes to anything of importance you will find that I get my own way." *

Miss Clifford, however, was unable to discern any point of contention which Bret thought it important enough to impose his will on Mrs. Bret.

The pleasant, easygoing atmosphere of the *Overland*'s editorial rooms was frequently disrupted by the imperious descents of Anna Harte bristling with wifely authority, as Miss Clifford recalled:

---

* There may have been a measure of truth in this claim, particularly regarding family finances. The records of the old First Unitarian Church — according to James deT. Abajian of the California Historical Society — show that Bret collected his wife's pay for her services as a choir singer, which continued after their marriage.

That the woman nearest him, his wife, was not always a pleasant companion for him is not a secret. Never has it been a secret since the days she was in the habit of coming to the Clay Street sanctum to order her husband for escort on a shopping expedition. It seemed so ridiculous that this high-strung, sensitive man should be at the order of a woman who seemed to share no aspiration with him, but simply regarded him as an agent for her convenience.

Bret's patience with his demanding wife was "beyond expression," Miss Clifford said. Even in the presence of strangers Mrs. Harte would "reiterate any command she laid upon him, or repeat any measure of negation she had imposed. 'Frank, you shall not do so and so'; Frank, I tell you I won't have it'; 'Frank, don't you do it' — all of which he bore as Socrates may have borne with the little infelicities of his wife's temper."

Bret's mother, who also made a habit of dropping around the *Overland*'s offices, though she had been less visibly clinging and maternal in his childhood and youth, was vigorously anti-Anna. "And what his mother told me," wrote Miss Clifford, "would explain, perhaps, what his enemies have said against him: that he was unreliable, and would fail to produce either the manuscript or the ready cash he had promised, in one direction or another." It was a curious situation indeed, the famous writer's mother airing her grievances against her daughter-in-law with two of her son's female associates; a situation which tends to develop a certain amount of sympathy for the maligned Anna.

"How my heart aches for the poor boy," Mother Harte was quoted by Miss Clifford.

They expect him to write something for the magazine every month. But how can he write? Through the day, in his office, he is always interrupted — he is never alone, and when he comes home at night, she (meaning his wife) just wears the life out of him.

He waits so pathetically till she and the children have gone to bed before he attempts to do any writing, but he gets no peace even then. It is "Frank, come to bed, the lights disturb me"; "Frank, if you don't put the light out, I'll get up again and sit down by you." And that, of course, always settled the matter. Oh, you don't know how I long to take him in my arms as I used to when he was little and always sick.

That was, said Miss Clifford, "the constant refrain of the gentle mother-heart . . . many and many a time."

In contrast, she added, Anna wore "a morose, stubborn expression on her face which invited neither cordiality nor sympathy . . . Mrs. Harte never seemed a lovable woman to me."

Out of Mrs. Harte's benumbing presence Bret's eye was inclined to rove, or, as Miss Clifford put it, "he enjoyed a bit of fun as keenly as any boy out for a holiday." Their home was located at San Rafael because Anna's parents had moved to that bayside community from New York, but occasionally it had other attractions for Bret. Among its frequent guests was

an interesting young widow of the style of drooping eyes and Madonna air. For this lady to live was to flirt, and the unfortunate fish dangling at the end of her line just then was her language teacher, a young man selected, I suspect, principally on account of his good looks . . . One day, when Mrs. Harte was absent, and there was no other figure on the chess-board to play against the language man, Harte was pressed into the service of the fair widow without ceremony. Entering into the spirit of the game at once, he applauded all the widow's views, hung upon her every word, cast angry glances at his rival, grew furious when the widow spoke to him, slipped into her white hand a bit of white paper . . . and acted the ardent lover to life.[12]

Before the first year of his editorship of the *Overland* ended, there were a number of changes in Bret's professional life. With a new administration (Grant's) entering the White House, he lost his cushy job at the Mint. Also his one-year contract with the *Overland* was expiring and a new management was taking over the magazine.

Officially Anton Roman decided to sell out because his health had declined and his physician recommended it. There was reason to suspect, however, that Roman was not entirely pleased by the way the "Golden Gate Trinity" had taken over the magazine and made it their own, a platform for the exhibition of their literary talents, when Roman had envisioned it as a medium for glorifying northern California and propagandizing on behalf of the state's brilliant commercial prospects. In a letter written more than thirty years later Roman recalled that Harte's enormous popularity had caused him to "fear that one of the main features of my plan for the *Overland Monthly* would be lost sight of. It would evolve, I apprehended, into a mainly literary magazine." When Harte decided to leave, as he eventually would, the magazine would "lose prestige" and wither away.[13] Events proved Roman to be a shrewd businessman. He sold his holdings to John H. Carmany for seventy-five hundred dollars.*

Bret came to terms quickly with the new publisher, who apparently realized that the magazine's success depended wholly upon Bret's continuance as its editor. Bret drew up an agreement which read as follows:

* His memories of Bret Harte were not particularly kindly. "He was a dandy; a dainty man, too much of a woman to rough it in the mines," he was quoted as saying in an article by Robert L. Fulton in the *Overland Monthly*, August 1915.

I will continue in the editorial charge of the *Overland Monthly* upon the following terms:

    1. That I have the exclusive control, as formerly, of its literary and critical conduct.

    2. That I shall be privileged to select and occupy, for that purpose, a private office as formerly — where rent shall not exceed thirty dollars per month chargeable to the *Overland*.

    3. That I shall receive as compensation two hundred dollars per month, payable weekly, and receive the same amount paid other contributors per page, for all contributions to the body of the magazine exclusive of Etc. and Book Reviews.

    4. That when the business or magazine shall justify the expenditure, I shall have exceptional editorial assistance.

    5. That this contract shall continue in force for one year.[14]

To supplement the income lost through the spoils-system seizure of his job at the Mint he subsequently was offered the chair of Professor of Recent Literature at the University of California in Berkeley. This post, too, was apparently a form of patronage and Bret would not have been expected to deliver much in the way of instruction. Despite the fact that a three-hundred-dollar monthly salary was attached to the offer, he turned it down on the grounds that he didn't have enough time for his writing as it was. California, though occasionally discomfited by his waspishness in print, his refusal to conform to its self-promotional standards, was eager to keep him against all temptations from the East.

He continued to attract attention to San Francisco as a cultural center with the publication of "Miggles" and "Tennessee's Partner," the latter ranking with "The Luck" and "Outcasts" in fame and quality, and would contribute four more tales to the *Overland* before his editorship ended. They struck the same artful note of tragicomedy, worked the same parallel veins of sentiment and humor. John Oakhurst and Jack Hamlin, gentlemen-gamblers, made their graceful and ironic bows; Colonel Starbottle roared on scene; Yuba Bill clowned on the box of his stagecoach; his sturdy ingenues and painted but redeemable women were becoming household figures. His stories, reprinted countless times (without compensation, thanks to the lack of copyright laws), were entertaining a nation largely dependent on reading material for escapism and amusement. While the west was still being won, half a dozen years before the showdown at the Little Big Horn, the matrix of its legend was being hammered into final shape; the Red Gulches and Sandy Bars of Bret Harte's imagined land — as mythical as Camelot or Cockaigne, as fabulous as Troy or Xanadu — were being imbedded forever in the American conscious. The changeless West in which men shot it out before breakfast, dealt out justice at the end of lynch rope, met with death or dishonor over a poker table, and struck it rich or starved to death digging for pockets of gold in the lonely hills had been created by a citified man who hated violence and risked nothing if he could help it. The wonder of it was that the country, and the world beyond, instantly recognized and seized upon Bret Harte's version of the myth they needed to account for all that had transpired since the white men began flooding across the Mississippi.

The eminent Fields, Osgood & Co. of Boston pressed him to sign a contract for publication of his stories in book form. It finally appeared early in 1870 to general acclaim, and included his first four stories in the *Overland*, "M'liss" and nine earlier sketches of life in California, under the title of *The Luck of Roaring Camp and Other Sketches*.

For all the prestige Bret was supplying as its editor and star attraction, the *Overland*, however, was not making money. The nation may have sobbed in unison over the loyalty-unto-death of "Tennessee's Partner," but it didn't put a dime into the till. Later the *Overland*'s publisher, John H. Carmany, was said to have grumbled that it cost him thirty thousand dollars to make Bret Harte famous.

SIX

Overland Monthly to Overland Express

THE way Mark Twain told it, Bret Harte was always tumbling into seriocomic predicaments, largely because of his arrogant nature. One incident related by Twain as the gospel truth, though it was probably hearsay, embellished by his vivid imagination, concerned a trip Bret made to Sacramento by riverboat. On the return trip, having forgotten to reserve a stateroom back to San Francisco, he arrived at the landing to find that a line of passengers stretching from the purser's office to the gangplank, over the levee and across the street was waiting to arrange for accommodations.

Harte elbowed his way to the head of the queue, hoping that presentation of his card to the purser would obtain one of those "half a dozen choice places always reserved to be conferred upon belated clients of distinction," since "his name and his praises were upon every lip." The purser had just informed a "vast and rugged" miner that no berths were vacant. On glancing at Harte's card, however, the purser immediately handed him a key and exclaimed, "Ah, Mr. Bret Harte, glad to see you, sir! Take the whole stateroom, sir!"

The large and truculent miner, overhearing this, "cast a scowl upon Harte which shed a twilight gloom over the whole region and frightened that author to such a degree that his key and its wooden tag rattled in his quaking hand."

Instead of repairing to his stateroom, Harte headed for the hurricane deck and hid himself behind a lifeboat until the boat cast off.

Just as he emerged from cover he came face to face with the miner whom he had hoped to avoid.

"Are you Bret Harte?" the miner demanded.

Harte, said Twain, "confessed it in a feeble voice."

"Did you write that 'Luck of Roaring Camp'?"

Harte admitted he had.

"Sure?"

"Yes."

"Son of a bitch!" the miner roared "fervently and affectionately," and added, "put it there," as he gripped Harte's hand "in his mighty talons." [1]

Hyperbole aside, it was probably a fair sample of the pangs and pleasures of celebrity Bret was experiencing at the time. That fame increased greatly in the fall of 1870 when, quite casually and without any expectation of the stir it would cause, he published sixty lines of humorous verse titled "Plain Language from Truthful James," which became more popularly known as "The Heathen Chinee." Published in the September 1870 issue of the *Overland*, it quickly established itself as the most quoted and recited verse of the post-Civil War years.

It was generally believed that the character of "Truthful James" was based on Jim Gillis, one of the brothers whom he visited briefly in the foothills, but the brothers were probably right in indignantly denying this.[2] This theory was based largely upon that visit and the fact that in one line Bret referred to "Truthful James" as living "upon the Stanislow." Actually the character, with all his contempt for veracity, was modeled after a young Münchausen of the typsesetting trade whom Bret met when he worked in the composing room of the *Golden Era*. One of his fellow printers was Jim Townsend, who was renowned as the "champion of all liars" west of the Mississippi. One expert said he was "one of the best storytellers I ever listened to." Definitely he was an oddball. He was twenty-three years old but claimed to be thirty-five and to have served in the British forces which quelled the Indian mutiny. His gift for hyperbole was given freer rein and wider circulation when he became the editor of the Homer *Index*, the pages of which were enlivened by his exaggerations. "It is so dark in the Table Mountain Tunnel," he once wrote, "that a piece of charcoal looks white." When people complained of the local prevalence of mosquitoes, Townsend consoled them in print by claiming that in Alaska the mosquitoes were so thick "you can swing a pint cup through the air and catch a quart."

"Plain Language from Truthful James" was the simple tale of a Chinese, Ah Sin, who outwitted two white gamblers at euchre, upon which Truthful James commented:

> *Which I wish to remark —*
> *And my language is plain —*
> *That for ways that are dark*
> *And for tricks that are vain,*
> *The heathen Chinee is peculiar,*
> *Which the same I would rise to explain.*

Perhaps it irked Bret all the more that the poem was so blazingly successful because it tended to confirm the prejudiced view of most people that the Chinese were notable for "ways that are dark" and "tricks that are vain." Bret had always been vigorously opposed to any form of racial prejudice and was especially, and outspokenly, disgusted by the harsh treatment of the Chinese in northern California. This undoubtedly stemmed from the brutal impression made upon him by the massacre of the Indians on Humboldt Bay, which brought to him the realization that prejudice can erupt from mere slander into mass murder. In his essay "John China-man," he had written: "I don't know what was the exact philosophy that Confucius taught, but it is to be hoped that poor John in his persecution is still able to detect the con-scious hate and fear with which inferiority always regards the possibility of even-handed justice, and which is the key-note to the vulgar clamor about servile and degraded races." [3]

Bret wrote the poem, then slipped it into a drawer and forgot about it until white space yawned in the dummy for the September issue and he sent "Plain Language from Truthful James" off to the printer to fill the hole.

Its impact was as great a surprise to the author as anyone else. Cheap reprints were sold on the streets of most cities. It was set to music. It was collected in anthologies published as far away as England and Australia. Every parlor in the coun-try echoed to recitation of its stanzas. Easterners were de-lighted with it because it depicted a couple of Western brag-garts being outslickered by a humble Oriental. Westerners were inclined to gloat over the line, the ironic implication of which they ignored or failed to grasp, "We are ruined by Chinese cheap labor," the bleat of one of the outwitted whites.

Several months after the poem's publication in San Fran-cisco, a New York newspaper described a mob scene on Broadway on New Year's Day. A crowd of hundreds "of high and low degree" had collected in front of a shop win-dow in which was displayed an illustrated version of "Plain Language from Truthful James." The newspaper account added that "In all our knowledge of New York nothing like this has ever been seen on Broadway . . . We have been obliged to produce it ['Plain Language from Truthful James'] twice in the *Globe* to answer the demands of the public, and we venture to say there is not a secular paper in the United States which has not copied it." [4]

Nothing better illustrates the freakishness of popular success than that accorded "The Heathen Chinee," or the vast ennui that greeted another "Truthful James" poem. Apparently hoping to capitalize on the success of the first, he wrote a subsequent fable in verse told by the same veracious character. It was titled "Truthful James and the Klondiker" and anticipated by many years the gold rush that was to swarm over the Yukon country. A young man who had prospected in the Klondike told his tale around a campfire "on the Stanislow":

> *He talked of snows, and of whiskey wot froze in the*
> *solidest kind of chunk,*
> *Which it took just a pound to go fairly around when*
> *the boys had a first-class drunk,*
> *And of pork that was drilled and with dynamite filled*
> *fore it would yield to a blow,*
> *For things will be strange when thermometers range to*
> *sixty degrees below.*[5]

Mining speculators would have found a lucrative tip in the prediction that there was "gold in heaps" awaiting discovery on the Klondike, but neither they nor the general public paid much attention to this second effusion from Truthful James.

At the beginning of a decade in which Emerson, Longfellow, Lowell, Dana and Holmes were still alive and producing, Bret Harte had become the most famous writer in America. Certainly not the best, nor the most distinguished, nor even the most promising, but the one whom even the semiliterate immigrant masses had heard of or listened to. And it was Truthful James's account of a three-handed game of euchre which had pushed him up past his peers and betters. Bret was not only astounded but disgusted; he thought of the poem as a bit of doggerel barely worthy of publication, and he wanted his career based on something more substantial, something that he could be proud of. Perhaps, too, he had learned to be as wary of mass popularity as he was contemptuous of mass disapproval. Afterwards he referred to it as "trash" and "the worst poem I ever wrote."

Nor did he want to be known principally as a humorist. In this his experience ran parallel to that of Mark Twain, who also wanted the weightier laurel of a "serious" writer, and who protested, when "The Celebrated Jumping Frog of Calaveras County" gained a similar notoriety, that it was a "squib" and a "villainous backwoods sketch." Both Harte and Twain apparently failed to realize that the humor they and others produced was a psychological necessity, a counterweight to the essential tragedy of frontier life. There was an even higher incidence of suicide than of homocide in the mining camps. Men had to laugh or go mad, thus the wild originality of their humor, their endless concoction of hoaxes, pranks and tall tales. In *Roughing It*, Twain gave a glimpse of the despair they combatted when he asked himself what had happened to the "young giants" he had known on the frontier. "Scattered to the ends of the earth, or prematurely aged or decrepit — or shot or stabbed in street affrays — or dead of disappointed hopes and broken hearts — all gone, or nearly all, victims devoted upon the altar of the golden calf."

In little more than a decade Bret Harte, more by luck and accident than by the long sustained intellectual labors of an Emerson, found himself one of the idols of Gilded Age America. It couldn't have happened in an earlier time; it was an indication of what kind of country this was becoming, that a few lines of humorous verse and a quartet of short stories could make their author so famous. Distrustful of mob worship as he was, Bret seemed to have realized that this kind of fame could be ruinous; what the mob makes it loves even more to break. Regarding the basis of that fame, he seemed to be utterly undeceived. "He said to me once with a cynical chuckle," Twain remembered, "that he thought he had mastered the art of pumping up the tear of sensibility. The idea conveyed was that the tear of sensibility was oil, and that by luck he had struck it." [6]

To enjoy the fruits of that fame, however unmerited, he had to go East. His decision to leave San Francisco was not long in coming. It was made long before the mob scene on Broadway. The proprietors of the *Atlantic Monthly* were offering him unprecedented sums for the exclusive rights to whatever he wrote, and in addition a new magazine in Chicago called the *Lakeside Monthly* was making extravagant offers to lure him into its editorship. On January 10, 1871, he made the formal announcement that he and his family were moving East.

The city was properly downcast; its bonanza millionaires, bullion magnates and stock speculators had attained a certain vulgar significance nationally but Harte was its first home-grown cultural celebrity, and it hated to lose him. Publisher Carmany offered to double his salary at the *Overland* and pay one hundred dollars for each story and poem he contributed to the magazine. But Bret was eager to be off. He had always been an Easterner at heart, and for years had kept an ear cocked for invitations from Boston or New York. He knew that he had more than a few enemies around San Francisco — men who envied him, or disliked his aloof manner or misunderstood his shyness, men who were still bitter about his role in keeping California in the Union, men (and a few women) who resented the way he edited the *Overland*, and others who were affronted by his refusal to go along with the belief that San Francisco was the new hub of the universe.

Thus he was not swayed by pleas that the *Overland* would expire without his magical touch — which it did, several years later. It was revived in the mid-1880's, when Ambrose Bierce called it the *Warmed Overland*, and eventually served as the springboard from which Jack London, much like Harte himself and writing about the new frontier to the north and its even wilder gold rush, launched himself to national prominence. The lingering bitterness Bret felt about the local enmity was expressed in his letter to Carmany in 1875 when the publisher pleaded with him to return and save the *Overland* from its impending collapse. Actually, at that point he could have used the job, but he wrote Carmany:

I can make here, by my pen, with less drudgery, with more security, honor and respect thrice as much as I can make in California at the head of the *Overland* — taking the peak as the estimate. As far as I can see the tastes, habits, and ideas of you people have not changed since you and I were forced to part company, because I could better myself here . . .

I do not see how I could make the *Overland* 'sanctum' the literary Mecca of the West, after the Prophet had been so decidedly renounced by his disciples. I think that even a California community would see the ridiculousness of my returning to a magazine that had, under the thin guise of literary criticism, abused me at *the expense of its own literary record.*

The "blundering malice" and "shameless ingratitude" of Californians, he said, would make it impossible for him ever to return there.[7]

He felt that California was indebted to him rather than the other way around. Hadn't he helped in great measure to introduce Charles Warren Stoddard, Mark Twain, Ina Coolbrith and many others to the audience they deserved? He had made the *Overland* a vehicle distinguished enough to attract General William T. Sherman (an article on his connection with the Vigilantes in 1856 while a resident of the city), Louis Agassiz, and Charles Kingsley as contributors. He had published the first short story written by Ambrose Bierce, "The Haunted Valley," a macabre tale of how a psychopath tried to frighten a miner to death. Doubtless he also credited himself with keeping Joaquin Miller and his chromatic gush out of the *Overland;* it was only after Harte left that the magazine began publishing Miller's effusions. In his definitive survey of San Francisco's contribution to American writing, Franklin Walker has written that the *Overland* contained "the best that Western journalism was to produce. In no later journal printed on the Pacific slope" could be found "the true pulse of a pioneer society."

In the last days he would spend in San Francisco, Bret managed to conceal whatever adverse thoughts he had about the city in which he had found the path to fame. Only the great charm, which even Twain conceded, was in evidence as he made his farewells.

The farewell dinner given for him was limited to eleven friends of the literary world, all but one of them San Franciscans. The outsider was Samuel Bowles, the editor of the Springfield *Republican,* who was one of Harte's greatest admirers and publicists in the East.[8] Among those present was Noah Brooks, who had been his assistant from the *Overland*'s first issue and who later recalled the occasion as one of the most gracious and companionable evenings he ever spent. Some time after dinner was served in a private room at Louis

Dingeon's restaurant, Brooks recorded, "I saw Bowles furtively slip out his watch and look at the hour. The involuntary wave of surprise that swept over his face as he pocketed his timepiece induced me to look at my watch also. It was twenty minutes to four o'clock in the morning." What seemed a very short time later another diner looked at his watch, Brooks recalled, and exclaimed, "Boys, it is almost five o'clock tomorrow!" and with that "the spell was broken" and the diners dispersed.[9]

The San Francisco *Chronicle* recapitulated his achievements as a writer and editor and concluded that except for "a few jealous ones, whose lesser flames have cast shadows where the brighter light of Harte's genius was introduced," all his fellow citizens "will regret his departure." Harte himself was supremely confident that his light would blaze up even more brightly and enduringly in the more sympathetic surroundings to which he was removing himself. How could the trajectory of his career help but go higher and higher?

He could not have known in those final days in the city at the Golden Gate that his fame would undergo one of the quickest and most curious transitions in American literary history, or that his friend Stoddard one day would write of his going East, "I have often thought that if Bret Harte had met with a fatal accident during that transcontinental journey, the world would have declared with one voice that the greatest genius of his time was lost to it." [10]

On the morning of February 2, 1871, Bret, his wife Anna and their two sons Griswold and Francis, eight and six years old, boarded the Overland Express for Chicago. It was a triumphal progress. Reporters and admirers boarded the train at cities along the way to interview him and pay tribute. They entered his compartment expecting to find a hairy-faced, whiskey-swilling frontiersman in red flannel shirt and muddy boots; instead they were confronted by a quiet-voiced man with a wry and cultivated wit, dressed in the height of fashion, with fine dark eyes, aquiline features and an elegantly sweeping mustache, surrounded by his equally fashionable wife and their well-mannered sons.

Mark Twain later wrote that he "crossed the continent through such a prodigious blaze of national interest and excitement that one might have supposed he was the Viceroy of India on a progress, or Halley's comet come again after seventy-five years of lamented absence." He was as famous as if his name "had been painted on the sky in letters of astronomical magnitude." In Harte's case, particularly, Twain thought it "a pity that we cannot escape from life when we are young," for Harte at that point "had lived all of his life that was worth living . . . There was a happy Bret Harte, a contented Bret Harte, an ambitious Bret Harte, a hopeful Bret Harte, a bright, cheerful, easy-laughing Bret Harte, a Bret Harte to whom it was a bubbling and effervescent joy to be alive. That Bret Harte died in San Francisco . . ." [11]

Still, it was a lively enough corpse that presented itself in Chicago, the pre-fire Chicago as growingly conscious of its importance as San Francisco, and even more eager to pay homage to greatness. It regarded Bret Harte as its prize catch, the man who would endow it with a cultural aspect to match its commercial and industrial prospects.

A few days after his arrival Bret was to be the guest of honor at a dinner given by his admirers at which he would be installed as editor and part owner of the *Lakeside Monthly*. At the appointed hour the guests assembled in a private dining room downtown. A check for fourteen thousand dollars was slipped under Bret's plate at the head of the table. They waited for his arrival, but he never appeared nor did any word of regret, apology or explanation arrive from him. Finally the diners dispersed after one of them carefully tore up the fourteen-thousand-dollar check.

What happened? For days afterward Chicago and the literary world were busy with rumor and speculation about his cavalier treatment of his backers and admirers. The mystery of his conduct has never been entirely explained. Less than a month later he wrote Josephine Clifford, one of his assistants at the *Overland Monthly*, a letter which left no doubt that he really wanted the *Lakeside* editorship but offered only the flimsiest excuse for his not appearing at the dinner — and none for not having sent his regrets to his supporters. "I presume you have read through the public press," he wrote, "how nearly I became editor and part owner of the *Lakeside*, and how the childishness and provincial character of a few of the principal citizens of Chicago spoiled the project. For many reasons — some of which we discussed in San Francisco — I wanted the Chicago magazine, although I have since found that financially, at least, I can do much better in New York, or Boston . . ." [12]

Somewhat later, he expanded on the "provincialism" of his Chicago supporters by telling Noah Brooks that they had promised to send a carriage and an official escort for him. Neither had shown up at the appointed hour, so he had sat down and had dinner with his family.

Was he really so helpless, or so insistent on protocol, that he had to be conveyed to the dinner in state? That seems even more doubtful than the suggestion that his hosts would have failed to send a carriage for him if they had promised to do so, since every effort was being made to propitiate him.

Francis F. Browne, a member of the *Lakeside Monthly*'s staff, later recalled that Bret had spent the afternoon in the magazine's offices, no doubt looking the property over and deciding on what improvements might be made. "There is no doubt he intended going to the dinner," Browne said. He left the offices at five o'clock "saying he was going home to dress for the occasion." A friend of Harte's told Browne he had offered to pick him up and bring him to the dinner but that Harte refused and said it "wasn't necessary." [13] Obviously something happened between five o'clock and the time he was supposed to leave his hostess's house to attend the dinner.

The Hartes were staying with a cousin of Mrs. Harte's; the cousin had not been invited to attend, perhaps because whoever was in charge of the arrangements simply didn't think of it or possibly didn't even know of her existence. Certainly Bret's would-be associates weren't obligated to include his wife's relations on the guest list; they were stretching a point in inviting Mrs. Harte herself.

Mrs. Harte, as Josephine Clifford later learned from an acquaintance on the staff of the *Lakeside Monthly*, was so enraged by what she regarded as a snub to her cousin and hostess, intentional or not, that "she would not go herself, nor allow her husband to go to the dinner party." [14]

Another San Franciscan alert to gossip concerning the Hartes' domestic affairs related in her book that "it is said on good authority that Mr. Harte was handicapped by a jealous spouse — jealous of his fame and jealous of the attention he attracted. She was not willing to accept submissively the position of being the wife of a genius nor to be absorbed in his greater light. Because she had not been included in an invitation to dinner, or because a carriage had not been sent for her, she frequently prevented him from keeping his engagements with the social world . . ." [15]

A wifely tantrum, apparently, prevented Bret from taking a job which might have made all the difference to his career. He didn't have the freelancer's temperament, the ability to withstand financial insecurity, fend off creditors with one hand and write with the other.

To do his best work he needed a well-paying job that would cover his substantial living expenses and allow him enough time to write his stories on the side. For years he had functioned at peak efficiency while holding down jobs at the mint and the *Overland*, or the *Californian* before that, with storytelling as a profitable sideline. He valued comfort very highly — too highly for a dedicated artist — and needed to be well housed, well fed, well clothed before the creative juices were willing to flow freely. His shabby-genteel childhood had made him excessively concerned about appearances, and the uncertainties of living from check to check at the whim of publishers must have terrified him, particularly since Anna Harte insisted on maintaining a middle-class standard of living whatever the toll it took on Bret and his creditors.

More was lost that night than a magazine editorship, it would seem. From then on Bret's relationship with his wife, though they continued to share the same home for another half-dozen years and brought two more children into the world, was never quite the same again. Even while yielding to Anna's demands that he scorn his Chicago supporters, he must have come to the realization that he would never be happy in an atmosphere dominated by his wife's whims and fancies. From then on he began slipping out from under her thumb; he was too much the worthy burgher to demand a divorce but opted for a cat-and-mouse situation with himself as the triumphantly elusive mouse.

"There is no doubt that the dinner-party fiasco was the proverbial last straw that broke the camel's back," in Josephine Clifford's opinion. After the Chicago episode, she said, he even seemed to change physically and "no other face has ever grown strange to me so quickly." [16]

The phenomenal luck of Bret Harte had begun to run out on him when he and his family boarded the train February 11 for the Eastern seaboard.

II Celebrity

SEVEN

An Apparition in Green Gloves

MUCH as he may have looked forward to the editorship of the *Lakeside Monthly*, he had no reason to despair as he and his family continued their journey eastward. There were other strings to his bow, principally an offer from the firm which published the *Atlantic Monthly;* the details hadn't been ironed out, nor had contracts been signed, but the *Atlantic* wanted him as a regular contributor and could afford to be generous. No doubt there would be other editorial opportunities. Meanwhile, his journey excited interest all along the way, with newspaper interviews at every stop, people clamoring to see him as though he were Wild Bill Hickok or General Custer. William Dean Howells, who had just been promoted to editor of the *Atlantic* and would soon play host, guide and interpreter to Bret in Boston, described it as a "princely progress" on reading the newspaper reports. Neither Howells nor any of his contemporaries could recall any literary man causing such a stir in the United States.

The Hartes interrupted their journey eastward for a visit with Mrs. Harte's relatives in Syracuse, then proceeded to New York and a five-day stay with Harte's sister, Mrs. Eliza Knaufft, in her home on lower Fifth Avenue. Then on to Boston and a glorious week of being petted and admired by the authentic top-chop guardians of literary excellence, of receiving the final assurance that he was worthy of the honors which had been bestowed upon him. To be received by the Brahmins of Cambridge and Boston was equivalent to knighthood in England or election to a place among the "immortals" of France. Howells, an amiable and astute Ohioan the same age as Harte, had invited Harte and his family to stay with him at his new home, 3 Berkeley Street, off Harvard Square in Cambridge, for a week. It was a week Howells would never forget and Harte would always remember as perhaps the social high point of his career.

On his part, Howells awaited his guests with considerable trepidation. Reports that Harte's imperious temperament had caused him to snub the Chicagoans eager to lay a magazine at his feet only reinforced Howells's fears that his hospitality could not match Harte's expectations. On his arrival February 25, Howells decided to engage the "handsomest hack which the livery of Cambridge afforded, and not trust to the horse cars and the express to get him and his baggage out, as he would have done with a less portentous guest."

On first acquaintance, Howells later recalled, Harte seemed "a fairy prince," so magnetic was his personality and so resplendent his manner. Howells was quickly disarmed by "that voice and laugh which was surely the most winning in the world. Before they came in sight of the editor's humble roof he had mocked himself to his guest at his trepidation, and Harte with burlesque magnanimity had consented to be for that occasion only something less formidable than he had loomed afar. He accepted with joy the theory of passing a week in the home of virtuous poverty . . ."

Howells noted with approval his guest's "jovial physiognomy" and playful sense of humor, with something less than approval his style of dress. To a man already accustomed to the staid and sober styles of Boston, Harte was "a child of extreme fashion."

That first day Harte was plunged into the politest society this side of the Atlantic, dining that night at the Saturday Club with his host and Henry Wadsworth Longfellow, Oliver Wendell Holmes, Ralph Waldo Emerson, Richard Henry Dana, Jr., James Russell Lowell and Louis Agassiz.

Even the irreverent and rough-hewn Mark Twain was abashed in such company, but Harte refused to be overawed. He was prepared to treat them as equals. When Howells tried to impress him with the fact that nowhere in this country were so many literary figures grouped so closely together, Harte robustly agreed: "Why, you couldn't stand on your front porch and fire off your revolver without bringing down a two-volumer!" [1]

Harte's breezy manner in Boston would, of course, have surprised his intimates in San Francisco. There he had been known as the most circumspect of men, rather aloof, always on his dignity, to the point that many considered him something of a stuffed shirt. In Boston his personality seemed to have undergone a radical change; San Francisco who knew him well would have considered it unbuttoned, if not unhinged. Perhaps, amid all the lionizing, he felt that he was expected to play the part of a Western child of nature; perhaps he was overcompensating for all the gentility and finely calibrated distinctions which characterized literary Boston (Thomas Bailey Aldrich's manner toward William Dean Howells, for instance, would be greatly different from the hushed approach he would make to a Longfellow or a Lowell). These distinctions Harte swept aside with a jovial disregard for long-established propriety. Boston, long poised against outland barbarians, took him in stride, with an amused tolerance.

Always punctual and precise until now, he suddenly developed a feckless inability to get anywhere on time. Howells wrote:

It cannot harm him or anyone now to own that Harte was nearly always late for those luncheons and dinners which he was always going out to, and it needed the anxieties and energies of both families to get him into his clothes and then into the carriage, when a good deal of final buttoning must have been done, in order that he might not arrive so very late. He was the only one concerned who was quite unconcerned; his patience with his delays was inexhaustible; he arrived smiling, serenely jovial, radiating a bland gaiety from his whole person, and ready to ignore any discomfort he might have occasioned.[2]

Presumably he was on time and buttoned-up for the catered party which Mrs. Howells gave for the Hartes two nights after their arrival and which, she wrote a sister-in-law, cost *"a dollar and a half a head!"* John Fiske, the noted historian, was one of the guests and listed Longfellow, Lowell, Aldrich, Agassiz, Henry James and other luminaries among those attending, "so many we knocked elbows. Everyone wore his best bib and tucker, the house is well arranged for entertainment, and the supper was delicious . . ."[3]

The Hartes, Howells recorded, were "entertained somewhere every night," among their hosts being Longfellow, Lowell and James T. Fields the publisher. And there was also the unnamed hostess "of towering social ambition, who, unhappily for herself, was not of the privileged order, and had never been able to force the gates that barred her from the reigning aristocracy of the city," as Mrs. Thomas Bailey Aldrich recalled. The lady succeeded somehow in snaring Bret as her guest of honor. The evening, from her viewpoint, was a smashing success and her "long and showy drawing room was well filled with representative men and women." The lionizing lady, however, came a cropper before the night was over. At the height of the festivities

Mrs. Julia Ward Howe was asked by Mr. Harte if she would not give him the privilege of hearing from her lips "The Battle Hymn of the Republic." Mrs. Howe had a beautiful and highly trained voice . . . After "The Battle Hymn" Mrs. Howe sang an Italian song and ended with an English ballad, full of pathos. At the finish Mrs. Howe slowly rose from the piano, and the eloquent silence was broken by her hostess's voice at the extreme end of the room saying, "Oh, Mrs. Howe, do now sing something comic!" [4]

Harte himself committed a faux pas almost as disastrous at a luncheon given by Ralph Keeler, who had contributed to the *Overland* and other California periodicals. Among the guests were James T. Fields and the two young men who edited his magazines, Howells of the *Atlantic* and Aldrich of *Every Saturday*, with Bret Harte and Mark Twain and others less celebrated. Harte was the guest of honor in one of Ober's private dining rooms. Twain had attained considerable prominence with the publication of *Innocents Abroad*, but he had not as yet, according to Howells, "hit the favor of our community of scribes and scholars as Bret Harte had done."

Twain, who was capable of harboring resentments with an Ozarkian intensity, undoubtedly was conscious of the gap that existed between his own reception in Boston, whose favor was much more important to him than it was to Harte, and the near-idolatry with which his friend and rival was received. It must have festered; eventually he was accorded a much higher place in Bostonian esteem, but it came about only after years of proving himself. In addition, he and

Harte had recently fallen out over a trifling matter. As Twain explained it in a letter to a mutual friend, Harte had read *Innocents Abroad*, indicated "what passages, paragraphs & chapters to leave out" and Twain "followed orders strictly." Harte had requested early copies of the book so he could review it in the *Overland* but never received them due to a misunderstanding with the San Francisco distributor. Harte then wrote him, Twain related, "the most daintily contemptuous & insulting letter you ever read . . ." [5] The misunderstanding had since been smoothed over, but Twain, with his keen sense of rivalry, had another matter over which to brood. While Fields and his editors were courting Harte preparatory to signing a breath-taking contract for his contributions to the *Atlantic* and *Every Saturday*, Twain would have to wait another three years before one of his own pieces was accepted by the *Atlantic*, and then for a niggardly sixty dollars.

Thus Twain, that noon at Ober's, must have felt that though physically he was seated next to the guest of honor professionally he was placed well below the salt.

And some of that salt was carelessly rubbed into whatever egotistic wounds he was concealing. Someone at the table remarked on the extraordinary openness of the Boston literary world that Twain, an uncurried Missourian, should be accorded a place in such Olympian company. That remark in itself was a little snide, even taking into consideration the "convivial" atmosphere of the luncheon as described by Howells. Bret embroidered on it by clapping Twain on the back and commenting, "Why, fellows, this is the dream of Mark's life!" [6]

As Howells recalled the occasion thirty-odd years later, Twain's only response was "a glance from under [his] feathery eyebrows." With that careless remark, Howells believed,

Harte searingly dramatized Twain's "mental attitude to-wards a Symposium of Boston illuminates." If that attitude came close to truckling, it wasn't something Twain would want jeeringly exposed.

Aside from being addressed so chummily, in the style of a whiskey drummer opening a smoking-car session, his fellow guests were taken aback by the suggestion that Harte considered himself a cultivated Easterner like themselves. Here they'd been petting and spoiling him as an exuberant and picturesque Westerner, and by inference he was including himself in their polished and exclusive company. They must have reflected on the perils of condescension. It took a long period of grooming, censoring and burnishing before they admitted Twain through the sacred portals.

Harte, however, was obviously incorrigible. The only one of "the old saints" — as James T. Fields referred to the older generation of Boston's poets and philosophers — whom Bret viewed with an unalloyed respect was Henry Wadsworth Longfellow. Their most intimate moment came when they walked home from a dinner at James Russell Lowell's house on a winter's night and talked of poetry and other matters.

Of that two-mile walk at midnight from the Lowell home on the Charles to the center of Cambridge Bret would recall a dozen years later his elder and idol

as he stood in the sharp moonlight of the snow-covered road; a dark mantle-like cloak hiding his evening dress, and a slouched felt hat covering his full, silver-like locks. The conventional gibus or chimney-pot would have been as intolerable on that wonderful brow as it would on a Greek statute, and I was thankful there was nothing to interrupt the artistic harmony of the most impressive vignette I ever beheld. I hope that the enthusiasm of a much younger man will be pardoned when I confess that the dominant feeling in my mind was an echo of one I experienced a few weeks before, when I had penetrated Niagara at sunrise on a Sunday morning after a heavy snowfall and found that masterpiece unvisited, virgin to my tread, and my own footsteps the only track to the dizzy edge of Prospect Park. I was to have the man I most revered alone with me for half an hour in the sympathetic and confidential stillness of the night . . .

As I was the stranger, he half earnestly, half jestingly kept up the role of guide, philosopher, and friend, and began an amiable review of the company we had just left. As it comprised a few names, the greatest in American literature, science and philosophy, I was struck with that generous contemporaneous appreciation which distinguished this Round Table, of whom no knight was more courtly and loving than my companion.[7]

Longfellow, according to Howells, was the one distinguished graybeard whom Bret did not mock and satirize in private. By then Howells was just a little weary of Bret's teasing comments on the men whom Howells admired wholeheartedly, his supposedly helpless unpunctuality, his "ironic impertinences" toward all that Howells held dear. A little on the stuffy side, perhaps, Howells was distressed by Harte's tendency to drink too much — this, too, was a startling departure, for Bret had been comparatively abstemious until now. Fame and alcohol often go to the head simultaneously.

Howells was even more concerned by the fact that Bret borrowed money from his newfound friends and admirers, a complaint familiar to his California days, and never paid it back. Bret at least was gentleman enough not to borrow from his host, but he seemed to be forever tapping anyone around him for cigar or cab money, apparently feeling it was the tribute mediocrity owed to genius.

So Howells was relieved when the Harte family's week at his home came to an end. Despite all his precautions, however, there was a last-minute brush with disaster. Howells took the Hartes to the railroad station "in as much magnificence as marked his going to meet" them, and in plenty of time to catch their train for New York. He boarded the Pullman with them to have a few last words with Bret. At the last moment Bret discovered that he was out of cigars and could not face the journey without his favorite brand. Together they hurried off the train and into the station. When they returned to the platform the train was just beginning to pull out. Howells leaped aboard to make sure Harte was settled down with his family. Then he hurried to the door and leaped for the platform while Bret waved goodbye with his cigar. Howells, in his hurried exit, was almost crushed to death between the train and an archway, which would have been an exorbitant price to American literature for a handful of perfectos. "Deathly sick" as he was at the thought of his narrow escape, disillusioned as he was at the signs of disorder in Bret's personal life, relieved as he must have been at his "belated guest's" departure, Howells would write of Harte's personality thirty-two years later that it was "the most winning in the world." [8]

The Hartes returned to New York and the home of his sister Eliza, which they were to make their headquarters for the next several months despite the fact that Mrs. Harte and her sister-in-law did not get along swimmingly. An aura of triumph still surrounded the author. In Boston his charm, as well as the giddy excitement which surrounded his movements, outweighed his occasional gaucheries and eccentricities, on balance, and the firm of Fields, Osgood & Co., publishers of the *Atlantic Monthly* and *Every Saturday*, decided to give him a contract said to be the most lucrative ever offered an American writer. The terms were contained in his letter of acceptance March 6, 1871: "I accept your offer of ten thousand dollars for the exclusive publication of my poems and sketches (not to be less than twelve in number) in your periodicals for the space of one year . . ." [9] That wouldn't have been a bad price today, considering the length of most of the pieces he submitted, but in 1871 it was a lordly sum, tribute as much to his name-value as to his literary ability. American publishers, however, could hardly refuse suitable recompense when Bret was the subject of an editorial in a leading English newspaper, the London *Daily News*, which observed:

The East and the West contend for the reflected rays of his celebrity; cities dispute for the honor of his presence; Chicago beguiles him from San Francisco; New York snatches him from Chicago, and Boston plots deeply his abduction from New York. His slightest movement is chronicled in every newspaper, and where he stops for a few days, a kind of "Bret Harte Circular" appears in the daily press.[10]

Bret immediately set out to feast himself on the joys of celebrity. Almost every night he was wined and dined. Daytimes, when he might have been occupying himself with fulfilling the *Atlantic Monthly–Every Saturday* contract to the best of his ability, he dawdled, spent long hours over luncheon tables or at the bar, drifted around the city and let himself be admired. He loved every minute of his brief hour of recognition; perhaps it was premonition that fame would not attend him everlastingly that urged him to enjoy it while he had it. One thing he most certainly did not regret was leaving California. He announced his intention of founding a Society of Escaped Californians. The only Californian whom he wrote to was Josephine Clifford, his fervently loyal assistant at the *Overland Monthly*. When Anton Roman came to New York, Bret avoided seeing him, drawing from Roman the observation that fame had come to Harte so swiftly that "the adulation disturbed his head."

In the West he had been "that Eastern dude," which he accepted as a compliment, but now he was back in the East he was equally pleased — and apparently was not conscious of the irony — with playing the brash and uncurried Westerner. Possibly he had quickly sensed that he was most acceptable in that role, and realized that a celebrated writer has to adopt a fitting public personality. Several times he returned to Boston that spring on visits more social than professional, and when he was a guest at the Thomas Bailey Aldrich home he fascinated his host and hostess, "sitting about the round table with the walnuts and the wine," talking endlessly about his experiences in California. Obviously, as Mrs. Aldrich catalogued his recollections, he did not spare the brighter colors:

The warehouses where the trunks and boxes of the early forty-niners were stored by the missing and dead owners . . . the gambling saloons and the gaudily dressed and painted women who presided over them. The principal gambling houses were in the heart of the city and were open every hour of the day and night; the atmosphere hazy with the scent of tobacco smoke and redolent of the fumes of brandy. The wild music and the jingling of gold and silver were almost the only sounds. Almost everybody played, and in fact the gambling-houses were as clubs for business and professional men. People staked and lost their last dollar, Mr. Harte laughingly said, with a calm solemnity and a resignation that was almost Christian.[11]

One of Bret's spring visits to Boston was for the purpose of accepting a signal honor, delivering the annual Phi Beta Kappa poem at the Harvard Commencement exercises. For an American poet of the time this was the most solemn of compliments, but Bret approached it in the same rather frisky and cavalier spirit in which he had met "the old saints." Since his poetry to date was anything but high artistry, "The Heathen Chinee" being vaudeville in verse and his other efforts unexceptional or derivative, it behooved him to put a considerable effort into dignifying the occasion. Instead he refurbished some old comic verse published in the *Golden Era* years before, and retitled it "Aspiring Miss De Laine." On Commencement Day, furthermore, he appeared in what Mrs. Aldrich called "gaudy raiment." Judging from a photograph taken of him during this period, "gaudy" was not too strong a word: the picture captured him in full blossom, a garishly patterned cravat with a huge knot, a suit of exaggerated cut with swooping lapels and fabric with broad stripes.

Worst of all, he wore bright green gloves.

The assemblage at Harvard might have survived the shock of his appearance if the poem he had read in a low shaky voice — he was never at ease on the public platform, never able to project the charm so visible around a dinner table — had not been so obviously something he dashed off. "Inappropriate" was Mrs. Aldrich's word for it, softened only by her suggestion that he "apparently did not recognize the dignity of the occasion."

"Clothes and the man were equally disappointing to Harvard," she wrote. "The poet fully realized the situation, and fled in dismay." [12]

A man with a ten-thousand-dollar contract obviously couldn't spend the summer sweltering in New York City. He still hadn't produced much in return for the *Atlantic Monthly* or *Every Saturday*, but he was confident that the money would keep coming in. There was little danger that income would exceed outgo, however, as both he and Anna were competent spenders.

They decided to spend the summer in Newport; it was the place to go then, not only for Gilded Age millionaires, still fat on war contracts, but had long been a retreat for artists and writers and intellectuals. The law that wealth follows the arts in watering-places as well as other matters applied to some extent to Newport.

Long before the first profiteer and his wife and daughters paraded themselves on Bellevue Avenue, Newport had been a summer resort for literary and artistic people from Boston and New York. Edgar Allan Poe, in a flush and sober period, had summered there. In the postwar years Dr. Oliver Wendell Holmes, Longfellow, Julia Ward Howe, Henry James and the noted historian George Bancroft were among those who lived in its hotels and cottages.[13]

Socially, Bret and Anna were a success that summer in Newport. They were entertained by the best, and sometimes by the richest people. Anna felt herself in her proper element; Bret was a star performer before and after the port and cigars were passed, his anecdotes charming, his wit scintillating. Of the latter, unfortunately, few samples survive; we have to take his contemporaries' word for it that it was little short of marvelous, that he was at least as fascinating in conversation as on the printed page, if not more so. He had the ability to mock gently, to "take off" other people even if they were present, without offending; to satirize without stinging.

All this, however, wasn't advancing his career. Most of the time he lazed about on the beaches and verandas. By the end of summer only one story, "The Poet of Sierra Flat," had appeared in the *Atlantic Monthly*. Both it and the short story he produced for the September issue, "The Romance of

Madrono Hollow," appeared in the back of the book — a curious relegation for a writer for whom the *Atlantic* had laid out so much money.

An equally curious footnote to that stylish summer might be inferred from a letter Bret wrote his wife from Boston, where he had journeyed for a meeting with James T. Fields, his publisher of the moment. He mentioned the fact that his mother had telegraphed him asking if she was invited to join them in Newport. "If she has received my letter," Bret wrote, "this is about as cool a piece of pertinacity as I know of." The coolness between mother and son, which had begun early in his youth and had only been widened by her continuing disapproval of Anna, had not been eliminated by his new prosperity.

That fall, while his family was establishing itself in a house called The Willows in Morristown, New Jersey, Bret continued to visit Boston frequently. Much as he affected not to be overwhelmed by the stately old men of letters, he sought their company, possibly as reassurance that he had indeed reached the top drawer. In October of that first year in the East, he visited Emerson at Concord and strolled with him beside Walden Pond, which disappointed him for being much too close to town. What an odd pair they must have made, the austere philosopher and the comparatively youthful Harte in the bright plumage of success. Later, when Emerson suggested a "wet evening," he poured Harte and himself each a small glass of sherry. They disagreed not only on what constituted a wet evening, but also on a more abstract matter. "Bret Harte referred to my essay on Civilization," Emerson wrote in his journal on October 18, 1871,

that the piano comes so quickly into the shanty, etc., and said, "Do you know that, on the contrary, it is vice that brings them in? It is the gamblers who bring the music to California. It is the prostitute who brings in the New York fashions on dress there, and so throughout." I told him that I spoke also from Pilgrim experience, and knew on good grounds the resistless culture that religion effects.

Bret probably did not press the point, but he had a rather low opinion of anything cultural, ethical and intellectual the frontier churches brought with them; many of the men involved in the massacre on Humboldt Bay and other backwoods atrocities he had known of or written of were proud to sit in the front pews.

The temptations of celebrity, of making the most of the social invitations extended him, continued to keep him from his writing desk. His relationship with Fields, Osgood & Co. was rapidly deteriorating. He was so late with his Christmas story for the *Atlantic* — "How Santa Claus Came to Simpson's Bar" — that it had to be published in the March issue, and a longer story, "Mrs. Skaggs's Husbands," which was to lead off a new volume of short stories published by Fields, Osgood, was eventually allowed to count for two stories under his contract. By the time the contract expired in March 1872, he had turned in only seven of the dozen stories and poems he had agreed to write. It was another six months before he had turned in the other five pieces he was supposed to produce for ten thousand dollars. These included a short story, "Lothaw," published in *Every Saturday,* another *Atlantic* story, "Princess Bob"; the poems "A Greyport Legend," "A Newport Romance," "Grandmother Tenterden," "Concepcion de Arguello," "Idyll of Battle Hollow," and "Half an Hour before Supper," also published in the *Atlantic.*

In addition to the lateness of delivery, the *Atlantic* editors evidently didn't consider Bret's output since his arrival in the

East up to the quality they expected of him. At least two of the stories — "Mrs. Skaggs's Husbands" and "How Santa Claus Came to Simpson's Bar" — were, however, up to his general standard; he couldn't be expected to produce a "Heathen Chinee" or "Luck of Roaring Camp" every time out. The Christmas story was a rather sentimental tale about an old miner's young son who had never heard of that holy day. In the midst of a drunken Christmas Eve celebration in the father's cabin, Dick Pullen decides to play Santa Claus, rides across the mountains to Tuttleville and buys a sack of battered secondhand toys. Pullen is confronted by a highwayman on his ride back, but escapes with a bullet in his arm and his sack of toys intact. "Tell him Sandy Claus has come," Pullen says just before collapsing. And the Christmas dawn "looked so tenderly on Simpson's Bar that the whole mountain, as if caught in a generous action, blushed to the skies."

Less sentimental but more melodramatic was "Mrs. Skaggs's Husbands," which rambled from Angel's Camp (the scene of Mark Twain's "The Celebrated Jumping Frog of Calaveras County") to Greyport, which was Newport thinly disguised. Its characters included Yuba Bill and an improbable society girl who glided "like a lovely and innocent milk snake," and all credibility vanished the moment the story traveled East. The sharpest writing in it was a description of the spoliation brought to the California foothills by the gold-hunters, the trail along the flank of Table Mountain littered with

oyster cans, yeast-powder tins, and empty bottles that had been apparently stranded by the "first low wash" of pioneer waves. On the ragged trunk of an enormous pine hung a few tufts of gray hair caught from a passing grizzly, but in strange juxtaposition at its foot lay an empty bottle of incomparable bitters — the chef-d'oeuvre of a hygienic civilization, and blazoned with the arms of an all-healing republic. The head of a rattlesnake peered from a case that had contained tobacco, which was still brightly placarded with the high-colored effigy of a popular danseuse.

Even before the contractual year expired it was apparent that Fields, Osgood had no intention of renewing the arrangement. Bret's work simply had fallen below expectations in quality and punctuality. Late in 1873, when Osgood was negotiating the sale of his interest in the *Atlantic*, the publisher wrote Bret expressing his dissatisfaction with the way the deal had worked out. "I confess I was considerably surprised by your note," Bret replied on December 12, 1873, "as you had given me no intimation, when I asked for my account in Boston a few days ago, of the position you intended to assume. Neither did I know anything of your plans to dispose of the 'Atlantic' . . . There seemed, however, to be some misunderstanding between us regarding the 'Every Saturday' material being applied to the contract, and I offered to furnish you at some future time a sketch or poem in addition without charge . . ." [14]

There was no disguising the fact that being dropped by the *Atlantic* represented a resounding failure, the first he had met since assuming the editorship of the *Overland Monthly*. His career was not, after all, to be a succession of triumphs. As with most writers, he would have to learn to roll with the punches, spoiled as he had been by too quick and easy success. He would be a long time in accommodating himself to the brutal truth that he wasn't as good — or as lucky — as he had been led to believe. The "princely progress" of his glory-haloed journey East was now replaced by the misadventures of Grub Street, the traditional picaresque episodes endured by writers since the days of François Villon; by flights from creditors, living by his wits, drinking too much, borrowing too much; scrabbling for an existence on the tattered edges of Bohemia. It must be said that Bret finally adapted himself to the catch-as-catch-can life with a nimbleness that indicated aptitude if not positive delight.

By the end of 1871, with the *Atlantic* deal petering out, he allowed himself to be seduced by the appeals of lecture agents. Apparently they were unaware of his abysmal lack of ease on the platform, and thought he might duplicate the triumphs of other humorous western writers on the lecture circuit. Actually this was the most forlorn of hopes; the only communication at which Bret was expert was on paper or in the give-and-take of conversation in a small group. He had no setpieces with which to exact laughter or tears from an audience. He lacked the acting ability of Mark Twain and Charles Dickens, who blossomed forth the moment they stood before a crowd. Nor did he have the showmanship of a Joaquin Miller, another literary eminence hugely successful on the lecture platform; Miller would appear in boots (or mukluks after the Klondike gold rush, in which he participated as a Hearst correspondent) and an overcoat with nuggets for buttons; pure ham, but it was what the public wanted. Years later Bret speculated that if he had appeared in "a red shirt and top boots" his audiences "would have felt a deeper thrill from my utterances."

Inhibited, half-frozen with fear at the prospect, he set out on the lecture circuit in December of 1872 only because bills from tradesmen and small loans from friends and acquaintances were piling up most alarmingly, he had published nothing but the volume led off by "Mrs. Skaggs's Husbands" and otherwise composed of stories written in California, and he had fathered a third child, Jessamy (his fourth and last child, Ethel, would be born in 1875).

Bret Harte
as editor of the *Overland Monthly*.

The House in Union
which he shared with his sister and her husband.

The Harte Home in Morristown
which Bret visited between lecture tours and other forays.

Mark Twain
in the days before Bret
was "the S.O.B."

Joaquin Miller
whose lyricism soared too
high for Bret the editor.

John Hay
who protected Bret's reputation
during his consular days.

William Dean Howells
Bret's host and guide among
"the old saints" of Boston.

Bret Harte
during the early years of his
expatriation in London.

A Family Reunion
in England a year or two before Bret's death. Seated, left to right, daughter Ethel and Mrs. Harte. Standing, Bret and daughter-in-law, Mrs.
Francis Bret Harte.

The first leg of his tour included, Albany, December 3, 1872; Boston, December 13; New York City, December 16; Washington, D.C., January 7, 1873, and Pittsburgh, January 9, with a swing through the midwest and Canada to follow. The subject of his first lecture tour was "The Argonauts of '49," in which he first sketched in the early, pre-Anglo-Saxon history of California, then the coming of the gold-rushers and the brawling life of the mining camps. Included in it were various bits and pieces of his writings, such as gambler John Oakhurst's wisecrack when he rose from the table after winning five thousand dollars in ten minutes: "To think some folks believes that cards are a waste of time!" The lecture was well larded with anecdotes, and his first audience, at Albany, his birthplace, found it acceptable.

He appeared in Boston a day or two before the date of his appearance at the Tremont Temple. Not only was he nervous about making a decent showing before a predictably critical audience, but by then a sheriff was on his trail with a writ of attachment sworn out against a long-overdue trades-man's bill. He had to slip into town like a fugitive, and appeared without warning on the doorstep of the Thomas Bailey Aldriches "late on a stormy December night as we were covering with ashes the too bright blaze of the cheerful logs of the living-roof fire."

Mrs. Aldrich heard him jovially calling from the hallway, "Are you home, Aldrich? I have come to make a night of it."

The uninvited but welcome guest was told to come up-stairs and join them before the fire.

And then the melodious voice as he ascended the stairs two at a time chanting, "Polly, put the kettle on; Polly put the kettle on, and we'll all have tea." He had been to a dinner and reception given in his honor, and coming gaily into the room he asked for the loan of our spare room for the night, saying that the hotel room was dreary, and that he was in a mood to be happy and gay.

We joyfully loaned him the room and the lights—the pajamas and the brushes—and in return he loaned us through all the small hours, until the coming of the dawn, the aroma of his host's choicest cigars.

The next morning, still arrayed in his evening clothes, he went unembarrassed and airily hotelwards.

Mrs. Aldrich suspected that he had stayed overnight with them more out of a desire to avoid the pursuing sheriff than in search of "gayety." [15]

When he appeared at the Tremont Temple the following night, however, the sheriff was waiting to pounce. The latter was insisting that the proceeds of the lecture be turned over to him, and meanwhile Harte's friends were scurrying around trying to bail him out of trouble. As usual, Harte appeared less perturbed than they, proper Bostonians unaccustomed to fending off the bailiff. "Hurried calls were sent to his publisher," as Mrs. Aldrich recalled, presumably the disillusioned Mr. Osgood, "who was dining out and difficult to find."

Meanwhile Harte and his faithful friend Howells were waiting in an anteroom off the wings wondering whether the show would, indeed, go on. The sheriff fumed nearby.

"Well, Harte," Howells said, "this is the old literary tradition."

Bret, he recalled, "slapped his thigh and laughed excitedly," and referring to the old English custom of clapping debtors — including its distinguished literary men — in the workhouse exclaimed: "Yes, that's it, we can see it all now — the Fleet Prison with Goldsmith, Johnson, and all the rest of the old masters in a bunch." [16]

Bret was so buoyed up by the romantic comparison that he went on to make an excellent impression on what Mrs. Aldrich said was a "great audience." It was one of his few triumphs as a public performer.

Mrs. Aldrich said the lecture "had to be lengthened until the rescuer came, and the cue was given that the last word could now be safely spoken." Bret bowed off to delighted applause.

His lecture was also a success in New York and Washington. The New York *Times* gave it a column and noted that the audience in Steinway Hall laughed frequently. These early successes gave him a measure of confidence, but he was never at ease before a crowd, hated travel, and frequently came down with illnesses which would probably be diagnosed as psychosomatic today. Most of his appearances brought him one hundred dollars or one hundred fifty dollars, but he had to pay his expenses out of that and support the growing household in Morristown, New Jersey. Mrs. Harte was no better at managing money than he was, and frequently he had to telegraph her money orders to keep the butcher, the baker and grocer from suing. Occasionally a creditor lost his patience and hauled Bret into court, as when the tailoring firm of Teats and Throckmorton obtained judgment against him in a New York civil court for unpaid bills totaling two hundred thirty dollars. The cost of maintaining separate livings for himself and for his wife and family was to be his lifelong burden, never giving him the time and tranquillity in which to experiment as a writer, to explore new paths, to leave — for once — the California foothills he had known in his youth.

If anything lessened the rigors of lecturing, of living out of suitcases and catching midnight trains that led from one lonely hotel room to another, it was the occasionally interesting people he met on the road. His letters to Anna were devoted largely to them (as well as to money matters, his illnesses and other complaints). In Washington he met the British minister, Sir Edward Thornton, and "had some talk . . . which I have no doubt will materially affect the foreign policy of England." His first glimpse of the Capitol, he added, was unexpectedly impressive. "It is really a noble building . . . I felt very proud until I looked in upon the Congress in session — then it was very trying to compare the house with its tenants." [17]

The Canadian leg of his tour took him to Toronto, Ottawa and Montreal, where the hazards of rail travel and the urgency of arriving at lecture halls on time vexed him no end, with no one but himself to worry over punctuality and buttoning-up. His train broke down and he had to engage a special train to rush him to Toronto. He had to climb into his dress suit while the train, an engine and one car rushed through the night at seventy miles an hour, "the most rapid and unsatisfactory toilette I ever made." Even so the Toronto audience had to wait an hour and a half before he made his appearance. It was an English audience, he noted in his letter to Anna, and their reception was "quite a pleasant forecast of the reception I should meet abroad." Already, it seemed, he was considering that the urbanity he valued most in life wouldn't be found even in the oldest Eastern cities of the United States but would have to be sought abroad.

When he came to Ottawa, he was suffering from a cold and loss of sleep and appetite. He had to appear at a skating rink, "a hideous, damp, dismal barn," and the turnout was small, the proceeds barely enough to cover expenses. He had a showdown with Kirby, his lecture agent, and told him that unless the Montreal receipts showed a decided upturn he would have to give up the tour. The only bright spot in his weekend stay in Ottawa was the invitation from the Governor General and his wife, the Earl and Countess of Dufferin, to spend two days at Rideau Hall with them until it was time to leave for Montreal. "Don't let this worry you," he wrote to Anna, "but kiss the chickens for me and hope for the best." He would have sent money, he added, but he was broke and "maybe I shall only bring myself back." The Montreal house was satisfactory, however, and he sent home "the greater part" of the one hundred fifty dollars he received.[18]

He lectured in several other Eastern cities that spring, but never with the insouciance which had captivated his audiences in Boston and New York; perhaps like most men with an easy-going and slightly Micawberish disposition he needed the prod of necessity to produce his best efforts, such as a sheriff squatting in the wings.

On his return to New York early in April 1873, with the results of his first tour far from exhilarating, he was enraged to learn that the *Golden Era* in San Francisco had dug out of its files the longer version of "M'liss" which he had undertaken, but never published, at the suggestion of the former proprietor. The *Golden Era* was now serializing this version, and in the present state of the copyright laws there appeared to be nothing he could do about it. Worse yet, somebody on the magazine's staff evidently was adding chapters to his work. "Of course this means a swindle on the public, or a *forgery*. I regret to say they are quite capable of doing either in California." He was also having trouble, as he wrote Osgood, still his American book publisher, with a Canadian who proposed to bring out a one-volume edition of his selected work. The Canadian had appeared enthusiastic during his appearance in Toronto, but Bret hadn't heard from him since.[19]

Perhaps he was so concerned over past writings because he was producing so little in the present. Much of 1873, 1874 and the beginning of 1875 was given over to his lecturing, and he wrote little in the off-season summertimes. The only story he completed in 1873 was the "Episode of Fiddletown," which ran in three parts in *Scribner's Magazine*. From then until 1875 he wrote five other stories, including "A Passage in the Life of Mr. John Oakhurst," and a juvenile for the *St. Nicholas Magazine*, titled "Baby Sylvester." Something ought to be done about the piety of most writing for children, he indicated in a letter to Mary Mapes Dodge, editor of the *St. Nicholas*. "I find that children thoroughly understand anything but sentiment and theology — which are unfortunately the two things they are oftenest dosed with . . ." [20]

Apparently he was a little fed up with the sentiment he injected in calculated doses in his adult stories, if the Oakhurst story written about this time was any indication. "A Passage in the Life of Mr. John Oakhurst" exuded sentiment only over the Sierras and "a sky so remote as to be of no positive color — so remote that even the sun despaired of ever reaching it, and so expended its strength recklessly on the whole landscape until it fairly glittered in a white and vivid contrast." It dealt with Oakhurst's ill-starred love affair with a married woman, "an invalid Puritan, a sick saint," and the deceit with which she rewarded him. The woman was depicted with a realism and insight rare in fiction of the period, particularly that dealing with the feminine character. His Mrs. Decker suggested that he was beginning to grasp the "power of sex," as Henry Adams put it, a motivation which other writers refused to grapple with. Instead of the happy ending most readers expected, Bret left them with the unfaithful Mrs. Decker forgiving her husband with a "graciousness" that stung, and John Oakhurst with his arm wounded in a duel fought over the unworthy creature. When asked about the wound, Oakhurst warningly replied, "It bothers my dealing a little, but I can shoot as well with my left." It may have irked some of his more meticulous readers that Bret resurrected Oakhurst, who was supposed to have died in an earlier story, just as later he revived "the late Colonel Starbottle"; they and other characters kept dying and coming back to life in his dream world of the Sierras, in which clocks and calendars were startlingly unreliable.

On the lecture trail in the South and Midwest in the fall and winter of 1873–1874, he again found that the proceeds from his appearances barely paid the expenses of maintaining himself on the road — he traveled by Pullman and stayed in the best hotels, of course — and his family back in Morristown. The South, the land of Colonel Starbottle and his gentlemanly gamblers, charmed him in passing. From the Virginia countryside he wrote Anna of meeting an old gentleman who came down to dinner in ruffled sleeves and shirt-front and a powdered wig, who spoke of meeting President Madison and President Monroe. He had, he said, met the "real Virginian Colonel Starbottle" and looked upon his fictional creation, by comparison, as an "utter failure."

The South, with the iron hand of Reconstruction still clamped upon every phase of its life and Appomattox only eight years in the past, not only fascinated him but won his sympathy. He found himself standing "by the bedside of a ruined and slowly dying people," and if he were in high public office he would devote his life to rescuing them from the aftermath of the Civil War — a sentiment which the late Reverend Thomas Starr King and the patroness of his youth, Jessie Frémont, might have found a little contradictory. The gentility of the Old South, disregarding the harsh inequities it masked so gracefully, had a strong appeal for him. It helped, perhaps, that his Southern audiences were so "thoroughly refined and appreciative."

As he headed across the bleak prairies to Kansas, however, he found the people less receptive, and a dull audience made him a dull lecturer; he came down with colds and fevers again, mind rebelling against body; and misadventure dogged him. Once his train broke down and he had to gallop fifteen miles across the countryside to keep an engagement. The Topeka *Republic*, he wrote home, called him a "handsome fop," and the Midwestern newspapers generally insisted on terming his "worn-out shirts" the most "faultless linen" and making his "haggard" face that of a "Spanish-looking exquisite." Perhaps he protested a bit too much when he wrote Anna that he was "hopelessly furious" over allegations that he got by on the platform because of "my good looks." At Atchison, after a distressing experience with Kansas railroads, "you can imagine the savage, half-sick, utterly disgusted man who glared at that audience over his desk that night, and d——d them inwardly in his heart." Despite "pressing claims," he sent Anna the one hundred dollars he received for the Atchison lecture to "buy 'minxes' with, if you want to," by which he evidently meant a fur coat.

The prairie Westerners, he found, were a great improvement over the California species. He praised their "strange good taste and refinement under that rough exterior — even their tact," and maintained they had "twice the refinement and tenderness of their California brethren."

In January he was doubling back, appearing in upstate New York towns and depressed over a "feeble drool of rain" that accompanied the January thaw. He wrote Anna that when she was worried or lonely she should think of him and "let your cerulean tint pale before my deeper indigo," and

asked her to indoctrinate the boys against becoming lectur-
ers, their daughter against marrying a poet.

In the college town of Ithaca he was cheered by an audience which rose to the "delicate points" of his lecture like "a
trout at a fly," and by his meeting with Professor Corson of
Cornell, a celebrated Chaucerian scholar and an admirer of
Bret's, "as sweet and gentle as the poets he lives among." He
was equally captivated by the student body and was impelled
to make an invidious comparison, perhaps in bitter recollection of the cold reception he had received at the Harvard
Commencement a few years back. "Harvard cannot show
such young *gentlemen* as met me in the committee room.
There was all the culture — without the conceit!"

During the 1874–1875 season he again lectured in the
South and was even more convinced that "the North is pro-
foundly ignorant of the real sentiments and condition of the
people." The state of Georgia particularly affected him with
its strange contrasts to the America he had known. "Since I
left Louisville, I appear to be travelling in a foreign land, and
among a foreign people. I am too full of it to talk about it; I
have done nothing — I can do nothing — but absorb." His
lectures — by now they alternated between the Argonauts
and "American Humor" — were so inappropriate when addressed to a South occupied by Federal troops and administered in part by Northern carpetbaggers that they seemed
"vapid." Georgians seemed "infinitely quainter and more
original, more pathetic, more ludicrous" than the gold-
hunting horde he told them about. He thought it little wonder that they stared hollow-eyed at "the profound statesmen
of the North who project themes for their well-being based
upon the temperature of New England." They were helpless
as children "who have suddenly been punished and brought
face to face with duty." There was a "strange, weird sym-

pathy and affection" between whites and newly freed Ne-
groes, he observed, which emancipation had not changed.
The prospects, he said with some sense of prophecy, were
"hopeless." Characteristically, it was the women who attracted his most sympathetic attention, and he considered
them "in manner, natural grace and gentle womanliness . . .
far superior to the New Englander." [21]

With a final swing through Iowa and Illinois, he came off
the lecture road for good, except for a few spasmodic essays
on the platform, and in another country, much later in life.
He now turned back to concentrating, as best he could, on
writing.

EIGHT

Hand to Mouth

"He was an incorrigible borrower of money; he borrowed from all his friends; if he ever repaid a loan the incident failed to pass into history."
—Mark Twain

ONE of Bret's more sober-minded friends in the literary world was John Hay, who had been one of Abraham Lincoln's two private secretaries and since then had turned to writing for a livelihood. They were on excellent terms despite the fact that their stories mined the same picaresque vein.* Once Hay complained to Bret that he had run out of money and didn't know where to turn.

Bret laughed, not unsympathetically. "It's your own fault," he said. "Why did you fool away your money paying your debts?"

None of his contemporaries, it seemed, would fault Bret on that score. They regarded him as one of the nimblest and most elegant defaulters of his time. Outwitting one's creditors requires a certain unassailable savoir-faire — the least

---

* One James Redpath had commented on the Harte-Hay vogue:
This is the day of the gambler unstained . . .
You may murder or steal, keep a house of ill fame
And still go to Heaven — if you only die game." [1]

[165]

flicker of shame or regret can bring the whole pack down in full cry — and that was a quality Bret had cultivated since youth. He refused to be intimidated by his creditors or the bills they flourished.

Lecturing, arduous as it was, barely kept them at bay. He insisted on maintaining his family in a large and comfortable house and, from the summer of 1875 on, keeping a small apartment in New York at 713 Broadway for his frequent flights from home and its problems. No matter how much he protested in his letters to Anna that he yearned for his own hearth, he was absent from it at increasing intervals and not only when he was on the lecture circuit. From 1872 to his departure for Europe in 1878, his family saw very little of him.

One factor in his absences may have been the fact that his mother and her aged husband had moved into the Harte home at Morristown. His wife and mother didn't get along too well, and doubtless Colonel and Mrs. Williams were given shelter because they had nowhere else to turn.* Bret did not linger where his tranquillity could be disturbed, particularly by those near and dear.

Perhaps Anna would have tried to put a stop to his frequent departures except that he always had the excuse of making a living for his increasing number of dependents. And besides, he wrote such affectionate letters — the longer he stayed away the more affectionate, the more expressive of domestic yearnings they became. His talent for eluding creditors was matched only by his quicksilver quality as a husband.

With two more persons to provide for — three, counting a new daughter, his fourth child, Ethel — Bret had chosen a rather inopportune moment to embark on writing a novel.

* Both his mother and stepfather died before Bret left the United States.

Not only was the form unfamiliar to him, but he had usually run out of inspiration and inventiveness ("M'liss" was a possible exception) whenever he attempted a story longer than a few thousand words. It was inevitable, however, that he would be tempted to try the longer form of storytelling; as inevitable as his attempts at playwrighting. Writers are seldom satisfied to stay in the field in which they have made a reputation — someone else's form always looks more interesting and profitable. A successful novel would lend him stature he could achieve in no other way, just as a successful play would give him financial security.

With his increased responsibilities, however, he picked a poor time for the experiment. He was in debt and would have to count on spending a year on writing the novel to the exclusion of all other work. And his creditors were becoming importunate, both those in New York and those closer to home in Morristown, the local tradesmen, who were not inclined to extend long-term credit to a man with so poorly visible a means of support as scribbling for a living. One of his early biographers dredged up a tale of how Bret paid off an impatient butcher. Supposedly Bret collected the return postage sent with letters requesting his autograph, and the stamps added up to enough to keep the butcher quiet.[2]

There were many other stories current on his debt-dodging; in fact it was the scandal of the literary world. Not the least assiduous spreader of these tales, subsequently, was Mark Twain. His favorite story of Bret's cavalier attitude toward his obligations concerned a wealthy admirer who couldn't wait to meet Bret. Soon Bret was borrowing money from him in varying sums which eventually reached the total of three thousand dollars. On Christmas Eve of 1877 his wealthy friend collected the notes and sent them to Bret with a note saying he was canceling the IOU's as a Christmas present and begged him not to be offended by the gesture. Bret, according to Twain, sent the IOU's back with a letter "all afire with insulted dignity" which "formally and by irrevocable edict permanently annulled the existing friendship. But there was nothing in it about paying the notes sometime or other." [3] (This story, unlike other of Twain's anti-Harte propaganda essays, was confirmed by a more impartial observer. Noah Brooks, who had worked for and with Bret in San Francisco, and who remained friendly to him throughout his life, investigated a number of the stories floating around about Bret's blithe attitude toward his creditors. He happened to be with Harte when the latter received the IOU's from the wealthy admirer. Bret, Brooks recounted, damned the man for his "impudence." Brooks asked him what he was going to do about it, and here his account varied slightly from Twain's as he quoted Bret as replying, "I have made a new note for the full amount of these and have sent it to him with an intimation that I never allow pecuniary matters to trespass on the sacred domain of friendship." [4])

Twain related that he himself was victimized by Bret-the-borrower — and evidently brooded over it for thirty-odd years. On July 31, 1905, he met Thomas Wentworth Higginson of Boston in Dublin and had dinner with him that night. Twain, wrote Higginson in his journal, said he "lent three thousand dollars in all to Bret Harte when he first came East, though knowing him to be laden with California debts. When Harte asked him for $250, he proffered $500." [5*]

Twain expanded on Bret's borrowing methods in his autobiography. Bret, he recalled, appeared on the Twain doorstep in Hartford uninvited and unannounced one night,

* Regarding the debts Bret was supposed to have left in California, an article appeared in the San Francisco *Chronicle* of Dec. 15, 1872, which termed him "a rascal in the higher walks of life" and a "loose and not infrequent borrower of large sums . . ."

much as he had materialized out of a snowstorm at the home of the Thomas Bailey Aldriches. "He said he was without money and without a prospect; that he owed the New York butcher and baker two hundred and fifty dollars and could get no further credit from them; also he was in debt for his rent, and his landlord was threatening to turn his little family into the street." Twain insisted on giving him five hundred dollars to satisfy the landlord as well as the tradesmen. Far from being overcome by gratitude, Twain wrote, Bret "employed the rest of his visit in delivering himself of sparkling sarcasms about our home, our furniture and the rest of our domestic arrangements."

Noah Brooks, hearing all the stories about Bret's financial difficulties, went to their mutual friend Samuel Bowles, the salty fellow who edited and published the Springfield *Republican*. Evidently he hoped Bowles might volunteer some idea for helping Bret out of his troubles. Bowles only laughed crustily and commented, "Well, it does seem to me that there ought to be enough rich men in New York to keep Harte a-going." [6]

Harte himself took a nonchalant position on his financial troubles and the gossip that was going around about them. Once he ran into Brooks on a New York street corner, told him he'd left his rooms without his purse and needed a dime for fare on the Broadway horsecars. Brooks gave it to him. The next time they met Bret handed him the dime, laughing as he remarked, "You hear men say that I never pay my debts, but you can deny the slander."

No matter how blandly he faced a world teeming with creditors, Bret could hardly have been unaffected by those pressures. Thus he worked away at his novel *Gabriel Conroy* under handicaps that were more burdensome than they would have been to a writer who luxuriated in adversity and flourished artistically in a garret. His talent blossomed only in a cozy, secure atmosphere, for which he had a cat-like appreciation. *Gabriel Conroy*, his first and only novel, reflected his lack of ease and domestic harmony. He had begun it in the summer of 1874, when he was resting between lecture tours, and it took him a month to produce the prologue, a vivid description of a wagon train caught in the snow-clogged passes of the Sierras on its way to California. He continued to work on it, in Pullman cars and hotel rooms, while on tour. The following spring, by which time he had come off the road, he wrote his publisher, Elisha Bliss, head of the American Publishing Company of Hartford and a friend of Mark Twain's, that "I find the book winds up slowly. It requires as much care — even more — in *ending* than in beginning." The novel was already being set in type and the illustrations were being drawn. "Try and make the artist think that his reputation is equally at stake with mine . . . if only he would read my text a little more carefully." Bret and Bliss had differed over the selection of a title, Bret insisting on *Gabriel Conroy*. "Believe me, the shorter the title, the better the chance for its quotation and longevity." [7]

As Bret himself described the plot in a sort of prospectus for the consideration of interested publishers, Gabriel Conroy, the hero, was

an uncouth but gentle giant, of superb physique, but modest and diffident in manner and sincere in character. He escapes from Starvation Camp in the Sierras with his little sister Olly, and takes a squatter's claim at One Horse Gulch, where he finds a little gold, and where he earns a reputation as a nurse for the sick. Mme. Devarges, a divorcee and adventuress, learns of the presence of gold in his claim, and assuming the name of Grace Conroy, his sister, who is the real owner of the property by inheritance from Dr. Paul Devarges, begins proceedings against

Gabriel, but, being saved by him from drowning, changes her mind and marries him instead.

The silver is found, and Gabriel becomes rich. He is accused of killing his wife's former suitor and accomplice, Victor Ramirez, and does all in his power to sacrifice himself in order to save her, whom he believes to be the guilty person; but on the testimony of Henry Perkins, alias Henry Devarges, he is acquitted. He had married simply to give his little sister a companion, but the birth of a child draws him toward his wife, who has loved him for some time, though her motives for marrying him were wholly selfish.[8]

The novel's "longevity," however, was one thing he needn't have worried about. *Gabriel Conroy* simply proved that Bret wasn't a novelist. It was an episodic grab-bag, a catchall with everything but a firm and consistent story-line. Instead of concentrating on his hero and a few other major characters, he introduced a whole parade of characters — interesting in themselves but tending to clutter up the plot — who kept popping in and disappearing without much motivation. He attempted a vast mural of the early history of California, Spanish and American, and it was too abrupt a departure for a writer adept at miniatures. One of his more severe critics (in San Francisco) demolished the work on the grounds that Conroy was a fool, his sister a weakling, and the major villain a nonentity.[9] In general this was the reaction of American and English critics, who had awaited his first novel in a charitable mood. The novel, oddly enough, attained its greatest popularity in Germany, where it went through several reprintings.

Actually, though written off by literary historians as an abject failure, *Gabriel Conroy* had a number of things to recommend it — particularly the vividness of its characterization (of the lesser characters, unfortunately, more than the major ones), and the brilliance of his scenic descriptions. It also demonstrated the tyranny of the small-town mentality in a manner not to be equalled until the publication of Sinclair Lewis's *Main Street*. Those bits and pieces, including the gripping prologue, did not compensate, however, for its larger and more destructive flaws.

Despite its eventual failure once the critics took after it with fang and claw, *Gabriel Conroy* made Bret a small fortune, considering the purchasing value of the dollar in the depressed seventies. It was to be published by subscription, the most profitable method for an author at that time, with a royalty of seven and one-half per cent. In addition, *Scribner's Magazine* also contracted to publish it before seeing a line and paid him six thousand dollars, the most ever advanced for a serial up to that time.

Bret was almost delirous with joy when he wrote Osgood, his other publisher, about the money pouring in from his unfinished novel. He would not hear of any criticism of Roswell Smith, his literary agent. "I reject with scorn the small shifts and brutal sallies aimed in your note at that truly great man." He totted up other advances secured by the agent:

One thousand pounds is the sum he is to get from the English publisher for me. I have, I fear weakly, consented to take five thousand pounds for the rights in Europe, Asia and Africa — reserving Australia and certain penal settlements in the Pacific, where my works are popular. I can imagine how your breast will dilate with envy when you read of Roswell Smith's presentation at Court with a copy of "Grabiel Conroy" in one hand and "Bonnicastle" in the other.[10]

Presumably the six thousand pounds he was to receive for the English and Continental rights would be divided evenly with the American publisher; still, in that day, it was a tremendous windfall.

While finishing the book, he nibbled away persistently at the treasury of the American Publishing Company. Before he turned over the final chapter of *Gabriel Conroy*, in fact, he had obtained thirty-six hundred dollars in advances surrendered by Elisha Bliss under constant duress from his star author. As Mark Twain testified, writhing in anguish over having led his friend Bliss into the sinkhole of Bret's finances, ". . . Bliss could get plenty of promises out of Harte but no manuscript — at least no manuscript while Harte had money or could borrow it. He wouldn't touch the pen until the wolf actually had him by the hind leg; then he would do two or three days' violent work and let Bliss have it for an advance or royalties." [11]

These spurts of effort, accompanied by a plea for another advance, would occur about once a month, as Twain recollected. No individual advance was for a large sum but to "Bliss's telescopic vision a couple of hundred dollars that weren't due, or hadn't been earned, were a prodigious matter."

Bliss's mistake, Twain believed, was overenthusiasm at the beginning of the venture. "In the beginning he had recognized that a contract for a full-grown novel from Bret Harte was a valuable prize and he had been indiscreet enough to let his good fortune be trumpeted about the country." The publicity could have been valuable in building up interest in the book only "if he had been dealing with a man addicted to keeping his engagements," but by the time the novel came off the press it had been delayed so long as to cause the public to lose interest. [12] Partly the delay of publication until 1876 wasn't Bret's fault — as Twain did not mention in his memoir — because the serialization deal with *Scribner's* provided for it.

Bliss finally realized he had a "white elephant," according to Twain, because "as a subscription book its value had almost disappeared." Twain added that the serial rights were sold to *Scribner's* for "a trifling sum" — actually the highest ever paid to that date for such rights — since it was the only way he could recoup part of his investment. Twain violently overstated the case against Bret, dilatory and vexatious though he may have been for any publisher; for with all the money raked in for serial rights in the United States and Britain, and the foreign rights, in which Bliss shared equally with the author, the American Publishing Company should have turned a profit even though the book didn't sell very well in the United States.

All the money that came to Bret as proceeds from the novel dribbled away almost as quickly as the checks arrived. It was paid out to creditors, used to maintain his family in Morristown, splurged on a summer on the beach at Sea Cliff, Long Island, spent with tailors to keep him at the peak of fashion. His respite from financial worries was brief indeed. Even before *Gabriel Conroy* made its appearance in the book stalls Bret was groping around for ways to make more money faster. Curiously enough it didn't occur to him, apparently, to return to writing short stories, the safe and sure way of maintaining a decent nineteenth-century income.

Playwrighting instead caught his attention. The theater had always fascinated him. So did the prospect of settling back after a play was written and letting the royalties flow in from Broadway and numerous touring companies. His ability to fashion dialogue, particularly in the authentic dialect of Forty-niners, had been highly praised on all sides — and what, he mistakenly thought, was a play but dialogue? It was keeping the actors in motion, and credible motivation, as well as having them declaim at each other and the audience, and he apparently did not realize this. The technique of play-writing usually has to be absorbed through long immersion in the theater, backstage as well as out front. Bret, however, believed it was simply a job of writing like any other and plunged ahead with his usual initial outburst of enthusiasm. Perhaps the fact that three different pirated versions of "M'liss" were playing around the country encouraged his optimism.

He began work on a play titled *Two Men of Sandy Bar*, which was to be packed with tested ingredients. The gambler John Oakhurst, Colonel Starbottle and a Chinese laundryman Hop Sing, the latter a fresh characterization but the first two almost household names in the United States, would be the principal roles in a melodrama about the Vigilantes in a foothill town.

As soon as he had several scenes completed he dashed up to Cohasset, the seaside summer colony in Massachusetts which was favored by theatrical people. Two celebrated actors, Stuart Robson and Lawrence Barrett, were convinced that Bret was a playwright of great promise and held readings of the completed scenes.

When the whole play was finished, Robson agreed to produce and star in *Two Men of Sandy Bar*, reportedly paying Bret three thousand dollars in advance with a royalty of twenty dollars for each performance. Much exhilarated, he wrote his Boston publisher friend Osgood that he was about to make Stuart Robson's fortune because "I have got tired of enriching only publishers."

The play was opened out of town and brought to New York and the Union Square Theater the night of August 28, 1876. The audience reaction, not always a reliable indicator on an opening night, was good, but the newspaper critics fell upon it with the enthusiasm of the Vigilantes who figured in the melodrama. The *Times* man was particularly outraged at Bret's temerity in attempting to write a play. Robson, he said, was "an object of public pity" for the first time in his career after essaying the role of John Oakhurst. Rarely had Bret received such rude comment. "The piece is utterly aimless, is without coherency of plot, definiteness of purpose, or actions, and lacking in any artistic symmetry in its model, or characterization in its *dramatis personae*. Its sentiment is maudlin and mushy, its plot shallow, its pathos laughable, and its wit lachrymose. All in all it is a proof that the ability to write a comic song does not qualify one to write a play." *

The other critics were equally unkind. Largely on the strength of Robson's drawing power *Two Men of Sandy Bar* held on for a month's run in New York, then ventured into the hinterlands. Eventually it expired in San Francisco, where the reviewers assaulted it with a predictable fervor. One said it was "overweighted with a ballast of rubbish." San Francisco would never forgive Bret for having skipped off the moment he won his first measure of fans, nor for the bitter comments he made about the city in the East, even less for his insistence on writing of northern California as though it were still overrun by red-shirted miners and their laundress wives.

Bret was never to be convinced that he wasn't capable of fashioning a play that would please the critics and public alike. It was one of the more consistent facets of his Micawberism. Almost to the end of his life he was intermittently

* The critic referred to "The Heathen Chinee," which had been set to music by other hands.

becoming involved in theatrical schemes, generally with a collaborator to help share the burden (and the blame).

The first of these theatrical collaborators was to be Mark Twain, and it was to be one of the most star-crossed and vexatious collaborations in the history of the theater.

Considering his opinion of Bret's working and borrowing habits, it was strange that Twain consented to enter into the arrangement. It was suggested by Bret on this basis: Bret would contribute Hop Sing, the most successful character in *Two Men of Sandy Bar*, and Twain would "put in" the other major character, Scotty Briggs, and they would work together on stitching the two characters into the fabric of the plot. They would, as Twain said, "divide the swag" evenly.

Twain was persuaded to join in the venture largely because he admired the "perfectly delightful Chinaman" Hop Sing. *Two Men of Sandy Bar*, Twain believed, "would have succeeded if anyone else had written it. Bret killed off his own chances in New York by having charged loudly and publicly before the opening that the newspaper critics never said a favorable thing about a new play except when the favorable thing was bought and paid for beforehand." Perhaps this time he could be dissuaded from making such pronouncements before curtain time. As for his work habits, it was true that Bret dawdled unconscionably until the direst pressures drove him to his writing desk, but then "he could sit down and work harder — until temporary relief was secured — than any man I have ever seen." [13]

At first the two men worked separately, Twain in Hartford, Bret in New York, and everything went well. When Bret had finished Hop Sing and Twain his Scotty Briggs, the two characters would, somehow, be joined together with the other characters. To say the least, it was an odd method of collaboration and promised considerable difficulties in smoothing out a playable final product.

Once during this period Bret made one of his unannounced descents on the Twain home in Connecticut. It was shortly before Christmas, 1876, as Twain later recalled. Bret had been forced to halt work on the play temporarily to grind out a long story, *Thankful Blossom*, which had been commissioned by Charles A. Dana for the New York *Sun*. The story was laid against the American Revolution, the centennial of which was being observed, and Bret had been promised a hundred-dollar bonus if he finished it in time for the Christmas special edition. Bret, however, was being hounded by his creditors and needed a refuge in which to finish the story.

Bret arrived on the Twain doorstep, characteristically, just in time for dinner. He told the Twains that he had to get to work immediately after dinner, but thereupon gave one of his more memorable exhibitions in the art of procrastination. He chatted away before the fireplace in the Twain library until Mrs. Twain brought them a whiskey punch, Twain's usual nightcap. Eleven o'clock struck, and Bret "kept on pouring and pouring and consuming and consuming" until one o'clock, when Twain announced it was two hours past his bedtime. Before he could escape, Bret asked that a bottle of whiskey be sent to his room to aid the process of writing the rest of *Thankful Blossom*, and Twain complied though "it seemed to me that he had already swallowed enough whiskey to incapacitate him for work."

Bret drank and labored through the night. Long before breakfast he had finished the first quart of whiskey and procured another. Yet when he came to the breakfast table,

Twain recorded with astonishment, Bret had finished his story *and* the two quarts of whiskey, and was "not even tipsy, but quite himself and alert and animated."

Twain wondered what kind of work could be turned out under such circumstances. He found out later that morning when a local girls' group, the Saturday Morning Club, gathered in the Twain library. Twain had agreed to give them a reading, but suggested instead that Bret read his just-completed *Thankful Blossom*. Bret fumbled the job and Twain snatched the manuscript away from him to finish the reading.[14] He was surprised, he said, at the quality of the story and years later still considered it "belongs at the very top of Harte's literature" — which only indicates that writers, even the best, are seldom possessed of acute critical faculties.

Shortly after the holidays Bret returned for a longer visit during which he and Twain proposed to polish off the play, which was to be titled *Ah Sin*. At first the collaboration proceeded without either personal or professional friction. Twain frankly admired the ease and swiftness with which Bret set about the task, his professionalism, his command of technique. First they discussed the characters and how they would be worked into the plot, then Bret took over the main effort of getting it all on paper, "began to sketch the scenario, act by act and scene by scene." Twain testified that Bret could accomplish as much in an hour or two as he could do in "several weeks of painful and difficult labor. It was a wonderful performance." When it came to writing the dialogue, Twain would dictate that for the characters he was responsible for. In two weeks they were finished, satisfied they had produced a "comedy that was good and would act"; Twain conceded that Bret's contribution was "the best part of it."

[179]

Toward the end of the collaboration, however, Twain became increasingly irked by Bret's "sarcasms" about a certain lack of elegance in the Twain establishment. Bret indicated, in his lofty style, that he was accustomed to greater luxury, refinement and comfort than was available under the Twain roof. Undoubtedly this was a perverse expression of just the opposite: Bret's haphazard and debt-ridden existence, both in Morristown and in his New York lodgings, couldn't compare with the serene domesticity with which Twain surrounded himself. At the age of forty Bret was becoming a bitter and sometimes disgruntled man; the struggle to make a living, on terms suitable to a man of what he fancied was his deserved position in life, was fraying the urbanity on which he had always prided himself.

Twain must have understood something of the reasons for Bret's attitude, but he had been irked beyond endurance and leveled a shriveling tirade against his old friend and present collaborator.

He told Bret he wouldn't stand for his habit of denigrating Mrs. Twain.

It does not become you to sneer at all; you are not charged anything here for the bed you sleep in, yet you have been very smartly and wittily sarcastic about it . . . you have made sarcastic remarks about the furniture of the bedroom and about the table ware and about the servants and about the carriage and the sleigh and the coachman's livery . . . but this does not become you: you are barred from these criticisms by your situation and circumstances; you have a talent and a reputation which would enable you to support your family most respectably and independently if you were not a born bummer and a tramp; you are a loafer and an idler and you go clothed in rags, with not a whole shred on you except your inflamed red tie, and *it* isn't

paid for; nine tenths of your income is borrowed money —
money which, in fact, is stolen, since you never intended to re-
pay any of it . . . Where have you lived? Nobody knows.
Your own people do not know. But I know. You have lived in
the Jersey woods and marshes and have supported yourself as do
the other tramps . . .[15]

Twain did not quote Harte's reply, if any, leaving the implication that his collaborator merely hung his head and slunk
away crimson with shame.

There are several reasons to suspect the accuracy of
Twain's recollection of this incident. In the first place, he
recalled it exactly thirty years later. Secondly, he supposedly
denounced Bret some time early in February, the last day of
their collaboration on *Ah Sin*. Yet on February 22 Twain
was writing Howells that he and Harte were plotting out
another play. After such a denunciation it seems doubtful
Harte would have been willing to continue the collaboration; and actually it was Harte who, on March 1, notified
Twain that he didn't think it "advisable" that they write another play together.[16] And it might be noted that Twain's
diatribe, as he quoted it, contained several unjustifiable low
blows. The crack about the state of Bret's clothing, for instance: Bret always dressed as stylishly as possible, even at
the cost of being sued by his tailors. As for his debts, Bret
was handicapped by an optimism that outran his income. He
had come up so fast that he was unable to believe that his
luck wouldn't suddenly take a turn for the better. The fact
he took a rather jocular attitude toward his indebtedness indicated only that if he had a choice of laughing or weeping
over the situation, he preferred not to weep. His meticulous
attitude toward the smallest debts later in life proved he was

not a congenital deadbeat, but a victim of temporary circumstances.*

Literary historians have speculated at length over what really ruptured the friendship besides unpaid loans and Bret's alleged criticism of Mrs. Twain's taste. The eventual failure of their collaboration on *Ah Sin* was undoubtedly a contributing factor, but Bret's letter of March 1, 1877, must have been the deciding factor. Bret had just received a statement from Bliss on the sales of *Gabriel Conroy* and was shocked to learn that, by Bliss's accounting, the novel had sold fewer copies in five months than the hastily hacked out *Thankful Blossom* in one month. (The sale of *Gabriel Conroy* in that period was only two thousand copies.) Bret hinted to Twain that the American Publishing Company's records must have been falsified and that Twain, as a silent partner of Bliss's, profited from it.[17] The extremity of that charge could be forgiven only on the ground that Bret was close to cracking up over the desperate state of his finances.†

Bret also mentioned in that letter Twain's offer of twenty-five dollars a week and his board if Bret would collaborate on another play. He had to reject the offer, Bret said, because Twain would despise him if he accepted it and besides he could make more than that working on his own projects.

Twain naturally was enraged by the letter, and scrawled on the margin that he read only the first two pages before his temper exploded and he was unable to continue.[18]

Despite their mutual grievances, however, they got together late in April to help put *Ah Sin* into production and

---

* Harte's lifelong friend John Hay, later Secretary of State in the Theodore Roosevelt administration, is quoted as stating that Bret paid off all his debts eventually. The Hay quotation is contained in John Erskine's *Leading American Novelists*.

† Twain himself, four years later, threatened to sue the same company on charges he also had been swindled.

work on revisions in the script at a theater in Baltimore
where rehearsals were being held for the May 7 opening at
Washington's National Theater. Twain even undertook to
direct the actors. Before opening night Twain suffered an
attack of bronchitis and returned to his home in Hartford.
Bret was left in charge of the play-doctoring, a process ham-
pered by the fact that he and the star Parsloe, a man of growingly arrogant temperament, didn't get along. Parsloe had
apparently decided to ally himself with Twain, to whom he
wrote lengthy letters of complaint. Parsloe's charges against
Harte didn't quite jibe, though evidently Bret had fallen into
one of his periods of lassitude. On the one hand Parsloe complained that Bret's presence at a rehearsal annoyed the company; on the other, he charged that Bret was loafing on the
job and leaving it to the actors to make revisions as they went
into the final rehearsals. No doubt Twain felt Parsloe's gripes
were justified. All the available expert opinion indicated that
the play could have been considerably improved by cutting
rather than any extensive rewriting, and this should not have
been beyond Bret's capacities.

The opening-night audience responded enthusiastically
when at Twain's telegraphed suggestion it was asked to vote
on whether the play was a success. The critics were cooler.
The Star's man thought the play was remarkable more for
"novelty" than for any intrinsic merit is possessed. Certainly
anyone who expected a masterpiece from the two foremost
American humorists of the time would have been disappointed.

Despite the fact that the whole idea had been Bret's to begin with, he lost interest in the project entirely and Twain,
unaided, had to labor over the necessary revisions that summer. Bret in fact was preoccupied by a promising new job
which had been offered him. Early in July, while Twain and

the *Ah Sin* company were struggling to revamp the production in preparation for the New York opening July 31, Bret still lingered in Washington discussing the new post with his prospective employers. When *Ah Sin* opened on July 31 at Daly's Theater, Mark Twain was in attendance, but his collaborator found that other business required his presence in Washington. Bret may not have mastered the technique of the playwright, but he had acquired one attribute of the theater professional: he could smell a flop across several state lines.

At that, *Ah Sin*, possibly because the critics felt kindlier toward Mark Twain, who was billed as having personally supervised the production, than toward his collaborator, was not lambasted as heartily as *Two Men of Sandy Bar*. The New York *Sun* considered the play "beneath criticism," with a feeble plot, occasionally coarse dialogue and characters who lacked dramatic emphasis. The other newspapers were much gentler but none advised their readers to stand in line for tickets. Whatever praise they accorded the work was given Twain, while Bret was showered with the blame for its ineptitude. Just how the men in the aisle seats were able to divine which collaborator was responsible for what, they did not reveal. Twain himself credited Bret with having provided the best parts of the work, and he was rarely suffused with false modesty.

"The piece," as Twain laconically recorded, "perished." It barely lasted a month at Daly's, then limped out on the road and expired months later on the kerosene circuit. In his wry account of what might have been a historic collaboration, Twain ended with an incident which he believed illumined the character of his late colleague.

About the time the script of *Ah Sin* was to be turned over to the producer, Twain came down to New York and that evening met Bret in the lobby of the St. James Hotel. The first thing he learned was that Bret, tardy as usual, hadn't delivered the manuscript. Twain proposed that they do so immediately, expecting that Bret would suggest they walk over to the theater a few blocks away.

Instead Bret, who looked shabby and wore a "crumpled little soft hat which was a size or two too small for him," stepped over to the reception desk and asked the clerk to send it around to the theater. The clerk looked him up and down, sniffed, and announced, "The messenger's fee will be ten cents."

"Call him," Bret demanded.

When the boy appeared, Bret turned to Twain and said, "Let me have a dollar."

Twain came up with a dollar bill and Bret handed it to the messenger.

"Wait," said the clerk, "I'll give you change."

"Never mind," said Bret with a regal gesture. "Let the boy keep it." [19]

NINE

Saved by an Election

"He hasn't any more passion for his
country than an oyster has for its bed;
in fact not so much and I apologize to
the oyster."
—Mark Twain on Bret Harte

B RET lingered on, month after month, in Washington.
Once again a bright vision of recouping his fortunes
bedazzled him. The habit of failure was becoming ingrained,
what with the disappointing reception of *Gabriel Conroy*,
and with *Two Men of Sandy Bar* and *Ah Sin* sinking without a trace in the provinces, but he refused to admit it.

What held him in Washington was the proposal of a
group of men headed by John J. Piatt to build up a magazine
called the *Capitol*, which resembled the *Overland Monthly*
in style and content. Bret was to write for it at one thousand dollars a story or article, and later was offered the post
of co-editor with Piatt.

Past forty now and growing anxious about the slipperiness
of the slope he was trying to ascend, he was becoming a desperate man. He suffered from dyspepsia. His wardrobe was
growing shabby with the disappearance of available credit.
The depression in which he floundered made the work of
writing doubly onerous; it took him weeks to turn out "The

Story of a Mine" for the *Capitol*. The potboilers he produced for the New York *Sun* at one hundred dollars a story during this period represented not only a financial but an artistic low point.

Usually he sent half the money he received for his Sunday-supplement fiction to Morristown immediately in hope of staving off the local tradesmen. He was also sending money to Eliza, his sister, who had recently been widowed and was struggling along as the proprietor of a boardinghouse.

He tried to keep his spirits up by writing a humorously archaic letter to a friend in Baltimore, reporting that "I am lying Ill of a Sore Distemper which cometh from the Fogs and vile airs that the fens and marches of the Capitol Exhale at Night . . ." He hinted that he might drop in to sample his friend's hospitality, or as he archly put it, "I shall Chance to Lie at yr. House . . ."[1]

A touch of hypochondria had become evident in his correspondence. Almost every letter he wrote home dwelled at length on the parlous condition of his health. His respiratory and digestive tracts, to judge from his complaints to Anna, were in a constant state of inflammation and rebellion.

One would have thought he was stationed at some tropical outpost. "I wonder how I stand it; but I am careful with my diet and expose myself but little to the direct sun." Anna evidently had suggested that the family join him in Washington, and he was having none of that. It was "very unhealthy in summer for children." The question of moving the family to Washington was "a little too large to be . . . settled at once."

At the moment Mrs. Harte was stranded in a resort hotel on the Jersey shore with their children, but he hoped she would be patient a little longer. "If I could do anything by being *there*," he replied to what must have been a complaining letter, "more than I am doing here, I would come." He dodged the obvious fact that for a family in their straits it would be much more sensible to maintain them in one home rather than two.[2]

Shortly after receiving a letter which apparently complained in strong terms of his living away from home and leaving her to stand off hotel managers and other creditors single-handed, he replied expansively regarding his prospects at the *Capitol*. The management of the *Capitol* had offered him five thousand dollars a year if he would share the editorship with Piatt. Aside from editing, he would be required to fill two columns of the weekly, a stint which would leave him plenty of time for outside writing. "Washington," he oddly enthused, "is the place for a literary man to make money." He added that he would try to rejoin the family for a few days the following week and "if the roads are blocked by strikers" — there was a nationwide Knights of Labor strike against the railroads — he would "come by sea."

Throughout the summer he continued to radiate optimism about his prospects with the *Capitol*, even though Piatt never quite kept his promises and paid him piecemeal for the work he was doing. From what he received he sent more than half home. Anna and the children evidently were drifting from resort to resort for some unexplained reason, and late in July Bret complained that he had to telegraph his sister Eliza in an effort to track them down. He was trying to cure what had been diagnosed as "gastric catarrh" by living on beef tea and broth and going on the wagon. "I had to be half killed before I could show my self-control."

By September 21, he was confessing that the *Capitol* apparently was unable to meet its obligations to him and begging Anna to "be patient a day or two longer." A month later he wrote Anna that he was hanging on in Washington "in the hope of getting something from the *Capitol*." [3] That proved to be a forlorn hope, however, as the weekly's creditors pounced a few days later and attached all its assets.

Bret stayed on in Washington, eked out a living and enough to send fifty dollars home at irregular intervals by grinding away at Sunday-supplement stories for the New York *Sun*.

There followed what Bret later called "that *awful, terrible* winter." He stayed on at Rigg's Hotel in Washington, somehow unable to face an emptyhanded homecoming. Not the least of the worries that confronted him was the realization that he could no longer make a living as a writer; he'd run out of fuel for the imagination; his stuff was trite, without a spark of animation, a reworking of old materials.

In his predicament he decided to turn to the Great White Father, the federal government, as his last hope. Other writers — Melville, Hawthorne, Whitman among them — had taken jobs with the government under similar circumstances. He himself of course had worked for the United States Mint, and with that sinecure to provide him with financial security had managed to produce a good deal of writing on the side.

Fortunately for him a Republican administration, headed by Rutherford B. Hayes, had won out in the controversial election of 1876, and now, in 1878, he had several friends well situated in the government. He had been a Republican back when Republicans were a lot scarcer, had vociferously supported the party in Lincoln's first touch-and-go election, so he had a claim to a return on his loyalty. Furthermore his record as a minor executive with the Mint showed that he had some grasp of administrative matters.

According to Mark Twain, however, in his sardonic footnote to Bret's Federal job-hunting, the latter characteristically hedged his bets. During the election campaign of 1876, Twain said, Bret avowed support of both Hayes and Samuel Tilden, the Democratic candidate, depending on whom he was speaking to. Twain recalled that Bret paid him a visit in Hartford the day before Election Day, November 8; it was the period during which they were collaborating on *Ah Sin*. He was surprised to learn that Bret intended to stay over Election Day, and asked him whether he didn't intend to vote in New York, where he was registered. Bret said he had no intention of voting, because "through influential friends he had secured the promise of a consulate from Mr. Tilden and the same promise from Mr. Hayes . . . He said that he could not afford to vote for either of the candidates, because the other candidate might find out and consider himself privileged to cancel his pledge." Twain, of course, professed himself shocked at such unabashed cynicism.[4]

What makes his recollection of Bret's maneuvering — though it was not entirely out of character, certainly — suspect in the extreme is the fact that in the fall of 1876, so far as can be ascertained, Bret had had no intention of seeking any sort of government job. His mood then was euphoric. *Ah Sin* would be a smashing success, and his other writing, benefiting from it, would also come up to mark. In the fall of 1876 he had not the slightest intimation that by early 1878 he would desperately need or want a government job.

A good share of that winter of 1878 Bret spent in the corridors and anterooms of the bureaucracy. His best hope of landing a position which would support him and his family while he struggled to get his literary career back on the tracks was John Hay, who had entered the State Department when the Hayes administration took over. A European consulate would fit both his capabilities and his need for spare time.

In an undated letter to Anna of that period, he wrote that President Hayes, Secretary of the Interior Carl Schurz and other high officials had assured him of a post in western Europe. President Hayes received him in the Cabinet room, he wrote, and promised that " 'he would unite with the Secretary of State' in giving me an appointment." A Colonel Laking in the State Department had also befriended him and saw to it that his name was on the list of appointments abroad. "No one could have been kinder to me than this noble Teuton; no one has ever, I think, received such uniform courtesy and intelligent appreciation as I have."

A few days later he was interviewed by Assistant Secretary of State Frederick W. Seward, the son of the wartime Secretary, and discussed which consulate would be his. At first he was offered the prestigious post of First Secretary of the American Legation in Russia, but that would have required private means to support the social demands of the position, and "I could barely keep up appearances on the salary." Seward then led him over to a map on the wall and said:

Mr. Harte, wouldn't you like to look at the map and look at some of the places talked of for you? You know, however, that you are not supposed to know anything about it — until you are offered some place. But here is Crefeld, near Dusseldorf, in Germany, on the Rhine, not much to do and it's worth about two thousand now and may be raised to three or four thousand. What do you think of it? Mr. Matthews was looking at it for you and we've stopped the application of others for it at present. It is vacant now, and has the advantage that you could take it at once.[5]

No matter how politely Mr. Seward put it, Crefeld, in the Rhineland, had been settled upon as Bret's post.

Bret was feeling expansive again, for the first time in almost a year, as he wrote Anna that a petition was being circulated in Congress on behalf of his appointment and bore the signatures of Republican and Democratic members alike. "One of the Senators told me that in the history of the American Congress, no such honour or compliment was ever before given to an illustrious citizen."

"Illustrious" though he may have been, he had to report that certain "enemies were trying to poison Mr. Evarts's ear with reports of my debts, extravagancies, etc. My friends took hold of the matter on the ground that Mr. Evarts [the Secretary of State] would be influenced by it, as this statement, if true, might show my unfitness for any financial trust. In this extremity I remembered that I had held a pretty responsible position in the Mint, honourably, for seven years. They were overjoyed at this news." His record was looked up, Bret said, and the snide criticism of his enemies was "demolished." * The prospect of a consulate was, he wrote Anna, "a glimpse of Paradise." [7]

Several days later he was able to write home that his commission was being drawn up by the chief clerk in the State Department. "It is *Crefeld* — and I am beginning to think that perhaps it is, as Mr. Seward says, the best thing for a beginning." Lest she be overwhelmed by the good news and the fact that "the long suspense was over and that I had a place at last," he was compelled to add that "I've been quite sick and my cold and cough has returned; but I'm ever so much relieved and hopeful now." [8]

On May 11, 1878, his appointment as consul at Crefeld

---

* Probably unknown to Bret was the fact that Mark Twain was one of those enemies. Twain wrote President Hayes decrying Harte's appointment. The President then queried William Dean Howells, whose wife was his cousin, and Howells replied that he knew of nothing about Harte which should prevent his appointment.[6]

was officially announced and he posted bond and wrote his letter of acceptance.

He went home to Morristown to spend a week or two with his family. When he said goodbye, he was presumably unaware of the fact he would never see Morristown, or his homeland for that matter, again. Nor that he would never be entirely reunited with his family, nor that Anna wouldn't see him again for almost a quarter of a century, and then only after she finally managed to cross the Atlantic and catch up with him, briefly, in England. His pseudo-bachelorhood, of which he had become very fond, would continue to the end of his life. In accomplishing this he was to play one of the longest con-games in the annals of matrimony.

While waiting to take ship in New York, he wrote William Dean Howells that he was sending a poem for the *Atlantic*, one of many he intended to write "when the soul that is in me shall germinate." Perhaps he was already considering the possibility of long exile in Europe, even more separated from the background of his stories and poems, for he wrote that "I find men and women pretty much the same on Fifth Avenue as in Dutch Flat" and there was "abundant material" for his writing wherever he went.[9] It was to be all too true of Bret that you could take him out of California but you couldn't take the California out of his writing.

On June 28, aboard the *Suevia*, he sailed for England, one of the earliest of America's literary expatriates, and one of those who would never return. Mark Twain, years later, thought it a small loss. Bret, he wrote in his autobiography, was like Edward Everett Hale's "The Man Without a Country." "He hadn't any more passion for his country than an oyster has for its bed; in fact not so much and I apologize to the oyster. The higher passions were left out of Harte; what he knew about them he got from books." [10] Many of his contemporaries would have agreed with that verdict, though they might have phrased it less harshly. They were one of the reasons he never cared enough about returning to this country to set foot on a gangplank. He loved America, but found he could very well live without Americans.

III Expatriate

TEN

A Disgruntled Watch on the Rhine

DESPITE Mark Twain's man-without-a-country characterization of him, Bret Harte sailed for Europe, undoubtedly, without the intention of expatriating himself for the rest of his life. He hoped to use the financial respite offered by his consular appointment to rehabilitate himself as a writer, then return home in triumph. He had long wanted to go abroad, particularly to England, not only to obtain a fresh perspective but to bask in the less adulterated admiration accorded his work overseas. His books and stories sold especially well in Britain and Germany. There would be less of the bitchiness, he was confident, among the more urbane and generous literary men abroad; the gossip about his debts and drinking and family affairs would hardly follow him across the Atlantic, and in both a personal and a professional sense he would be making a fresh start in the old world.

That malignity stemmed chiefly from Mark Twain and, whatever Bret's hopes, followed him overseas. Twain was sojourning in Heidelberg when he received the news of Bret's appointment to the German post no great distance away. Twain wrote Howells immediately, on June 27, demanding to know which German town Harte was about to "filthify with his presence." He was indignant over the fact President

Hayes had "silently ignored" his offer to produce evidence of Harte's unfitness for a government appointment, and admitted that he felt "personally snubbed."

In his letter to Howells, Twain categorized Harte as a liar, thief, swindler, snob, sot, sponge and coward. He also charged Harte with concealing the fact of his quarter-Jewish ancestry. (If so, it was a pretty feeble attempt at concealment. It was generally known that Harte was partly Jewish, and there is no evidence to suggest that he ever denied it. James Russell Lowell exhibited a distaste for Harte, in Howells's belief, because he knew of Harte's ancestry. Oddly and ironically enough, Lowell kept himself aloof from Twain because he wrongly suspected that Twain also had Jewish blood. The old saints were not entirely saintly. Bret, incidentally, returned Lowell's dislike in equal measure.)

Twain also made the groundless accusation that Harte, while editor of the *Overland*, had pocketed money that was supposed to have been paid contributors. Harte, he further declared to Howells, would not be allowed to "swindle" the Germans if he could help it. He proposed to write the authorities of whatever town Bret "filthified" and warn them against lending him money.[1] Apparently he didn't carry out his threat.

Fortunately Bret was unaware of all this ill-wishing.

It would be a drastic oversimplification to suggest that he was eager to leave his native land because of the crass materialism of the "wild seventies," the decade in which he won fame and lost it almost as quickly. True enough the United States seemed to be in the grip of the Goulds, Fiskes, Vanderbilts, Drews and lesser predators; that the Gilded Age often seemed to a sensitive man unbearably vulgar and money-grubbing; that the West was being stolen rather than won by the land sharks and crooked entrepreneurs who followed the frontier regiments over the graves of the Indian nations; that financial success was the sole criterion of a man's worth, and anyone who had to be badgered by his butcher and sued by his tailor was beneath contempt. But Bret wasn't so much affronted by the materialism and amorality of the times as depressed by his inability to share in their bounty. He absorbed all he could of their comfort and luxury, spent his substance on fine clothes, good cigars and whiskey and food. All his life, actually, had been spent in a money-centered society, whether in the cities or the gold-bearing foothills. Going abroad wasn't an escape but a chance at making a comeback.

For all his hopes, however, England initially was something of a disappointment. His friends there had assured him of a warm welcome, but "nobody has been to see me yet — it takes a long time, I suppose, for people to find you are in London." He had sent a letter of introduction from the playwright Dion Boucicault to Charles Reade, along with his card, but Reade hadn't responded. It appeared that he would have to proceed to Germany without having seen anyone but his English publisher. At first glimpse London seemed a "sluggish nightmare." [2]

About Germany — then much admired by Americans, especially, for its scientific achievements, its music and philosophy, and by some for its quick victories over Austria and France — his impressions were less vague. He didn't like Germany or the Germans, and never would. In the first place he couldn't speak the language except for "one or two little phrases." The people themselves seemed more alien, somehow a little frightening in their crude vigor and vitality, than what he had glimpsed of the English and the French. Their capacity for food and drink was downright dismaying. Even the architecture was disturbing: "those impossible houses — those unreal silent streets."

His complaints about the crudity of German life were a constant refrain in his letters home. The second night he spent in Crefeld he attended a festival "in an artificial garden, beside an artificial lake, looking at artificial flowers." The beer and wine flowed endlessly into seemingly bottomless gullets. "Here as in Paris, everybody drinks, and all the time, and nobody gets drunk. Beer, beer, beer — and guzzle, guzzle, guzzle, food and drink, and drink and food again." Beside the lusty Germans, he thought, Americans were "but insubstantial spirits." [3]

By that time he was feeling better about his reception, or lack of it, in England. Charles Reade had written him and the letter had been forwarded from London. James Anthony Froude, the venerable biographer of Thomas Carlyle, whom he met during one of Froude's American visits, had also written and invited him to visit at his country place in Devonshire. Even so he believed that he had not received a warmer welcome because, as he had learned, "the French and English papers copied all the ugly things" which had been published in the United States about him.

During his first days in Crefeld he felt that he'd be lucky to stick it out for a year, and only his wife's disappointment at another failure would make him endure Crefeld that long. It was a small city in the Rhineland, with the damp misty climate of the Rhenish lowlands, certainly not the best place for a man with an ultra-sensitive respiratory tract. His office was small and cramped. The people with whom he had to do business were only "a little kind." Crefeld exported a considerable amount of silk, velvet and other textiles to the United States, so the American consulate was kept fairly busy licensing this trade. Practically all this sort of detail, however, was handled by a young German named Schneider, whom he engaged as vice-consul at five hundred dollars a year and whose proficiency in English, French and German made up for Bret's incapacity as a linguist. Bret's duties were largely ceremonial and supervisory; thus he would be able to devote most of his energy to writing, which he hoped would bring in another twenty-five hundred dollars a year, provided he was able to surmount his physical and psychological problems. With his second letter home there resumed the familiar and never-ending catalogue of his woes — "incessant" headaches and a desperate loneliness at this point — with which, it seemed, he was determined to get the jump on his wife and her own complaints.

He made it very plain to Anna that, if she was left at home with their children and creditors, life was anything but pleasant in this backwater of the Rhineland. No mention of the medieval charm of its architecture or of the magnificence of its setting, which had enchanted travelers for centuries. Not a word about its cultural aspects. All he could see was its provincialism and vulgarity.

Bret evidently had left home promising that Anna and the children would be brought over almost immediately. Now he made it clear that they must save up "at least eight hundred dollars" in addition to their ship and train fares before a reunion could even be considered. He explained that there was no choice but living like a gentleman in Germany, which he considered due his position, if not his income, or living like a "petty shopkeeper." The first would take three thousand dollars a year, the second one thousand dollars, but even at the cost of keeping the family separated a while longer he must insist that they live on the gentlemanly scale.

He had been at his post only two weeks when he began

making plans for an immediate vacation in France, England and perhaps Switzerland. To Anna he explained that he simply had to get away from Crefeld and its lack of amenities. His hotel was encrusted with history; it was over four hundred years old and had sheltered soldiers during the Thirty Years' War, but his room was "the most uncomfortable hole I ever was in." The city now seemed to him like a shrunken Philadelphia but without its neatness. Its houses were so small that "a man, two blocks away, looms up like a tree." German cooking was "damnable."

He continued to look upon the populace with unabated distaste. Although his own capacity for whiskey compelled Mark Twain's reluctant admiration, he professed himself disgusted with the local custom of wine-bibbing. Every man, he said, drank a couple of bottles of wine with dinner. None of them seemed to get drunk from their exertions but many had red-veined cheeks and purple noses. "God help me," he piously added, "from ever becoming one of these fat-witted rosy satyrs." [4]

One of his more winning qualities was his concern for children and animals, and even here the Germans let him down. It shocked him that the Germans made dogs work as beasts of burden, such as drawing milk carts through the streets (then common to all western European cities). Dogs, he held, should be valued for their "lawless, gentle, loving uselessness. . . . I fancy the dog seems to feel the monstrosity of the performance and in sheer shame for his master forgivingly tries to assume it is play." German children, he found, were too "serious" and "grave." When he stopped to talk to two little blonde girls, they seemed unable to comprehend his playful intentions. That they may have been inhibited by the fact he couldn't speak German didn't seem to occur to him. Perhaps like the mythical Englishman he fancied that the "natives" could understand him if he simply raised his voice. It was hardly strange that the only native he approved of happened to be the "very sweet German wife who speaks English well" and who was married to the American consul in Barmen.

Exactly fourteen days after his arrival in Crefeld, having arranged affairs in the office so his presence wouldn't be unduly missed, he took off on a month's vacation in France and England. A sinecure, obtained through political influence, meant exactly what it said to Bret. He literally fled from Rhenish provincialism to luxuriate first in the cosmopolitan graces of Paris, where he negotiated with the editor of *Figaro* for an article about his impressions of the French capital.

By August 11 he was writing Anna from London that his hair was still standing on end from the wickedness of Paris. He complained that his health was still miserable — hacking cough, poor appetite, sleeplessness — even though he had escaped the bad advice of German physicians. One practitioner, he claimed, had prescribed valerian to help him sleep, but when he opened the bottle he smelled chloroform and threw it out the window. Few German doctors, he added, believed in the homeopathic theory of medicine, of which Bret was then a devoted follower.

This time London was much more receptive, if not quite as open-armed in its welcome as he had hoped. One of its most distinguished periodicals had commented, on learning that he had been appointed to the consular post, "It is to be hoped that his duties will not prove so engrossing as to prevent him from continuing to write," [5] and the English literary world regarded him as one of the contemporary greats.

It may have galled him that some of the warmth of his welcome was due to Joaquin Miller, whose florid verse Bret had kept out of the *Overland Monthly* with all the determination of a knight defending his keep. Miller since then had been widely published, not only in the *Overland* but in England, which regarded him as the epitome of the American frontiersman. Then and on earlier visits Miller had made himself the darling of London society with his flamboyant dress and manner. On his first visit early in the seventies he had sent a delicious shudder through the ranked hostesses of London by appearing everywhere in a bearskin cape thrown over his shoulders, red flannel shirts and high boots. His voice roared out, quoting his own poetry, from beneath a broad sombrero. Social historians of the time recorded with awe his habit of smoking three cigars at once, and of biting debutantes' ankles when he felt frolicsome. His tall tales kept the most fashionable dinner tables enthralled, even though, as his fellow Americans knew, he had "borrowed the events of the dime novel for his past."

Shuddering much less deliciously than the hostesses, no doubt, Bret allowed himself to be taken in hand by Miller on his arrival. Presumably Miller had not heard of Bret's remark, a half-dozen years earlier when Miller was making his first splash in London society: "Joaquin Miller is the greatest liar the world has ever known." Nevertheless he suffered the exuberant Miller's presence and allowed him to arrange an introduction to George Eliot, who, without specifying which, told Bret that one of his poems was "the finest thing in our language." Miller also escorted Bret on a pilgrimage to Charles Dickens's grave. Then, perhaps with some relief, Bret detached himself from that traveling vaudeville show.

Despite that brief thaw, he and Miller were never again on friendly terms. A quarter of a century later, at a banquet at the Bohemian Club in San Francisco, Miller appeared in his usual bearskin-and-boots costume, ate and drank with relish, and appeared to be in high spirits until the chief speaker of the evening launched into a lengthy tribute to Bret's literary accomplishments. Miller got up from his chair, glowered at the speaker and stomped out of the banquet hall. A short time later, the speaker having consented to a question period, someone asked, "What has become of the old, picturesque Wild West?" The speaker got a roar of laughter by replying, "Haven't you noticed? He just walked out." [6]

Perhaps Bret's reception on his second visit to England was rather tepid because he refused to emulate Miller and behave as the English expected of any man who had made his mark on the far frontiers. Later he was to cater somewhat to this expectation, expanding, as he grew older, on the more picturesque aspects of his life in the mining camps, but initially he resented the indignity of the situation. He was a writer, not a road show. Whatever was colorful or extravagant about a minnesinger of the Wild West would have to be found in his writings.

In his first letter to Anna from England during that visit he complained that James Anthony Froude, who had invited him to his country home, was the only Englishman who had "treated me with any particular kindness." Lord Houghton had extended a vague invitation to dine with him, but there had been no follow-up.

The visit to Froude's home, however, made up for London's coolness. He thought Froude's place on the Devonshire coast the most perfect country house he had ever visited, with lawns and terraces sweeping gracefully to the seawall, a splendid walled garden, and a bountiful peach orchard. He was impressed by the fact that this had been the seat of the Earl of Devon, whose name was inscribed on the door of the room Bret occupied.

Even more satisfying was the way he hit it off with Froude and his family. Himself a noted historian, Froude would soon begin work on his epic biography of Carlyle. Froude, Bret wrote Anna, was a "dear noble old fellow . . . democratic in the best sense of the word." He was properly awed by the fact that Froude was Tennyson's best friend as well as Carlyle's most trusted intimate.[7]

Froude was a widower with two daughters and a son, and Bret was considerably amused by the childen. "The eldest girl is not unlike a highly educated Boston girl . . . There is the usual sly grimace, with the usual much 'put-upon' look . . . The youngest daughter, only ten years old, told her sister in reference to some conversation Froude and I had 'that Mr. Bret Harte was inclined to be *skeptical.*' Doesn't this exceed any English story of the precocity of American children?" Froude's fourteen-year-old son, he related, acted like an American boy of eight and talked like a man of thirty. He admired the manners and breeding of the Froude children but was disturbed by the probability that they were imposed on them through "some discipline that I don't like." He was also disquieted by the rigid class structure of English life; the tendency to become more American in outlook the longer he was away from his native country was to grow, often rather wistfully, with the passing years of expatriation. Somehow he found the respect shown him by the Froude children rather depressing. "I can easily feel how this deference to superiors is ingrained in all." [8]

Not at all depressing was the English attitude toward writers of Froude's stature: "they are kings." Undoubtedly Bret was beginning to view England as the place where he could continue his literary career in an atmosphere of dignity and tranquillity.

On leaving the Froudes, he journeyed to Newstead Abbey near Nottingham, where Lord Byron had lived. For this also he was grudgingly beholden to Joaquin Miller, who was visiting at the Abbey when the invitation was forwarded to Bret at the Froudes', but, as he hastily added in his report to Anna, "after I arrived here, and since I have been here, all the kindness and excessive cordiality shown to me I think I won for myself." Mrs. Webb, his hostess at Newstead Abbey, insisted that he was to think of the place as his English home and the Webbs as his English first cousins.

He was overcome by the melancholy beauty of the Abbey, with "Byron's genius instinct in every line of the ruined chapel." As he wandered through places the poet had known as a boy Byron became a reality to him. Byron, the perverse romantic, had never greatly appealed to him but now he felt that he could weep for his tormented life; "I walk here alone in a dream." He accounted it a privilege to be allowed to sleep in the room reputedly haunted by Byron's ghost. There was no spectral visitation, but he wrote a poem to commemorate the occasion which he presented to Geraldine Webb.[9]

Although he professed himself to be disturbed by the class distinctions upon which the English placed so much emphasis, his head was ever so slightly turned by meeting the Duchess of St. Albans, who flattered him by attempting to kidnap him from the Webbs and whom he characterized as a woman of grace, sympathy and intelligence. It was the beginning of a friendship which was to cause considerable tongue-wagging in England, with trans-Atlantic echoes. That the duchess should attempt to steal him away from the Webbs and take him to her home, Bestwood Lodge, was frankly overwhelming. He couldn't affront the Webbs' hospitality by permitting that, but promised to visit her on his next trip to England. Although she was the wife of the second-ranking duke of the realm, he informed Anna, he felt more at home with her than among any American women he could recall. Perhaps to mollify any resentment Anna might have felt over his single-handed conquests in the highest and most glittering society while she remained in stodgy Morristown, he added that the Webbs wanted her to visit them as soon as she came to England. He also hastened to add that he was "heartsick" over being separated from his family.[10]

Some of the heartwarming quality of his reception by the Froudes and Webbs sustained him on his return to Germany, and he wrote a long letter to his son Frank about the history of Newstead Abbey and the outsize achievements of his host, Colonel William Frederick Webb, who was a celebrated African explorer, friend of Livingstone, owner of a coal mine that "runs under half a county."

By early October, however, the Teutonic malaise apparently had gripped him again. He had a bad cold and his dyspepsia was "terrible." The only treatment he could find for the latter was a goblet of hot milk and cold seltzer-water taken on rising and occasional glasses of Bordeaux wine the rest of the day. In spite of these ailments he was beginning work on a story commissioned by the English magazine *Belgravia* and a number of sketches which he hoped *Scribner's* or the *Atlantic Monthly* would publish.

Only a month later he was taking another vacation in England. Obviously he could not wait to accept the Duchess of St. Albans's invitation, and hastened through London to Bestwood Lodge. This time he emphasized the duchess's "noble-souled" quality in his letters home. The duke, not unexpectedly, he found less attractive, an aloof and reserved gentleman with a "cold, grave" passion for gambling. The chill dampness of November in England was so depressing that he could easily understand why the suicide rate rose so abruptly in England during that month.

It was almost a month before he returned to his post in Crefeld, "very nervous over your long silence," as he wrote Anna. While he was disporting himself with the lovely and amiable duchess and her friends, it seems, Mrs. Harte was having money troubles at home and he had to cable her one hundred and fifty dollars. Henceforth, he wrote, he would send her regular semi-monthly checks on the first and fifteenth. He had completed two short stories, "Great Deadwood Mystery" and "The Heiress of Red Dog," and felt that his literary career was waxing again. To keep the money rolling in, he was considering various lecture offers in Germany and England, much as he detested platform appearances. On December 2, in fact, he lectured before four hundred persons, mostly English, in the Kursaal at Wiesbaden, taking a Rhine boat to the spa and finding the scenery spectacular but "slightly theatrical." He needed the one-hundred-dollar fee to send home for Christmas. From then on, it appears, he devoted about half his income, or perhaps a little more, toward supporting Anna and his four children, with the balance spent on keeping himself in style, if not luxury, and amusing himself generally.

Just how grim his life in Crefeld was it is hard to judge on the only available evidence, his letters home and occasional glints of reminiscence from people who knew him in Germany. The tenor of his correspondence with Anna — unfortunately her letters to him have not been preserved, but judging from his replies they must have contained frequent complaints of their continued separation and the difficulty of maintaining a home in Morristown on half his income — was unremittingly plaintive. Rheumatism was added to the list of his complaints; the German winter was "black and bitter"; the red tape of running a consulate, despite the best efforts of his German assistant, occasionally caught him in its snarls, and Anna must understand that he was "very, very lonely." The loneliness could have been relieved by bringing over his family, but diphtheria was "frightfully prevalent" and the Duchess of Hesse-Darmstadt, in a nearby province, had died of the disease after kissing her stricken child. He emphasized that there was no pleasure to be found in Germany that couldn't be obtained in the United States with "less trouble and expense."

Balanced against this recitation of woe, however, was his fairly active social life. He had made friends at last with a number of Germans and regularly attended concerts, the theater and the opera in Dusseldorf and Cologne. On such occasions and at dinner parties he was always seen in the most aristocratic company. The general commanding the military district of Dusseldorf — though a stiff-backed Junker seems about the least likely specimen of humanity to win Bret's approval — was one of his closest friends while in Crefeld.

There was a small mystery about the Christmas holiday of 1878 which would certainly have aroused Mrs. Harte's interest if she had ever learned about it. A letter to a Crefeld resident named Jengtes exists, though not in the family-published collection of Harte letters, in which Bret politely turned down an invitation to spend Christmas with him and his family. He and his cousin, "Miss Cooper," Bret explained, had already accepted an invitation to spend the holiday with a Madame Fay in Dusseldorf.[11] The mystery: who was Miss Cooper? He had no cousins by that name, and he didn't refer to her in any letters to his wife. And if she wasn't his cousin, why did he feel it necessary to designate her as such among the righteous burghers of Crefeld?

His letter to Anna during the Christmas season was a brief and uninformative one paragraph wishing her and the children a happy new year.

The need for money to support two establishments, which continued relentlessly until his last breath, drove him to resume lecturing. Many offers had come from lecture agents in England, and he finally agreed to make a limited tour starting late in January. Before leaving Crefeld he wrote Roswell Smith, his New York literary agent, that he was sending him a long poem titled "A Legend of Cologne," which *Belgravia* of London was publishing and which he hoped *Scribner's* would buy. Earlier he had completed a short story, "The Legend of Sammstadt." Both were attempts to break away from California locales and make use of material gleaned during his months in Germany.

His best writing of the period was in his letters to his sons, Francis and Griswold. To the former he wrote of finally seeing a stork perched on its chimney nest, a sight he had expected to be more common from his recollection of German fairy tales. He described how three little children joined hands and began singing to the stork:

> *With the legs so long-like*
> *And the knees so short-like,*
> *Virgin Mary has a child found*
> *That was all in gold bound . . .*

He wrote down the verse in German and English and suggested that Francis teach it to Ethel, the youngest child. He also wanted Francis to start learning German. "Papa has begun to study German like a child . . . and has broken his heart and has worn his eyes out . . ." To Griswold he also advised a study of languages, citing the fact that German children learned French and English until they could speak them fluently. He still thought Crefeld was no more interesting in itself than Morristown or Newark, but reported on a trip to a village outside the city, dreaming away behind its ancient arched gateway, with a sudden and breathtaking view of the ruined castle which once had been the seat of the Archbishop of Cologne.

He also described the constant military presence in German cities and towns, every one of them a garrison filled with marching and counter-marching, blaring trumpets and crashing boots. To Bret's sturdily civilian mentality it was all rather wearying, yet he had to concede that beside the gorgeous Hussars and splendiferous Lancers even the finest American regiments looked drab indeed. When he attended the opera in Dusseldorf with his friend General von Rauch and another officer, both glittering with stars, crosses, ribands and medals, he felt like "a crow who had suddenly got into a cage with some tropical parrots." The general, he said, once paid him the supreme compliment of stating that Bret looked more like a Prussian officer than an American or Englishman. Bret gallantly responded that von Rauch reminded *him* of General Ambrose Burnside — a double-edged compliment considering Burnside's military record.

He also set down the strict rules governing the conduct of German officers, particularly the one against carrying parcels, even for a lady he was escorting. "I have seen the wife of one, loaded down with shawls, traveling bags, etc., etc., and her husband strutting solemnly at her side, with nothing heavier than his long sword trailing at his heels." [12]

Bret was at his splenetic best in describing for Anna, a day later, his experience of a performance of *Tannhauser* at the Dusseldorf Opera, which he characterized as "diabolically ludicrous" and "stupidly monotonous," with the orchestra pounding away like a "boiler factory" in full production. The singers sounded to him as though they were declaiming the multiplication table. He had grumbled about the crashing dissonance to General von Rauch, he said. The general, who had a lively and witty appreciation of German Puritanism, asked him if he knew the story of *Tannhauser* and the reason for its sword-swinging climax. Bret admitted he didn't. "The story," General von Rauch informed him, "is that three minstrels are all singing in praise of love, but they are furious at Tannhauser who loves Hulda, the German Venus, for singing in the praise of love so *wildly*, so *warmly*, so *passionately!*" Bret had to conclude that he didn't understand anything about Wagner but he was beginning to understand the Germans. He was also impressed by the fact that German audiences were so undemonstrative. "The opera audience at Cologne looks like an American prayer-meeting." [13]

The high spirits evident in those letters home were dashed a week later when he journeyed to England to keep his speaking engagements. He had viewed them with dread, as he said, and they lived up, or down, to his expectations. The blame, he felt, was largely D'Oyly Carte's, who booked the tour.

Instead of opening in London, Carte booked him into the cavernous and echoing Crystal Palace at Sydenham, with its patrons more accustomed to music-hall and concert-party entertainment. On the evening of January 18, 1879, he appeared backstage at the Crystal Palace, rather horrified to find himself imbedded in what Americans would call a vaudeville show. A pantomime artist opened the bill, then would come Bret, followed by a magician!

No one introduced him. He simply walked onstage, cold, and began delivering his lecture on the Argonauts in a low, tremulous voice. There were repeated shouts for him to speak up — that indignity at least had never occurred in America — and a bearded heckler rose to interrupt him at length. Bret managed to quiet him only by inviting him to sit on the platform. He stumbled through the rest of his lecture and left the stage feeling as though he'd been placed on the rack. *Punch*, he reported to Anna, gave him a "brotherly" review and the London newspapers were not unkind, but he was determined to cut off the tour then and there. Only the advice of a solicitor that he had to fulfill at least four of the engagements for which he was scheduled, or face lawsuits, kept him on the road. The other engagements would be "postponed." On his return to consular duties at Crefeld, he found that he had received only two hundred dollars above expenses for the lectures, or about forty dollars a lecture. In the bargain, he said, he was certain that he had been "swindled" in not receiving a fair share of the proceeds.[14]

The bureaucratic detail of his office, after that experience, was almost welcome. He worked hard at his consular post the first months of 1879 and so simplified the routine of issuing invoices for the export of Crefeld's silks and velvets to the United States that the volume of trade during his first year increased from six hundred thousand dollars to eight hundred thousand dollars. Nevertheless he was already thinking of appealing to the State Department for a transfer. The longer he stayed in Germany, the more he was convinced there were more salubrious places for his health, his literary efforts and his comfort.

At the end of March he returned to England for more lecturing, lured by the promise of eighty-five guineas (then $425) for an appearance in Manchester. Engagements at Brighton and Birmingham were added to the list. This time he was received with greater enthusiasm, perhaps because he was more comfortable discussing the origin and development of American humor than in describing the manners and mores of the California pioneers, possibly also because he gracefully credited the English with having provided its original inspiration.[15]

American humorists, he told his audiences, "stand in legitimate succession to their early English brethren." It was an English judge stationed in the Colonies, he said, "who first detected how much sagacity, dry humor, and poetry were hidden under the grotesque cover of Sam Slick of Slicksville," and to him "the world first owed the birth of true American humor." Its subsequent development owed much to the South and West for "that humor which is perhaps most characteristic of our lives and habits as a people." Southern humor flowered "among conditions of servitude and the habits of an inferior race . . . It abode with us, making us tolerant of a grievous wrong, and it will abide with us even when these conditions have passed away." The Western contribution was brevity. As an example he cited the story of a California gambler's funeral.

During the funeral service the hearse-horses became restive and started off prematurely, with the rest of the mourners in pursuit. When the horses had been stopped and the last sad rites were concluded, the friends of the deceased wrote his widow a letter acquainting her with the fact that they had given her dead husband a good send-off, and that although the unpleasant occurrence, which they described, somewhat marred the solemnity of the occasion, it gave them a melancholy satisfaction to inform her that "the corpse won."

The audiences in Manchester and Birmingham, he reported home, even broke into applause when he stopped to take a drink of water. In Brighton a committee presented him with a illuminated scroll which, he related in ironic amusement, resembled a patent of nobility. Again the financial rewards were slender, with agents' fees and expenses eating up most of the proceeds. The less tangible compensation for those dreaded appearances was a widening of his English friendships and even warmer relations with the Froude family, the Webbs, the Duke and Duchess of St. Albans. He also finally managed to regain contact with the unpredictable Lord Houghton, whose taste for brandy made him an amiable but somewhat vague companion.

Undoubtedly it was these burgeoning friendships, in part, which resulted in an invitation which both delighted and terrified him. The President of the Royal Academy, Sir Frederick Leighton, asked him to accept the high honor of responding to the toast to Literature at the annual banquet in early May. First he half-promised to make the response, then was overtaken by pure stage fright at the thought of raising his voice among the most distinguished assemblage in Great Britain. After-dinner speaking, for some reason, terrified him more than lecturing. His English friends begged him to make a firm commitment to attend, but finally he sent a curt telegram to Sir Frederick stating that the press of consular business would detain him in Crefeld. In a letter home he found a variety of excuses for turning down an honor which would have added considerably to his prestige — it would have cost him seventy-five dollars to make the trip, he feared that someone in Washington would object to another absence from his post, his study of the German language would be interrupted, and besides his vice-consul had been taken ill.

Instead he attended a state banquet of the Rhenish provinces in Dusseldorf at which he was presented to a Hohenzollern prince and was unspeakably bored by long speeches in German and the excessive wine-guzzling of his fellow banqueters. The latter were somewhat taken aback by his failure to wear a consular uniform for the occasion, as the consuls of other countries did, and he was irked by the fact that the British consul, in particular, looked down his nose at him for appearing drably in a dress suit.

That summer he decided to spend his vacation in Switzerland — the ocean voyage home to New Jersey would, perhaps, have taken up too much of his month off — in hopes that the mountain air would improve his health. His fervent sampling of German medical opinion had left him completely at a loss to account for the reputation German science had acquired with the rest of the world. For an eye disorder a celebrated oculist had given him a "rare prescription" identical with a homely remedy he had used in San Francisco fourteen years before; a local dentist had attempted to kill the nerve in one of his teeth and given him the pain of forty toothaches instead. "D——n Germany!" he concluded.

His journey to Switzerland produced a number of letters which indicated, in the privacy of those communications, that he might have made a fine, if somewhat bilious, writer of travel sketches. The letters have more bite and personality than anything he published at the time. As Wallace Stegner has commented, "the letters give evidence that if he had chosen to, he might have become a lively, biased, and outrageous travel reporter in the jingoist tradition of Mark Twain." [16] Travel did indeed bring out in him a chauvinism — a nostalgia even for California — seldom exhibited in any other circumstances.

Very little of that journey late in July up the castle-crested Rhine seemed to meet with his approval. The famous Strasburg Cathedral was "very ugly," an impression hardly relieved by the fact that a skeleton trundled out to strike the hours. Nor was he overcome by Zurich, its lake and girdling of mountains. "I wish I could say that the hills were finer than the California Coast Range at Oakland, that the waters of the lake were bluer than Lake George, or that the sky was fairer than any American sky — but it is not."

A concert of yodelers under his window in Zurich reminded him of fifty alley cats yowling on a back fence, "with an obbligato from a donkey." There was "nothing in Switzerland *grander* than the Sierras," though he would concede that some of the Alpine peaks were "more singularly *beautiful*." The fabled glow of Alpine snowfields was a "cold, ghastly, bluish white . . . Death made visible."

When it came to the Swiss themselves, he really let himself go. That they were reputedly "hardy" and "liberty-loving" was humbug; the Swiss were "the biggest frauds I ever met." He considered them the most "intolerant and bigoted" of any people he had come across. "How the mountains must despise 'em so that all the mountains every now and then take a shy at 'em with an avalanche."

He was equally disrespectful of "their sham sentiments, their sham liberty, their sham chamois (an ugly cross between a goat and a jackass), their sham *jödel* — that awful falsetto as musical as a cat's serenade; and nothing real about them but their hideous goitres." [17]

Aside from these blistering memories, all he returned to Crefeld with was a case of neuralgia. His regularly catalogued list of complaints now included, in addition, rheumatism, dyspepsia, bronchitis, biliousness, bad teeth, and hay fever. On October 11, finally taking a German doctor's word for something, he wrote the State Department formally requesting a transfer on grounds of health and citing the supporting opinion of a Dr. von Kohlwetter.* It would

* On one of his trips to England he had learned that the U.S. consul in Bradford, a much smaller place than Crefeld, earned $8,000 a year, almost four times what he was receiving. An English appointment, he said, would have saved him from the "filthy fat and vinegar" of German cooking.

be months before the transfer came through. Meanwhile, he had given up trying to use German backgrounds for his stories and sketches. "A Legend of Sammstadt" had been accepted for translation and publication by the *Berliner Tageblatt* as the first of a series of pieces in which Bret, whose popularity in Germany was growing, would give his frank impressions of the country.* The reaction of the newspaper's readers to his frankness was such that, even though the editors deplored the thin-skinned qualities of their countrymen, it was decided to drop the series forthwith. Bret thereupon returned to California — or his private vision of it — for such stories as "Jeff Briggs's Love Story" and "The Twins of Table Mountain." Often his facial neuralgia bothered him so much he was able to write only a page a day. The stories were far from his best, and most of his output in this period was published in the New York *Sun*. Osgood, his Boston publisher, had agreed to bring out another volume of his short stories but was paying an advance of only one hundred and fifty dollars.

There was a pathos about his summation of his current literary efforts, his weariness and disillusionment, that would strike a sympathetic chord in any writer who knows the despair of working a vein that once glittered with promise but now looks more like iron pyrites. "I sometimes wonder what kind of work I am doing. I never see anybody whose opinion I value; I never hear any criticism. I grind out the old tunes on the old organ and gather up the coppers, but I never know whether my audience behind the window blinds are wishing me to 'move on' or not." [18]

* A dangerous proceeding for a comparative newcomer in any country, doubly so in a Germany growingly nationalistic and chestily conscious of its new hegemony in western Europe, triply so for an official representative of the U.S. government who, though not a diplomat, would be expected to be diplomatic.

Yet he was not so overcome by physical and creative debility that he could not flick a contemporary (or rival) with the unbuttoned tip of his rapier, given the occasion. The Duchess of St. Albans begged his opinion of Henry James as a person and a novelist, and elicited a reply that was both frank and slightly malicious. If he seemed to treat James as a fashionable and transitory phenomenon, Jamesians may be consoled by the fact that writers seldom make reliable and unbiased critics.

As a man, Bret replied to the duchess, James impressed him as an American who had lived abroad long enough to be critical of his fellow nations and to be taken aback "in a nice ladylike way" at the unconventional spectacle they made of themselves against a staid European background. James, whom he had met during his season of triumph in Boston, was too superficial to understand the cause and meaning of that unconventionality. Nor did James understand the significance of the "women-reverencing" tendency of American society. Bret himself believed that placing women on a pedestal was an excellent idea, never more so than among the Germans and their views on masculine supremacy. He felt like flapping his wings, he told the Duchess of St. Albans, over a country which believed as much in free women as in free men.

In consideration of that feeling, Bret believed James had been much too harsh with his heroine in *Daisy Miller*, the only work of James's he had read. Daisy's fate, he said, was illogical. She could have gone to the Coliseum in a perfectly conventional manner and on an innocent errand, and yet have succumbed to a fatal onset of malaria. "You cannot believe her dying for love, any more than you can believe the cold-blooded hero . . . as a lover . . ." He had come across the Daisy Miller type several times himself, he added, but "they did not culminate in that fashion." [19]

Shortly after writing that critique he met its subject again, this time in London, where he journeyed just after New Year's 1880, on a leave of absence granted for reasons of health. (He had pondered whether to come home, in fact gave the impression that he would, until the last moment. Finally he indicated his health was too delicate for a midwinter crossing of the Atlantic, and went to England instead. For whatever consolation that would be to Anna, he added that "I cannot hope to be less lonely than I am" — though he would allow such lovely hostesses as the Duchess of St. Albans and Mrs. Webb to try to alleviate that condition.) James displeased him on reacquaintance, as he wrote Anna. "He looks, acts, and thinks like an Englishman, I am sorry to say."

American writers circulating in England generally displeased him, as his contemporaries would note. Bret was becoming established as the doyen of literary Americans; in time he became the most honored and flattered and universally accepted of all his countrymen in England. Greater reputations — Twain for instance — came fluttering down, and were briefly honored, but Bret stayed on and basked in an admiration that continued to grow despite the calcification of his talent. In England a writer was generously remembered for his best work, while in America he was judged mainly on the basis of his last published story or book. Recognizing that greater kindness, Bret was now beginning to regard England as his spiritual home.

On that January visit he was presented to a number of literary celebrities and, except for James, was charmed by them. George Eliot (Mrs. Lewes in civilian life) invited him to her home. It was not true that she looked like a horse, he averred, though she did have a long face and large white teeth. "She reminds you continually of a man — a bright, gentle, loveable, philosophical man — without being a *bit* masculine." Bret was proud of the fact that he was the first person she had received since the death of her husband, and that she complimented him on his work.

He also met Thomas Hardy and considered him a "singularly unpretending man," with nothing of the literary in his speech or manner. George DuMaurier, then an illustrator for *Punch*, impressed him favorably. A new club, the Rabelais, had just been formed and Bret was not only invited to become a member but the president, Sir Frederick Pollock, nominated him to succeed him to the presidency.[20]

He was so braced by all this that, several months later, he steeled himself to appear at the Royal Academy dinner. Once again Sir Frederick Leighton invited him to respond to the toast to Literature, and the honor was all the greater for the fact that James Russell Lowell had just been appointed American ambassador to England and might well have been selected in his place.

On May 1, 1880, at Burlington House, Bret found himself seated among the high and mighty of the British Empire at the head table. Among those present were the Prince of Wales, the Duke of Cambridge and other members of the royal family; Prime Minister Gladstone and members of his Cabinet; the Lord Mayor of London; numerous Members of Parliament, and such less official luminaries as Robert Browning, Arthur Sullivan (of Gilbert &), James Anthony Froude, T. H. Huxley, Anthony Trollope. In making the toast to Literature, Sir Frederick introduced Bret in terms that exceeded anything ever said about him:

"In coupling a name with literature, I propose to take a

rather unusual course; for I shall call upon a writer who owes us no allegiance save that of friendship to the country in which he is now a guest — an English writer, nevertheless, for English is the tongue in which he delights the innumerable host of his readers; English is the tongue in which he has clothed a humor racy and delicate at once, and has married it to a most subtle pathos — a pathos so deep, so tender and so penetrating that we rise from his pages half believing that wrong is an untoward accident in the world, and goodness the one abiding, inextinguishable thing. This company will be glad, I am confident, of the opportunity thus offered it of welcoming in its midst the great American humorist, Bret Harte."

Bret's response was short and graceful, and raised one hearty laugh when he remarked, "I presume I am selected to answer this toast as a native of a country which reads more English books and pays less for them than any other nation." The applause when he sat down indicated a modest success, confirmed when the Prince of Wales asked that Bret be presented to him.

In that lordly company, for those few hours, he must have felt the greatest triumph. America, always two-faced about success, had never given him such recognition; Boston's attempt had been half-hearted by comparison, and in New York he had never been anything but a curious striver from the West. That night, if not before, he must have been confirmed in expatriation.

ELEVEN

A Not Altogether Happy Glaswegian

"I cannot help feeling that I am living by gaslight in a damp cellar with an occasional whiff from a drain, from a coal heap, from a moldy potato bin, and from dirty washtubs."
—Bret Harte on Glasgow

O N April 2, 1880, had come word from the State Department that it was agreeing to his request for a transfer. His new post would be Glasgow, a sizable promotion, with his pay raised to three thousand dollars annually. "Other emoluments" would probably bring in another thousand dollars, and he would be able to raise Anna's allowance to two hundred dollars a month. He hastened to quench any hopes that the family would be brought over to join him in Glasgow, not by any direct statements but by repeated hints that they wouldn't much like it there. In a succession of letters he cited Glasgow's disadvantages: "sea fogs," "cold and sincere winters," "a rather *expensive* place," "very smoky, very damp." Furthermore it appeared that the Republican James A. Garfield would be elected President that autumn, but if a Democrat got in Bret couldn't be certain of keeping his consulship. Anna evidently had written expressing her strong desire to reunite the family that summer of 1880, but he thought it better to wait until the change of administration the following year; meanwhile he would certainly come home for a visit. Furthermore, all he heard of the Scottish people was "dreadful." Seldom has an unvisited city been painted in such bleak and disagreeable colors.[1]

The Scots in prospect could hardly have been more menacing than the Germans in retrospect. The moment it became known that Bret, at his own request, was being transferred to Glasgow the German press reacted with sorrow and indignation, but more of the latter than the former. *Zeitung* of Cologne was mildly reproachful and published a poem appealing to Bret to change his mind, to seek spiritual sustenance in Germany rather than *gelt* among a nation of shopkeepers. A Berlin newspaper, however, boiled over with outrage at the thought of anyone preferring Britain to Germany. It reported that Bret was leaving because he was "sick of Germany"; he had been sent to Crefeld (to "this land of swilling sots," as Bret commented) to cure him of his addiction to alcohol. The cure hadn't taken, however, and the "genial poet" was determined to find a place where he could "indulge himself more freely." While in Crefeld, the paper added, Bret had become notorious for his ungovernable thirst for *feuerwasser* (brandy).

Bret, through a lawyer, forced the newspaper to publish a retraction, which was reprinted by other papers. "But," Bret concluded in his account to Anna, "I knew — what I didn't dare tell my friends — that paragraph — *that slander came from America!*"[2]

With the taste of that affair still bitter in his mouth, he left Germany on June 18, 1880, and headed for England, even though he wasn't scheduled to take up his new post until a month later. Almost at once he began complaining of Scotland almost as harshly as he had of Germany. The people were dour, forbidding and bigoted; it rained for three weeks straight, and only the "general civility" was superior to German boorishness. Evidently Glasgow was afflicted with a nineteenth-century forerunner of smog: "the vapours from chemical factories and the thick mists made a compound that is simply diabolical." His transferring from Crefeld to Glasgow for reasons of health, he added, had turned into "a ghastly farce."

Despite all the despair he poured into his letters home, he apparently was enjoying himself during his first months in Scotland. He and William Black journeyed to Brighton, to the East Riding and to the Scottish Highlands that summer, just after Bret took over his new post, and according to Black's biographer Bret was a fountain of jokes, anecdotes and repartee. Black described him to a friend in terms that suggested something gayer than the long-faced hypochondriac of his letters home. "He is the most extraordinary globule of mercury — comet — aerolite gone drunk — flash of lightning doing catherine wheels — I ever had any experience of." [3]

And when autumn came Bret was out on the grouse moors with all the other sportsmen. He was invited to an estate at Innelan for the shooting. One mid-September day a hare streaked across the moor and Bret blasted away with his shotgun. The gamekeeper had overloaded the gun, it recoiled sharply and struck him on the upper lip. Bret was helped back to the house and a surgeon was summoned to take a number of stitches in his lip. His host's twelve-year-old son tiptoed into the room while these repairs were being made, and piped up, "Tell Mr. Harte it's all right. He killed the hare."

That autumn and winter Bret performed diligently in his new post. The new administration might conceivably want a new consul in Glasgow, unless he solidified his position as best he could. It could hardly have hurt his cause to have written the introduction to a campaign biography of the Republican candidate, particularly since Garfield won. His reports to the State Department included every phase of commercial and industrial life in the Glasgow and Clydeside area which might conceivably interest the people in Washington, but which probably served only to gather dust in the files. He reported on the price of wool and the founding of sugar refineries at Greenock, on warships being built on the Clyde for the Royal Navy, on engines being made for the Italian merchant marine, on Scottish labor conditions, on new inventions and industrial techniques. He dealt briskly with the affairs of the American bark *Bessie Wittich,* the crew of which signed a protest against their captain's drunkenness and brutality and their ship's unseaworthiness. He persuaded the Duke of Argyll to allow construction of a memorial on the duke's estate to the nineteen American seamen buried there after a shipwreck many years before.

Yet he still worried over being kept on as consul at Glasgow. He was certain, as he wrote Anna early in April, 1881, there were only "two or three men in America who are loyal to me." A letter from someone in Washington had indicated there were "thousands of people clamouring for Glasgow — that every little paragraph about my being un-American (think of ME being un-American when I get into quarrels every day defending my country) is made capital of and poured into the ears of the State Department and Congressmen and Senators." Also his frequent absences from duty were being discussed, and his informant in Washington had suggested that "as a matter of selfish interest it might be a matter of selfish wisdom to hang around there [at his Glasgow post, that is] and kick up dust for a while until the pressure subsides." [4]

He consoled himself by frequently rereading a letter from John Hay, his guardian angel in the State Department, who had written, "I do not know what Heaven meant by creating so few men like King and you.* The scarcity of you is an injury, not only to us, but to yourselves. There are not enough of you to go round, and the world pulls and hauls at you until you are completely spoiled. Such times as I have seen since the 4th of March. You would have got lots of fun out of it. I, only vexation of spirit. They have even asked for Glasgow — never more than once in my presence." [5]

Despite his forebodings, Bret was continued in his post. Later in the year, of course, he suffered a renewal of anxiety when President Garfield was assassinated. Garfield's successor, Vice President Chester A. Arthur, did not make any consular changes, however, and Bret really had nothing to worry about except the advent of a Democratic administration.

From the late spring of 1881 to the late fall his health was so poor — rheumatism and dyspepsia — that he didn't write home until November 11. The two-hundred-fifty-dollar monthly payments for support of his family continued, however, and he was able to concern himself with the professional futures of his two sons. Griswold was now eighteen and Frank sixteen, and he hoped they would take up careers that promised more security than his own. He wanted Griswold to attend a business school and Frank to enter the United States Naval Academy; on the latter's behalf he was trying to maneuver an appointment to Annapolis through Lieutenant John A. Tobin, who was on special duty in Glasgow to report on the Clyde shipbuilding facilities. Both sons sadly disappointed him in their choice of careers and decided

---

* Clarence King, an associate of Bret's in the *Overland Monthly* days, had just resigned a consular post in England.

on the riskiest of semi-professions. Griswold was set on becoming a writer and eventually became a newspaperman in New York, but died in 1901, at the age of thirty-eight, without ever seeing his father again. Frank disregarded the paternal advice — "I think it is a *safer* thing to be a Lieutenant of the Engineer Corps, U.S.N., than a clever stock actor" — and launched himself on a not very successful theatrical career.

Bret's own career, aside from the competent administration of the Glasgow consulate, had come to a full stop in 1881. No stories came from his pen, nor were any collected volumes of his stories published. (The following year he changed publishers, joining the list of Houghton Mifflin in Boston. That company immediately reissued *Gabriel Conroy* and promoted him much more aggressively than the conservative Osgood.) His concern about hanging onto the Glasgow appointment, and his various ailments, undoubtedly kept him from his writing desk; but he was also suffering from a deep and self-critical lassitude. The psychological impediment of "writer's block" had not yet been discovered, or dignified, but he was definitely floundering in uncertainty. Was there really much point in turning out the "old tunes"? Whenever he was praised, it was for work he had done a dozen years ago. Was he going to be one of those trapped-in-amber writers renowned for early success but never able to expand on it, develop and grow? It must have looked that way. None of the work he had turned out since leaving San Franciso could have inspired him to renewed effort.

He simply could not, or would not, break out of that near-perfect little pocket of creation in the California foothills. His creative imagination was polarized there, and travel did not broaden his artistic vision as it did, for instance, Mark

Twain's. He had made desultory attempts to use different
backgrounds and characters, and in the future would occasionally break away, but he had always returned to the mining camps, the Sierras, and Yuba Bill, Colonel Starbottle,
Jack Hamlin and John Oakhurst. There was no evidence
that he resented them for their obsessive hold over him as
Conan Doyle, for instance, was said to have come to detest
Sherlock Holmes and Dr. Watson.

The "picturesque localism," the "regional" writing of
which he was a pioneer held him enthralled. He lacked the
venturesomeness to experiment, to risk everything for a try
at real greatness. Above any possible attempt to scale new
heights he valued the coziness of his life in Britain, the self-
insulated joys of rewon bachelorhood, the self-indulgence of
good clothes and Havana cigars, the respect due him as a representative of the United States government, the flattering
association with titled aristocrats and untitled celebrities who
accepted him as one of their own. It would have cost him
dearly to attempt an artistic rehabilitation at the age of forty-
five. He would have been forced to give up his consulship,
reunite with his family in grubby circumstances, forget his
rather convenient ailments, and yield himself up to lonely
concentration on finding a new direction for his talent. But
he had never possessed the single-mindedness, the self-
absorption of genius. Writing was a craft, an occupation;
something, in fact, rather impersonal.

Thus there was an extraordinarily small part of his own
personality in the body of his work. He held himself asepti-
cally aloof as a scientist isolating microbes in a laboratory.
There was hardly the faintest trace of autobiography in anything he wrote. His characters were composites of people he
had met long ago. He put nothing of himself except his intel-

ligence in his writing. Whether it was a matter of inhibition, discipline, or inability to confront the reality of his inner substance and risk self-examination, he rigidly withheld himself from his work. The public was entitled to know him only as an impersonal storyteller. The lurid self-revelations of a later literary generation, from D. H. Lawrence onward, the gleeful brandishing of dirty linen and dredging up of sexual memories would have shocked him immeasurably. It was fortunate he died before Freud's influence spread to the literary world; he would never have survived it.

He began writing again early in 1882, largely because of the influence of a woman who was to be closer to him than any other until the end of his life.

Whether he was seeking a patronness or a mistress, he always was on more intimate terms with the female members of the families which for so many years took him in as an inveterate guest. He was more at ease with women than men; he found it easier, obviously, to charm and impress them; and thus it was that he was closer to the Duchess of St. Albans than to the cold-eyed duke, to Mrs. Webb rather than to her big-game-hunting husband. Women appreciated him, coddled him, catered to his whims, and were more interested in him as a writer; the sportin' talk of the Victorian country gentleman largely bored him, and when the port and cigars were passed he must have yearned to join the ladies in the drawing room. So it was with the Belgian couple, the Van de Veldes, with whom he became acquainted first during his early visits to England. He almost literally joined the family circle during the summer and autumn of 1881 when he spent much of his time at their London town house in St. John's Wood and at their summer home in Bournemouth. In both houses a room was set aside for Bret to occupy whenever he came down from Glasgow, and thus began a relationship that caused a long-playing scandal in Victorian and Edwardian society.

In a diary Bret kept from 1881 to 1888, with most entries in Marguerite Van de Velde's handwriting, a curious intimacy in itself, he recorded that he first dined at the Van de Velde home on January 18, 1881.* A week later the couple accompanied him to Edwin Booth's performance as King Lear. From then on, the association with the Van de Veldes as traced by diary entries grew closer and more fervid. By the end of that year the threesome was the gossip of fashionable London and the country houses beyond.

There was no doubt that the three of them were soon made aware of society's disapproval, all the more intensely reflected by the Van de Veldes' closest friends. On January 1, 1882, Bret noted in the diary, though the handwriting again is Madame Van de Velde's, that the Van de Veldes had "broken off" with the Miles family because they "supported the Taubners' view of our friendship." [6]

Tongues would wag despite the fact that Marguerite Van de Velde was the mother of nine children, despite the fact that Bret's apologists maintained that he was her "tenth child," so all-encompassing was her maternal nature. The gossips insisted it was a *ménage à trois*, resulting from the indulgence of Monsieur Van de Velde, bizarre though it would have been with nine children romping on scene. Bret's position in the household may have been entirely platonic, as his early biographers, family and friends insisted, but it was certainly dubious by the standards of the 1880's and was rendered downright suspect ten years later when Monsieur Van de Velde died and Bret stayed on, more or less fulltime.

* The red morocco-bound diary with clasp and lock was acquired in recent years by the Berg Collection of the New York Public Library.

The Van de Veldes, however, considered themselves above and beyond the reach of gossip. He was a Belgian, the chancellor of his country's legation in London. She was the daughter of Count de Launey, a diplomat who had served in most of the European capitals; she was intensely interested in writing and writers and herself had written a book of reminiscences of the Spanish and French courts as well as a volume on the French novel in which she praised the realistic attitude of French writers toward love. She was independent, strong-minded, "intensely un-English," as Bret characterized her. Conventional attitudes were a challenge to her. There was a masculine quality of forthrightness about her — she signed herself bluntly as M. S. Van de Velde — that often attracted Bret as much as the subtler feminine traits in a woman; he had a definite aversion to the feline type. She was a great admirer of Bret's writing, and in later years, to the displacement of his widow, she would assume the role of defender of his literary reputation.

When this relationship was well under way, Anna apparently wrote demanding to know the exact details of his mode of living. Perhaps the association with the Van de Veldes, gossip of which already had crossed the Atlantic, had rung the first alarm bells. "You ask me how I live," Bret replied. "I thought I told you. The nearest approach I have to a home is, naturally, not where it ought to be — at Glasgow." In the same casual yet explicit vein he related that he was spending as much time as possible at the Van de Veldes' homes in London and Bournemouth; that it was a refined, simple, elegant and unaffected household. The Van de Veldes, for reasons he couldn't fathom, had taken him into the family circle as though he had known them for years.

Their friendship and hospitality, he added, was a warm and beneficial contrast to the comfortless quarters he occupied in Glasgow. He had taken a two-room suite in a hotel which had recently been taken over by a creditors' committee, causing him to wonder whether the guests were also creditors and the surly waiters were creditors in disguise.[7]

The easiness of his relations with Arthur and Marguerite Van de Velde was indicated by diary entries for the early summer of 1883. On June 4, after a visit to their London home, they accompanied him to Glasgow and stayed in the northern city for almost six weeks. On July 16, according to the diary, M. Van de Velde returned to London "leaving Marguerite with me." That information was confined to the morocco-bound volume with entries dictated by Bret to Madame Van de Velde; in none of his letters home did he mention the Van de Veldes' presence, together or singly, in Glasgow during this period.[8]

The relationship with Madame Van de Velde, at any rate, gave him a zest for life lacking for many years. There is no evidence that it ever encouraged him to seek a divorce from Anna. Judging from an aside he penned in the short story "Jeff Briggs's Love Story," any marriage in his belief tended to become an emotional dictatorship. "It takes the legal matrimonial contract," he commented in that story, "to properly develop the first class tyrant, male or female."

The most beneficial aspect of his new relationship was that Madame Van de Velde believed in his genius and managed to convince him that it had merely been lying dormant. More than anything else at the moment, he needed someone who could revive his ego as a writer, and she served that purpose admirably. She was his literary audience, his kindly critic, his goad to whatever ambitions survived in him. Under her influence and at her urging he started writing again early in 1882, only a few months after he met the Van de Veldes. He turned out a short story, "Found at Blazing Star," then succumbed again to the lure of the theater and its illusory promise of quick rewards.

During the next few months he adapted *The Luck of Roaring Camp;* collaborated with Edmund About, a French novelist, in dramatizing the latter's *Germaine,* and worked with Madame Van de Velde on a dramatic version of his short story "A Blue Grass Penelope." He also labored over dramatizing *Thankful Blossom,* the Revolutionary War serial he had hacked out for the New York *Sun.* All, in the end, testified more to a rebirth of creative activity than any innate talent for writing for the theater.

Of those four efforts, the dramatization of *The Luck of Roaring Camp* was the only one that came close to being produced. (One trouble may have been that Bret had the curious notion that a play was pretty much like a novel stripped to its dialogue, and his characters tended to talk at rather than to one another.) Daniel Frohman read *The Luck* and proposed to produce it at the Madison Square Garden Theater the following autumn. A contract was signed providing that Bret would receive a royalty of ten dollars per performance (it would be many years before the Dramatists Guild erased such inequities and made producers a little poorer, playwrights a lot richer.) Then Frohman had second thoughts about the script and decide it needed doctoring. Bret agreed on the condition that Dion Boucicault, then the theater's number one craftsman, make the necessary revisions. Boucicault apparently was unavailable, and the project died in the producer's office.

Bret's theatrical projects had the unfortunate effect, from his standpoint, of spurring on his son Frank's ambitions to become an actor. No doubt Bret was irked by the youth's refusal to accept his help in getting into Annapolis, and was further annoyed by Frank's rejection of his advice on the insecurity of a theatrical career. The young man wanted him to send a letter of introduction to Frohman, when *The Luck* project was still on the producer's schedule, but Bret refused. "I should not like your success as an actor to hang upon my success as a dramatist," he wrote Frank, apparently forgetting that he himself had used every available handhold to advance his own career in San Francisco. "It would be much more businesslike to consider your affairs and the play separately." [9]

Young Frank, however, was determined that his father make up for his years of absenteeism by aiding his theatrical ambitions. He did manage to persuade Bret to give him a letter to Boucicault, and it may well have been that Frank was allowed to read for the Irish playwright, who was also an actor and director. It also seems likely that Boucicault reported to Bret that his son was not exactly bursting with talent for the stage.

That would explain, at least in part, an episode which came to the attention of Mark Twain, always alert to anti-Harte gossip. According to Twain, and other sources, Frank Harte approached John McCullough, the celebrated tragedian with whom Bret had formed a friendship in his San Francisco days, with a letter from his father recommending that McCullough do anything possible to advance the youth's ambition to become an actor.

McCullough, Twain recorded, read the letter and then told Frank, "I was expecting you, my boy. I know your errand, through a letter which I have already received from your father; and by good luck I am in a position to satisfy your desire. I have just the place for you, and you consider yourself on salary from today, and now."

What he didn't tell the young man, Twain said, was that the other letter Bret sent separately from England read:

My boy is stage-struck and wants to go to you for help, for he knows that you and I are old friends. To get rid of his opportunities, I have been obliged to [equip] him with a letter strongly recommending him to your kindness and protection, and begging you to do the best you can to forward his ambition, for my sake.

I was obliged to write the letter, I couldn't get out of it, but the present letter is to warn you beforehand to pay no attention to the other one. My son is stage-struck but he isn't of any account and will never amount to anything; therefore don't bother yourself with him; it wouldn't pay you for your lost time and sympathy.[10]

A slightly different version of Frank's interview with John McCullough may be glimpsed in a letter Bret wrote his son December 15, 1882. Bret was apparently upset by a letter he had received from Mrs. Harte saying that McCullough had told Frank about the separate letter he received from Bret (despite Twain's claim that McCullough kept it to himself). Mrs. Harte had written Bret that McCullough told their son the separate letter advised him, "Be rude to him if necessary, but keep him off the stage." Bret denied having written such a thing. "It is scarcely worth while repeating that I never *could* nor *did* say anything of the kind or write anything like it to McCullough," he wrote Frank. "I told him that if it were true that you were physically not up to the active requirements of the stage, he ought to dissuade you from it." Bret added that "I have no desire to keep you off the stage from principle or taste, but if you must go on I should prefer you to go on properly. I do not see any urgent necessity for the haste that may produce a failure." [11]

Whether he was as devious and brutal in his methods as Twain asserted or not, he was determined to discourage his son's acting ambitions. It may have been because the stage was not entirely respectable, or because he had been advised that Frank wasn't exactly brimming with talent. In any event, the youth never made anything of the opportunity given him by McCullough and soon was dropped from the company following appearances in Cleveland and Chicago. Later he explained to Anna that he did not suggest that Frank come to England and begin his theatrical career more or less under direct paternal guidance because "I do not think the country is fit for young Americans to try their callow wings in." He insisted that both of the sons were "better in your hands" and that "you could help each other." If Anna felt that Bret was abdicating his paternal responsibilities, she was probably quite right. It must have galled her that, while shrugging off the hopes and aspirations of his sons, he wrote so glowingly of his enjoyment of the Van de Velde children. He described all nine of them as "very sweet children," perfectly disciplined in the nursery, who rose at seven in the morning and began their studies without intruding on the affairs of their parents. He enthused over the eldest boy's "perfect manners," and reported that they were "absurdly grateful" for any little attentions Bret gave them.[12]

Perhaps because of her uneasiness over his evidently growing attachment for the substitute family which had "adopted" him, he was once again forced to dodge around the issue of a family reunion in the summer of 1883. He put off until autumn the proposal that the family come over to Europe. Then he hinted that it would be best if he went to join them in America. By November, however, he advised Anna that he thought it best if his visit was "*postponed* until spring." More money might be available then because he had heard that the State Department was considering the possibility of raising his salary by one thousand dollars annually. Furthermore, if he came home, he would find himself involved in the financial difficulties of his widowed sister Eliza.

It would be hard for him to resist Eliza's appeals if he were on the scene (though until the end of his life he sent his sisters money from time to time). Meanwhile he professed himself more disappointed than Anna and the children by the postponement of their reunion. Spring came and summer passed without an appearance by Bret. Finally he wrote that a visit to America was out of the question for the time being. The presidential campaign of 1884 was under way, there seemed a strong possibility that the Democrats might return to power, and he did not want to be pinned down as favoring either of the candidates.[13]

Instead his son Frank descended upon him that fall with what Bret characterized as "sudden energy and impatience of display" after being dropped from Lawrence Barrett's repertory company. Bret sent money for both Frank's and Griswold's passage, but at the last moment, for undisclosed reasons, his eldest son decided against making the trip. Just before Frank arrived Bret wrote Anna that the boy mustn't expect that he would find employment in England. The most Frank could hope for, he indicated, was the opportunity of seeing London's best actors perform and "profit by it — *in America!*"

One did not have to read between the lines to divine that Bret and his nineteen-year-old son failed to hit it off after six years of separation. Scotland seemed to bore Frank, his father observed. Bret was alarmed by "his want of self-control and his habitual intolerance of any restraint" and his need of wine or beer to arouse his appetite at mealtimes. Bret considered his son a "most singular" mixture of man and boy, "with the thoughtlessness of the one and the independence of the other."

By then he had something besides paternal dissatisfactions to worry about, since the November election saw the Democratic candidate, Grover Cleveland, swept into office. That meant Bret's displacement, sooner or later, as United States Consul in Glasgow. He was working "breathlessly," as he wrote Anna, to get enough of his stories published to make up for the prospective loss of his three-thousand-dollar salary from the government. He had signed a contract with the *Illustrated London News* for a long story to be published in its Summer 1885 issue, had sent "Ship of '49" to Dana for publication in the New York *Sun*, and had just finished "An Apostle of the Tules," which he hoped would find a place in one of the better magazines. Dana, he complained, was paying only half what he had two years before, "another cause why I must work harder and quicker." He had to make the most of his remaining popularity with the reading public.[14]

A few weeks later the prospect of losing his consulship came closer when James Russell Lowell was recalled as ambassador to England. Though it foreshadowed the loss of his own position, he was rather glad to hear it had happened. "Lowell made himself vastly popular here by doing the Boston-English style, and by judicious truckling, and I am not sorry he was recalled." The more intelligent English, he thought, weren't fooled by such exhibitions. He had observed, he said, "the amused and self-satisfied contempt for these feeble Americans who are trying to ingratiate themselves by their ludicrous imitations of small things."[15]

In a brief essay on Lowell, generous as he usually was toward other writers, Bret criticized him for being "more of an Englishman than an American," a charge often leveled at Bret himself and with perhaps equal justification. Lowell epitomized that haughty provincialism of New England which tended to ignore the rest of the American continent as a moral and spiritual vacuum, and which now aroused his disgust as it had once inspired his admiration.

"The race," he wrote of New Englanders, "that had been intolerant of Quakers and witches in colonial days were only inclined at best to a severe patronage or protectorate over the Gallic mixtures of the South and Gulf, with their horse-racing, dueling, and reprehensible recklessness of expenditure; over the German millions of the West and Middle States, slow and sure in their thoughtful citizenship, but given overmuch to wicked enjoyment of the Sabbath; the Irishman of the great seaboard and inland cities, developing the conservatism of wealth in his mature years, but perplexing and perturbing in his youthful immigration; the Spaniards of the Southwest and the Pacific Slope, gentle and dignified, full of an Old World courtesy unknown to the Atlantic States, but hopeless in their Latin superstitions and avowed Papistry." [16]

Thus, with Lowell as his whipping boy, he wrote off his youthful yearnings to win recognition among the old saints of Boston and Cambridge.

The thought of leaving Glasgow, judging from everything he wrote, pained him no more than departing his earlier post in Germany. Regarding the physical aspect of living in Glasgow, he commented, "I cannot help feeling that I am living by gaslight in a damp cellar with an occasional whiff from a drain, from a coal heap, from a moldy potato bin, and from dirty washtubs." In such stories with a Scottish background as "Rose of Glenbogie," "Young Robin Gray" and "Heir of the M'Hulishes," in which Glasgow was identified as St. Kentigern, he laced into everything native to the country but its whiskey, woolens and wild Highland scenery. Especially the people, "the righteous St. Kentigners of the tribe of Tubal Cain." Their rigid Calvinism was as repugnant as German Lutheranism. Their drinking habits differed from the Rhinelanders in that they favored whiskey over wine, and alcohol never softened their natures. "There is no gayety, no brilliancy, no sense of enjoyment visible, but a stern, stupid aspect of business in it all as if they were intoxicated from a sense of duty." Their manners, except among the high-born, lacked the slightest suggestion of grace or civility. "Here in this lodging of mine even the table-girl cannot hand me a plate except in a spirit of aggression." And he would never forget the landlady whom he had asked to unpack his bags and who confronted him later to demand, "I've unpacked yer kists — and whaur's yer Bible?"

He prided himself that he had administered the Glasgow consulate efficiently and honestly, and quoted Vice-Consul Gibson as complimenting him on the fact that "the office had never been as purely administered as under me. I 'fished' to know why, and it appeared that all the other Consuls used to cheat the Government in small ways by taking certain fees that were 'official' and calling them 'unofficial.' " [17] Thus it irked him all the more that the New York *Tribune*, in an editorial paragraph, called attention to his frequent absences from his post. Presumably he was even less amused by the story making the rounds that once after he had been stationed in Glasgow for several years he arrived at the city's railroad station, put his head out the car window and asked someone on the platform, "What station is this?" * Close to the end of his consulship he received a letter of warning from the State Department on his reported absences from duty. He was in London when the warning arrived.

With doom impending, he could still be friskily humorous with his vice-consul, Gibson, a somber Scot who had also become his friend. It seemed odd to Bret that when indigent

---

* "Bret Harte is a wandering comet," quipped his friend William Black, equally in truth and jest. "The only place he is sure not to be found in is at the Glasgow Consulate."

Americans appeared at the consulate for passage money back to the United States, the men always appealed to his sympathy while the women instinctively turned to Gibson for help. ". . . Why is it," Bret wrote Gibson from London,

that no sooner is my back turned upon Glasgow than I find you surrounded by distressed women and babies appealing to you for succor? Why is it, as I pass out of one door, they appear to you at the other with dishevelled locks and mute pledges of affection in their hands? Why do they . . . fly when I approach? Why are you — so stern and uncompromising to masculine indigence — melting towards feminine mendacity — either with or without child, or obviously gestating?

Perhaps in the interests of propriety I had better return promptly to the Consulate. There — tho' I may succumb to impoverished tramps, who have never seen America or the salt water — tho' I may give largess to bachelors for the support of imaginary wives; though I may restore unhappy orphans to their fathers, and succor starving men with whiskey for passage money to the next port — I will at least uphold the unimpeachable moral integrity of the flag, and keep it from becoming the swaddling clothes of illegitimate posterity, and the advanced banner of vague paternity.[18]

What would he do when his consulship was officially terminated? The sensible, money-saving and talent-nurturing approach to the future would have been to return to America and resettle himself with Anna and their daughters — their sons having gone out into the world — as modestly and comfortably as possible. It was obvious from young Frank's visit that the children needed their father, and his replies to their letters indicated that they had made that need known. Back home he could gather up his creative resources for a new assault on fame, critical and popular esteem; here in

Britain he would have to keep scratching away, reworking the old formulas, just to keep the creditors off the doorsteps of both establishments.

Apparently he still felt a strong, if occasional tug of nostalgia for America. Just after his old publisher visited him in England, he told a friend, "I dare not go to Liverpool with Osgood for fear I shall get on the steamer with him and return."

On the other hand he had written Anna quite frankly some time before that he had an indefinable fear of returning to the United States. It was a "strange feeling," he said, threaded in all "my longings and all my desires to return." It wasn't exactly dread, nor was it a "presentiment" of disaster. "Perhaps it is because I have been *singularly lucky while I have been here in Europe*. My affairs have prospered; I have a market for my wares; I am not dependent upon publishers' whims or caprices . . . I have for the first time in my life known what it is to be independent." [19] Yet that independence was largely based on his government post. It was also true, as he admitted in another letter, that his primary market as a writer was the United States, that he received almost twice as much from American periodicals for his stories as from the British papers and magazines.

The first of August, 1885, the blow finally fell with official notice from the State Department that he was being relieved of his post, an item which had been leaked to the press two weeks earlier. It could not have been a surprise, but the official announcement carried an unexpected sting: Bret was being removed, not because he was a Republican appointee lingering under a Democratic administration, but for "inattention to duty." That, said Bret, was a "gratuitous insult." It was indeed gratuitous, but the charge was undoubtedly justified.

He was so irked by it that for once the bland, even-tempered, considerate tone of his letters home was broken by a harsh note. He wrote Anna that "it would have been some satisfaction . . . to have had a line from you of explanation or sympathy," since the news of his removal had been published two weeks before in the American newspapers. He was embarrassed and ashamed when his friends in Britain asked him, "But what do you hear from America and what do your friends say?" because he was unable to answer them.[20]

For the time being, he briskly added, he would recover from the bruises inflicted on his pride by visiting the Duke and Duchess of St. Albans at their Irish estate and the Van de Veldes at their country home. After that, he said, "we shall see." Two weeks later, after his Irish visit, he informed Anna that he would be staying on in England because Americans there had advised him he was no longer "a popular visitor in America." He quoted the United States Minister in Berlin as having told a mutual friend he was surprised at Bret's popularity in Germany "as I was completely 'played out' in America." He was afraid that if he returned home American publishers would think he had become "dependent" on them. As usual — for the hundredth time — he tossed a sop to wifely feelings by adding that in due time "we could . . . consider the question of *our all living here*."

His literary career had been responsible for obtaining the State Department posts and, it seems, ironically, was also partly responsible for his removal. According to the story Noah Brooks heard circulating in Washington, President Grover Cleveland had gone on a fishing trip to the Adirondacks early in the summer of 1885 with his private secretary, Daniel Lamont. While trolling for fish on the lake, the President idly picked up a copy of the New York *Sun*. By chance he read one of Bret's stories. Cleveland was no literary aficionado but he knew what he liked. He tossed the paper overboard with a grunt of disapproval and told Lamont, "Be sure and remind me to have *him* removed when we get back to Washington." [21]

TWELVE

A New Resident in Grub Street

"They say. What say they? Let them say!"
—Motto of the Mareschals of Aberdeen

INEVITABLY Bret chose to stay in England. Even without the prop of a government salary, even though he
would have to maintain two households, or at least one and a
half, on the proceeds of a free-lance's intermittent income, it
was preferable to returning to the States, always haunted as
he was by the memory of his struggles to make a living during his last few years there. Whatever emotional ties bound
him still to his family exerted little real pressure on his conscience. Perhaps not even to himself would he have admitted
that he no longer desired the role of husband and father; he
was enough a man of his times to regard the family as "the
Ark of the Victorian Covenant," but he placed the highest
value on the freedom he had enjoyed now for more than half
a dozen years.

Aside from personal freedom, England offered him a respect and constancy that he could never know in the United
States. When you achieved fame in America you were all
but consumed by blasts of adulation while in England you
were continually warmed as from a steadily glowing hearth.
A Poe or a Melville could die neglected and forgotten in
America while in England a man of talent or genius gradually

slipped into the role of Grand Old Man, surrounded by the utmost tolerance and indulgence.

Since he was nearing his fiftieth year, these were matters worth considering with care. So was the fact that the hostility toward him in America was unabated. Nowhere was this hostility stronger than in San Francisco, the capital of his creative world. As the San Francisco literary historian E. S. Cummins would write several years hence, "Ordinarily Californians do not like Bret Harte and Bret Harte returns the compliment. They do not like the wrong impressions that people get abroad from these queer, foreshortened, out-of-focus pictures of our land. They resent having the outside world believe that California has not changed in forty years — that we are still in the days of '49." The historian added that few San Franciscans bothered to buy volumes containing his stories; that women readers, in particular, found them abhorrent in the way he described Californians' crudities.[1] And this attitude was reflected in other parts of the country where, Bret knew, he was regarded as something close to a traitor for staying away so long. They didn't want him back but they resented his not coming back.

About this time, too, the financial aspects of writing took on a more encouraging tone. This was due largely to acquiring an English literary agent in A. P. Watt, whose firm was preeminent in its field. Watt saw that for Harte to make a decent living as a writer he needed to be published to greater advantage in both Britain and America. The only criterion as far as Watt was concerned was the price the publisher was willing to pay for a story; no more sentimental dependency on the New York *Sun* as Bret's American outlet, simply because Bret and the editor, Charles A. Dana, had been such good friends. His stories would be sold to the highest bidder. Henceforth, to the nourishment of both purse and prestige, Bret would be published in the *Illustrated London News*, *Macmillan's Magazine*, the *Strand*, and the *English Illustrated Magazine*,* among English publications. In the United States he would be published in *Harper's*, the *Saturday Evening Post*, *Scribner's* and *Lippincott's*.

Watt also saw to it that the stories were regularly brought out in book form by Houghton Mifflin, most of them slender volumes containing only a few stories, sometimes only one long story such as *Maruja* in 1885, which had appeared first in the *Illustrated London News*, then in *Harper's*.†

Thus Watt wrung every possible financial advantage from Brett's writing and soon made it possible to survive without a government salary.

At the same time Bret began an association with A. S. Boyd, an illustrator, and his wife, Mary, which was to endure to the end of his life. Bret had always taken a keen interest in the illustrations which accompanied his stories; they seemed almost as important to him as the text they adorned. Thus the year before, he had truckled to the artist Millais in hopes that he would consent to illustrate one of his magazine stories. The effort was successful, and Bret wrote Millais that his drawing pen conveyed to the reader a more exact impression of the "naughty little American girl" who figured in the story than Bret's several thousand words on the subject.[2] With A. S. Boyd, however, he formed a permanent collaboration, and no longer had to fret over whether the illustrations would capture his meaning. Mr. and Mrs. Boyd, in ad-

---

* In a typical year, October 1883 to September 1884, the *English Illustrated* published pieces by William Morris, Swinburne, Hardy, William Black, Edmund Gosse, Robert Louis Stevenson, Henry James.

† In the five-year period from 1885 to 1890, in addition to *Maruja*, Harte's books included *By Shore and Sedge*, 1885; *The Crusade of the Excelsior* and *Frontier Stories*, 1887; *A Phyllis of the Sierra*, 1888; *Cressy* and *The Heritage of Dedlow Marsh*, 1889.

dition, became his closest friends in England, and whenever he was away from London he wrote them more faithfully than his family.

The only real drawback to his continued stay in England was the weather. By this time Bret's respiratory complaints had become chronic and he really needed a warmer and dryer climate. The English damp raised continual havoc with his breathing apparatus from bronchia to sinuses. Much as he valued the companionship of William Black, the Scottish novelist — particularly, perhaps, because Black roared continually at Bret's jokes — he turned down an invitation to go salmon fishing with Black. He couldn't understand, he wrote Black, how anyone in the dripping British climate would want to make himself damper by sojourning along the banks of a Scottish stream. He shuddered at even hearing a river mentioned, he said, and got a chill contemplating a fish that wasn't dried.[3] Many parts of the United States would have been kinder to his health.

Balanced against this single drawback, however, was the cordiality with which he was surrounded in England. Losing his consulship, as he wrote Anna, had not diminished the respect in which he was held. His position as a writer won him much greater esteem than any attached to a diplomatic post. He was regarded with greater respect than James Russell Lowell, the former ambassador to the Court of St. James's, because Lowell took himself much too seriously as a diplomat.[4] This was not mere boasting. Regarding Harte's social acceptance, Justin McCarthy wrote in his *Reminiscences*, "No one is made more cordially welcome in literary society . . . both Bohemian and Belgravian."

Though neither his letters nor memoirs of the period mentioned it, several doors at which he was previously most welcome were now closed to him. The reason was his decision to make his home with the Van de Veldes at 15 Upper Hamilton Terrace, N.W., in London. The gossips and Mother Grundys for some years had been muttering and whispering over his intimate place in the Van de Velde household, in which he regularly installed himself whenever he visited London, which was frequently, and in their country home during the summer months. A *ménage à trois,* if it could be considered that in the adulterous sense, simply was too great an affront to the Victorian sense of propriety. The Van de Veldes were Continental aristocrats and Bret was an American writer, so a certain amount of unconventional leeway might have to be granted them. This was too much.

Bret no longer visited the Duke and Duchess of St. Albans and the Webbs of Newstead Abbey, and since the estrangement dated from the time he moved into a room in the Van de Velde house that was probably the reason. The St. Albanses and the Webbs were above petty gossip and easy moralizing, but as fairly representative Victorians they had an unyielding regard for appearances. The name, not the game, was their concern. If Bret and Madame Van de Velde were more than platonic friends, that was their business; it only became a matter of outside concern if and when they flaunted the relationship.

The Victorian era today is regarded as one long frigid winter in which the sexual instinct was all but done to death by the prevalent morality, by restraints imposed from above and accepted by the masses below. Actually it was far from strait-laced, except in public view. Bret's friend, the literary Lord Houghton, for instance, was an assiduous collector of erotic books. At his country seat, Fryston Hall, Lord Houghton and his guests, including statesmen and industrial magnates as well as the more Bohemian types, spent much of their time closeted in his library and discussing his collection.

[251]

There the lyric poet Swinburne, also known as "the swine-born," who luxuriated in a cult of sin "of the most refined and Parisian brand," and Richard Burton would spend hours discoursing on pornography and the sexual practices of the Middle East. The discussions often were punctuated by Swinburne's screams of eldritch laughter, the wild pitch of which was graphically described by Henry Adams.

Prostitution was conducted on such a vast scale in London, particularly with girls barely out of puberty, that the celebrated journalist W. T. Stead crusaded against the system in a series in the *Pall Mall Gazette*. Stead bought a thirteen-year-old girl from her parents, installed her in a house of assignation, and had himself arrested to dramatize the case against underworld procurers and their well-born clients. Only after his scalding articles appeared was the age of consent raised from thirteen to sixteen. The Stead exposé, it was noted, was welcomed not only by such reformers as George Bernard Shaw and General Booth of the Salvation Army but "by all amateurs of the salacious." Prostitution continued unabated; the only result of Stead's crusade was to make it illegal for a girl *under* sixteen to be sold to the procurers.

It wasn't sin but the open enjoyment of it that caused an offender to be blackballed by Victorian society, as one penetrating social historian of the era has divined. The Victorian upper classes, wrote Esmé Wingfield-Stratford in *The Victorian Sunset*, were determined to "confront the world with a façade of unsullied respectability." Thus "the penalties for any sort of association with any sort of scandal were so terrific that few were hardy enough to run the risk. Many a marriage that would have been wrecked in our day [1932] on the rock of incompatibility resolved itself into a not unhappy partnership, because both parties realized that there was no tolerable alternative to making good."

The cocksureness of the Victorians that they inhabited the best, and possibly the purest, of all possible worlds rested on "a tacit convention that no one was to blackleg by making too close an examination of the things he was certain about." If this was conducive to hypocrisy, it did "tend to enforce a high standard of conduct." Victorian morality, Mr. Wingfield-Stratford has remarked, reposed on "the belief that if you could not be virtuous, you could at least be respectable. Though the streets of London swarmed with harlots and a male virgin was regarded in the smoking-room as a rather poor-spirited fellow, the pretence of chastity was to be kept up. A conspiracy of decent silence was maintained, under the direct penalties, regarding any infringement of the sexual taboo . . ."

Thus Bret violated the most sacred of Victorian taboos. Not against sin, but the appearance of sin. The more top-lofty of his friends considered themselves obligated to turn from him. Yet he wasn't placed in Coventry, even among the more "Belgravian" types. The Boyds certainly were respectable people, and he was frequently bidden to the homes of Lady Lindsay, the Froudes, and Mrs. Henniker, the daughter of Lord Houghton; his traveling companion on the Continent usually was Colonel Arthur Collins, and he was often invited to Compton Wyngates, the country seat of Lord Compton in Warwickshire. He was still a member of such clubs as the Beefsteak, the Kinsmen, the Rabelais, and in later years the exclusive Royal Thames Yacht Club.

To his wife Bret maintained that his position in the Van de Velde home was "unexceptional." Unvaryingly he kept up the pretense that there was nothing in the least odd or reprehensible in his becoming a permanent guest of the Van de Veldes. Gossip to the contrary, he indicated, was hardly worthy of recognition. In his later years, as the relationship with Madame Van de Velde became even more ambiguous, he was fond of quoting the motto on the crest of the Earl of Mareschal of Aberdeen: "They say. What say they? Let them say!"

The woman who shared this obloquy with him was obviously as strong-minded as she was nonconventional. Madame Van de Velde cared even less for poisonous gossip than Bret did; the attitude of her husband was unvaryingly complaisant. Earlier biographers maintained that she looked upon Bret, in a way, as her tenth child; that his illnesses aroused only her maternal instincts. Her interests, however, were much wider than the typical Victorian wife and mother; she was more fascinated by the studio than the nursery, and the corseted life of a dutiful matron was not for her. She helped Bret with his manuscripts and eagerly assumed the role of his buffer against the world. Nor did she hesitate to advertise her position by acting as his spokesman. At the time it was fashionable for the daughters of wealthy Americans to hunt down husbands among the English and Continental aristocracies, and Madame Van de Velde gave vent to his scornful opinion of such alliances in a letter to a London newspaper in which she announced that Bret "severely satirized those of his fair compatriots who, dazzled by the lustre of lordly alliances, have too closely assimilated with the land of their adoption, and apparently forgotten their own country. To such he has not hesitated to apply the term of 'apostates.' " [5]

In none of the letters which have been preserved does Bret give more than an inkling of the attraction, platonic or otherwise, which Madame Van de Velde had for him. The way he explained matters to Anna, it was her kindness and Monsieur Van de Velde's hospitality which caused him to become their permanent guest. Monsieur Van de Velde is mentioned even less in the letters, but Bret often wrote Anna about the Van de Velde children and proposed that his daughters correspond with them. He seemed to stress her usualness in his letters to Anna and offered the observation, in writing of Madame Van de Velde, that experience had taught him that grand dames and plain dames were very much alike.[6]

In her independence of spirit and her contempt for public opinion, at least, Madame Van de Velde resembled the gallery of heroines Bret created in his stories. Bret as a writer had little use for the pallid, drooping, languishing female who supposedly epitomized the Victorian years; the type for whom a vial of smelling salts always had to be kept handy; the girl who bridled under her layers of whalebone and crinoline at the unabashed mention of the human limb. His were girls of spirit and enterprise.* They were frank, direct in speech and action, eager for anything new and untried. In his story "The Great Deadwood Mystery," the heroine was eager to lead the way into the "trickless, uncharted *terra incognita* of the passions." Other girls of his creative imagination, some of them possibly based on living models, were equally venturesome as they played their parts in his episodic saga of the California frontier. His girls were more likely to trail sequins than sentiment; some were respectable enough schoolmarms but often they pleaded guilty to a dubious past with a theatrical troupe; they were halfbreed mermaids found frolicking on the beaches, cultivated Bostonians with whom young Spaniards fell in love; they sang or danced for their supper in mining-camp deadfalls, were redhaired and freckled nymphs of the redwoods, were bold country girls who gave shelter to dashing bandits, and sometimes they appeared in later years as shopworn and raddled Mother Ship-

* Van Wyck Brooks has commented that the "brilliant Bret Harte heroines" generally "expressed as they reflected the atmosphere of risk and excitement" which pervaded his tales of the California mining country (*The Times of Melville and Whitman*).

tons and Cherokee Sals. They always stood out as individuals and — rare in a male writer of his time — they were often as interesting, complex and forceful as his masculine characters, if not more so.* There were no wallflowers in his portrait gallery of American womanhood. They were the mothers and grandmothers of the suffragettes, the flappers of World War I, the career girls of the years after that, and of today's blue-jeaned adventuresses touring Europe and Asia with guitar and pessary or leaving college to join the Peace Corps.

From then until the end of his life Madame Van de Velde provided the domestic ease and tranquil atmosphere he needed if he was to function as a writer. They were as essential to him as whiskey to Poe or applause to Twain; perhaps what he dreaded most about America was a return to the feverish disorder, the flights from creditors and writs of attachment, the monetary demands of his wife and sisters which had characterized his last years on American soil. Cozily established in the bosom of the Van de Velde family he was relatively free of financial worry; all he had to earn was the two hundred fifty dollars a month he continued to send to Anna plus a much more modest amount to keep himself clothed and entertained. He enjoyed the comforts of a well-appointed and smoothly managed town house most of the year and a country retreat in the summer. Madame Van de Velde acted as his amanuensis, nurse, confidante, propagandist . . . if nothing more. He was fond of the Van de Velde children, especially admiring their European manners in contrast to those of American children, and was able to immerse himself in the joys of family life whenever he was in the

* The best of his early biographers, H. C. Merwin (*The Life of Bret Harte,* 1911) rightly observed that his heroines resembled those of Turgenev and Hardy in that they "obey the instinct of love as unreservedly as men of an archaic type obey the instinct of fighting," and were characterized by a "magnificent forgetfulness of self."

mood, or retreat to his own quarters when he wasn't. The loss of a few disapproving friends, the accelerated gossip of the busybodies were more than compensated by all he gained as an ex-officio member of the Van de Velde household. Only an angry and determined descent by his wife could rupture this tranquil design.

For the first time in his life, and from then until the end of his life, Bret was devoting all his time and energy to writing. In San Francisco he had juggled two or three careers at once; in New York, too, he had flitted between writing and less worthy distractions; and in the past several years he had been forced to spend much of his day at consular duties. Now, on the verge of fifty, he became the complete professional, the resident of what George Gissing would make famous as Grub Street, the home of the hack and the genius alike. Most of the day he spent at his desk, slowly writing his stories in a small, barely legible hand, on sheets of notepaper about four by eight inches. When a number of sheets had been collected, he or Madame Van de Velde would paste two together to make one fair-sized sheet of copy. He wrote slowly, painstakingly; no more dashing off several thousand words in a night with the aid of whiskey. The longer he worked at his profession, in fact, the more deliberate and painful seemed the process of creation, the more dedicated his efforts to convey exactly the impression he wanted. Often it took him a full month to turn out a short story.

At the head of each story he made a businesslike note, like any efficient production manager: "*A Knight Errant of the Foothills*, 8881 words; Feb., 1889," "*Young Robin Gray*, About 7000 words; Begun 20 October, 1893; Finished 17 November 1893." [7]

Mostly they represented a dredging of his memory of events he had witnessed or heard of thirty years before when he was a young dude in cracked patent-leather shoes wandering the settlements of northern California. Occasionally he would write a story with an English background, as when he produced "The Desborough Connections" or "The Ghost of Stukely Castle," but at the same time he was writing "The Passing of Enriquez" and "Jack Hamlin's Mediation." The land of his green years was more real to him as a writer than the island on which he was to spend the last third of his life.

An integral part of the Harte legend is that he never wrote anything worth a damn after he left San Francisco. The truth is that there was no decline in his power of creation, no failure of the imagination; only a refusal, or an inability, to branch out, to explore new ground, to seek new forms. He was a painter of miniatures intent on perfecting himself on his limited canvas who would leave the murals and full-length portraits to others. Weariness and ill-health would increase, but his stories always retained a freshness, a nervous vitality, a marvelous compactness. He could say in a few quick flashing sentences what other writers would take several pages to convey.

The quality of many of the stories he wrote in England very nearly equaled, in parts exceeded, that of the first stories which captivated the reading audience of the late sixties and early seventies. It was just that they had lost their novelty. Two stories written just after he had settled in at 15 Upper Hamilton Terrace showed that his work was benefiting from the new professionalism of his approach, "Snowbound at Eagle's" with its riproaring leadoff of a stagecoach robbery and "An Apostle of the Tules." The latter impelled John Hay, his former protector in the State Department and a lifelong champion of Bret's, to write him that he was just arriving at the peak of his creative powers.

"An Apostle of the Tules," one of the few Harte stories

bearing an exact date, began at a revival meeting in Contra Costa County October 10, 1856. It was based on his observations of frontier evangelism while tutoring the sons of a rancher in the Sycamore Valley outside Oakland when he was twenty years old. The hellfire brand of religion had always struck him as unhealthy, overemotional; thirty years later he remembered exactly how the ranting of the preacher and the frantic response of his back-country audience had affected him. He recalled also that the drab garments of the women somehow made the homely girls homelier and the pretty ones prettier.

In a number of other stories he contrasted the febrile atmosphere of the open-air revival meetings and the grim proceedings in the wooden tabernacles of backwoods Protestantism with the cool and stately Roman Catholicism which had preceded them in the California hills. The contrast between Anglo-Saxon fundamentalism and the relaxed charm of the Spanish friars, though he may have exaggerated both, was conveyed in some of his most cogent and sardonic passages. In that respect civilization, in Bret's opinion, had gone downhill when American replaced Spanish influence. Thus in one story a cowboy evangelist spewed threats of brimstone over his parishioners despite a lurid past in Arkansas; in another a circuit-riding preacher in an old mission town was converted to Roman Catholicism by the organ-playing niece of his Mexican gardener.

In addition to a steady production of short stories — most of which appeared in English magazines, then American, then in book form in Britain, America and Germany — Bret compulsively flirted with the theater during the next half-dozen years. Adaptation of his stories for the stage would provide yet another source of income, almost "found" money. In the winter of 1885–1886 he labored once again over adapting "The Luck of Roaring Camp" for J. L. Toole, the eminent West End actor-manager, who had high hopes for it.

Perhaps Toole was influenced by an incident which had occurred several years earlier when he met Bret on the street with three other men. Bret introduced them as Count Bismarck (son of the German Chancellor), the Duke of St. Albans and Sir George Trevelyan. Toole insisted Bret was "joshing" him; he didn't learn until later, to his embarrassment, that Bret had been perfectly serious.[8]

Bret wrote a scenario, actually an outline or treatment, indicating how "Roaring Camp" might be transferred to the stage. The actor-manager found it an acceptable ground plan for the play itself, but on reflection Bret withdrew from the project. He decided that the play, as blocked out, would be too violent a departure from the story on which it was based. Toole was a farceur and the comedy aspects of the story would necessarily be stressed to the detriment of the pathos, which Bret considered equally important. People who came to see the play, he wrote his son Frank, would be the ones who had read and admired the story, and they would be let down by the emphasis on its farcical elements.[9] Instead of proceeding with the adaptation of "Roaring Camp," he agreed with Toole to attempt an entirely new project, a comedy from the start, with the leading role tailored more exactly to Toole's measurements.

The two-act farce he eventually turned out for Toole also failed to reach the production stage. Subsequently, in his spare time, he also worked on adaptations of *Gabriel Conroy* and, once again, *M'liss.** He did not, however, make his

---

* The pirated version of which played in stock and touring repertory companies for decades.

previous mistake of stopping work on his short stories to concentrate on pie-in-the-sky theatrical ventures. The stories, as he candidly said, were his "bread-and-butter" work. Sick or well, cheerful or despondent, he wrote Anna, he kept to his task of turning out approximately a story a month. It was the regimen to which he would be bound henceforth. There would be no further blessings from Kismet to allow him a respite of more than a few days or a week or two in the summer. He was now reconciled to the fact that his portion of luck had come a little too early in life for him to have made the most of it.

Communications between Bret and his scattered family — Anna and his two daughters in New Jersey, Frank touring with a theatrical company, Griswold involved on the fringes of New York journalism — often broke down in a way that frightened him. Sometimes months would go by without word from Anna, and he would have to appeal to her to let him know she and the girls were alive and well.

Not unexpectedly he and Anna were often out of sympathy, superficially for financial reasons. She refused to live within the generous enough allowance of two hundred fifty dollars monthly, a sizable sum in that day for the support of a wife and two daughters; partly it was because she had always mismanaged money, a trait Bret had formerly shared, and partly perhaps as a means of claiming his attention. In a letter he wrote her in the spring of 1886 he referred to her resentment over his recent cautioning her about being more careful with the money he sent her. He had never asked her for an accounting of her stewardship, he wrote, and never would, but she must realize that his occupation was a risky one dependent on a constant production and sale of his stories. If he fell sick or was disabled, they would have nothing to fall back on. He begged her not to be angry when he reminded her of the uncertainty of his income.[10]

His efforts to keep in touch with his sons' careers were not entirely successful. He worried over the "artificial excitement" of Frank's theatrical life and his tendency to resort to drugs and drink for relief from his physical (and probably neurotic) symptoms. He was so far removed from events in the States that he pronounced himself pleased by the fact that Griswold had joined the editorial staff of *Town Topics* in New York. Obviously he didn't know that *Town Topics*, edited by the notorious Colonel William D'Alton Mann, was a society gossip sheet which combined keyhole journalism with blackmail; its victims escaped the colonel's malicious exposures only by buying large amounts of advertising. Even after reading that journal because of his son's connection with it, Bret declared that it seemed more refined than most society weeklies. Unlike the other children, Griswold made no attempts to solicit his father's help in advancing his career, though as a writer of sorts he was the one whom Bret should have been able to help the most. He seldom, in fact, corresponded with his father and drifted farther away from the rest of the family than his brother Frank. If one could judge by his absence from the figurative hearth — figurative in that Mrs. Harte and her daughters drifted from house to lodgings to summer hotel — Griswold seemed to have washed his hands of the lot of them.

In the breakdown of communications with his family Bret himself was partly to blame, judging from his replies to his wife excusing himself for not having written for some time. William Black, his novelist friend, had obtained a guest card for Bret at the Reform Club and told of his astonishment at the fact Bret allowed stacks of mail to accumulate at the club without opening or answering any of it. "He is a mystery," Black said, "and the cause of mystification." [11]

He was considerably shocked in November of 1887 to read in the English newspapers an account of how his son Frank had almost died of an overdose of laudanum. For twelve hours Frank lay in a coma near death. According to the newspaper accounts, the drug, an opium derivative then widely used (without prescription) as a painkiller, had been administered by Mrs. Harte. At first he believed the accounts exaggerated, as so many stories about himself had been when they reached print. He told his friends the story must be a "gross fabrication."

Three weeks passed before Anna got around to writing Bret and telling him about the incident. Bret lost his composure, as he rarely did, as he could rarely afford to do, and berated Anna for having kept the news from him so long, especially since she must have known the English papers would pick up the stories from the New York papers. He learned from Anna that she had given Frank a dose of medicine which she believed to be one of the homeopathic remedies the family used. Then Frank noticed that his mother had poured the liquid from a bottle marked with a death's-head indicative of poison. Before going under from the overdose of opiate he was able to persuade his mother to send for a doctor.

After expressing his indignation over being kept in the dark about Frank's mishap, Bret confessed his worry over a son still in his twenties who had to resort to such powerful anodynes for relief of comparatively minor ailments.[12]

The gossip that sped around London regarding his son's brush with death embroidered considerably on the facts, speculating that Frank had attempted suicide because his father had refused to support the family and left them in desperate straits. In the same letter to Anna, Bret related that he had heard of a group of visiting Americans who spread the gossip at their hotel and at the American embassy; that an English bank official who knew of Bret's regular remittances home had overheard the talk and informed the Americans that Bret supported his wife and daughters in a style that exceeded that of British officers' families and the younger sons of the nobility. He asked Anna to try to trace the gossip to its source in New York. "Let them say!" may have been part of his borrowed motto, but he was sensitive enough about what was said of him in the States, then and later, to try to combat the slanderous whispers.

One source of the vilification, by his own confession, was Mark Twain, whose attitude toward Bret was as inimical as ever. Indelible in Twain's mind was the picture of Bret as he had known him in the late seventies, drinking hard, scrounging for money, dodging his obligations; he refused to believe anyone who told him that Bret was supporting his family in America. He recalled that Bret had told him once that during his early days in California "he kept a woman who was twice his age — no, the woman kept him," and added in his autobiography that in England Bret "was kept, at different times, by a couple of women — a connection which has gone into history, along with the names of those women." [13] Even so, Twain was mindful enough of the libel laws not to repeat the names wafted around by international gossips.

In the autobiography Twain related a seriocomic incident that stemmed from his conviction that Bret could never be up to anything good. He dropped in at the Players Club one night and joined a group of men drinking whiskey punches and idly conversing. The name of Bret Harte cropped up. Its mere mention, Twain recalled, fired a young man named

Henry Milford Steele with enthusiasm. Steele took the floor
for ten minutes straight telling about Mrs. Harte and her
daughters and the blameless lives they led in a New Jersey
town, how they eked out their income with Mrs. Harte
teaching music and the girls assisting, Ethel with her embroi-
dery, Jessamy with her drawings.

Twain listened without comment to the eulogy because, in
his opinion, Anna Harte was a living saint for putting up
with Bret. He grew restive, however, when young Steele
launched into an equally enthusiastic tribute to Bret's self-
sacrificing exile in England. The way Steele told it, Bret was
the most faithful of correspondents and sent a letter home by
each steamer. Bret had not come home for many years because it would have meant reducing the amount of money he
could send for the family's support.

Doubtless this was the explanation Mrs. Harte gave for his
prolonged absence. With steamship fares as low as they were,
however, Bret could have made it home almost anytime after
his first year in Germany.

Twain stood as much of the eulogizing as he could, then
took the floor himself and delivered this diatribe:

"Oh, that be hanged! There's nothing in it. Bret Harte has
deserted his family and that is the plain English of it. Possibly
he writes to them, but I am not weak enough to believe it
until I see the letters; possibly he is pining to come home to
his deserted family, but no one that knows him will believe
that. But there is one thing about which I think there can be
no possibility of doubt — and that is, that he never sent them
a dollar and has never intended to send them a dollar. Bret
Harte is the most contemptible, poor little soulless blather-
skite that exists on the planet today — "

At that point one of his companions tugged at Twain's

sleeve and managed to divert him by whispering, "For goodness' sake shut up! This young fellow is Steele. He's engaged
to one of the daughters." [14]

Despite Twain's aspersions on the prospective father-in-
law, young Mr. Steele subsequently married Bret's eldest
daughter, Jessamy.

There is nothing on the record to show that Bret ever
spoke harshly of Twain except for that one outburst in
which he accused Twain of having participated in a plot to
siphon off his royalties on the novel *Gabriel Conroy*. Bret
was as wrong in that instance as Twain was in charging him
with nonsupport.

Except among Americans visiting London and those English who objected to his being an anomalous fixture in the
Van de Velde household, Bret was fairly untouched by that
sort of slanderous gossip in England. Undoubtedly it was
one of the reasons he did not chafe in exile, being a man who
valued his dignity more than most, and was accounted a leading Anglophile.

His love of England and the English was tempered, however, by the insight he had gained into the lordly attitudes of
the upper class. He was almost snobbish in his preference for
their company, and in his frequent references in his letters to
the time he spent with the knighted and titled. That did not
prevent him from seeing them with a clear and skeptical eye
— any more than his position as a guest in the Twain house
had inhibited him, according to his host, from criticizing Mrs.
Twain's taste in decor.

In the winter of 1885–1886 a mob of derelicts had run wild
in the West End, assaulted people on the streets, smashed
windows in the clubs of the Strand and Pall Mall and broken
into shops. It was an explosion of resentment from the slums,

the doss houses of Whitechapel, that had never occurred before, and it broke through the crust of Victorian smugness with an alarming impact. Until then the purple-cheeked gentlemen in their clubs, who had to take refuge in the sculleries and wine cellars until the mob had vented its fury, had assumed that the proletariat was — and damned well better be — content with its lot. Yet for hours the police were helpless to contain the rioting of a few hundred unarmed and rachitic creatures boiling out of the East End.

For all the hospitality he had known in those same clubs and in the country houses of their members, Bret wrote of their confrontation with the lower elements with a savage sort of delight. He quoted one of the rioters as saying, "I suppose they will kill us — but it's better than sheer starving." He described how the clubmen had fled from their shattered plate-glass windows and cowered in dismay at the explosion of resentment, face to face for once in their lives with people they had despised for generations. "For once their sacred police could do nothing! For once they saw these terribly famished creatures, whom they had patronized in workhouses, petted in hospitals, and kept at a distance generally with good-humoured tolerance, absolutely breaking their bounds and clamouring for Heaven knows what!" It was hard for anyone in America to understand, Bret said, how hopeless was the ditch that had been dug between the classes "by centuries of class government." Bret believed that ditch might be filled with many corpses before a measure of social justice was attained in Britain.[15]

Several years later, while spending a weekend at a country house in Cirencester, he delivered himself of a lengthy and surprisingly bitter commentary on the lives, manners and morals of the upper class. Apparently he saw nothing paradoxical, or ungrateful, about unburdening himself on the subject while luxuriating in the midst of its comforts and pleasures.

An American, he said, had complained to his wellborn host, "You are too damned comfortable over here." To Bret's mind that was the pith of the matter. The privileged class, he said, thought of nothing but their own amusement, even arranged the meetings of Parliament so they would not interfere with time-honored institutions — hunting, shooting and racegoing — to which they apportioned their lives with a "ridiculous formality."

The solemnity with which aristocratic Englishmen went about slaughtering grouse particularly irked Bret. As sportsmen, he contended, they were ostentatious vulgarians who insisted on publicizing their exploits on the moors with the pomp of a Court Circular, "not only how many brace they shot but *who* shot and what Lord So-and-So did." The obsession with sport was ridiculous to Bret, who cited the fact that fashionable society turned out en masse for the Eton and Harrow cricket matches. The parents of public-school boys had no interest in how they did in their studies but prided themselves inordinately on their sons' prowess at rugby or cricket. He found it equally ridiculous that snobbish Americans sent their sons to be educated in such an atmosphere of crazed athleticism.

Even the English tolerance for eccentrics — certainly one of their more charming traits to most non-English — was somehow unattractive to Bret. The maddest sort of foibles were smilingly tolerated among the upper class, he observed, even though they conflicted with the canons of good "form." Some of the people he met in the best drawing rooms and manor houses behaved like lunatics or imbeciles, and their peers simply ignored their behavior. When he commented on their outlandish conduct, he said, he would be told, rather pityingly for his lack of comprehension, "Oh, that's only Lord A . . ." [16]

He recalled dining with a group of distinguished persons, none of whom thought it odd that the host fell asleep and snored halfway through dinner, none of whom would consider awakening him. Next to Bret was seated a gentleman whose entire conversation consisted of "Ah, Ho, Hum." The "Ah" was interrogative, the "Ho" confidential and the "Hum" contemplative. Bret considered that was reducing the language to something less than its essentials. At another gathering he was startled when "the most extraordinary apparition" glided into the drawing room. Her face was painted pink and yellow and she wore bright yellow ringlets, though she was about sixty years old; her costume was also hideously inappropriate, suitable for a young girl, if anyone, with a blossoming of bows, ribbons and sashes. Bret thought the family lunatic had escaped from her room, but he was informed that she bore a name and title familiar to anyone who read the society columns. What outraged Bret was that "the mere possibility of her appalling anyone outside that sacred circle never occurred to them, and they *didn't care!*" Nor did it occur to Bret, who became more pro-American the longer he lived abroad, that many of his blustering countrymen were even more curious to the English when they trooped down the gangplank at Southampton.

THIRTEEN

The Drudge of Lancaster Gate

AS the decade of the nineties wheeled into place, the world
began changing at a pace dismaying to anyone of Bret's
generation. Victoria was still on the throne but most of what
she represented was rapidly becoming anachronistic. The
florid elegance of the *fin de siècle* was replacing the prideful
dowdiness of the Victorians. Stovepipe hats, Dundrearys and
crinolines were seen no more. The iron steamers were junked
for steel ocean liners racing for the Blue Ribbon of the Atlantic. Electricity was slowly gaining popularity over the
mellowness of gaslight. In 1896 the sportive would be climb-
ing off bicycles and onto the first automobiles. The tele-
phone was intruding on the peace and privacy of many
homes. And politics was turning to more radical measures for
overdue reform. The Fabian Society, founded in the winter
of 1883–1884, was exerting considerable influence now toward reshaping the world and curbing the spirit of individu-
alism which had expanded the British Empire and built the
American nation. In 1897 the Empire would reach its apogee
with all the panoplied display of the Diamond Jubilee —
quickly followed by the Boer War and the significant lesson
that it required a marshaling of all the forces of the empire to
put down the revolt of a few Dutch farmers pioneering the
techniques of guerrilla fighting.

The new luminaries of the literary world in England were Kipling, Hardy, Meredith, Stevenson, Wells; in America Stephen Crane would soon be lighting the way with his brief incandescence, and Jack London, Frank Norris and Theodore Dreiser were waiting in the wings. Literature whether on the printed page or in dramatic form was making a startlingly effective attempt to penetrate human behavior and expose long-enduring social evils and inequities. In 1893 six Ibsen plays were running simultaneously in London theaters, and the works of George Bernard Shaw and Henry Arthur Jones were converting the theater from farce and melodrama to a proving ground of the intellect and the social conscience. For those to whom this strident modernity was disturbing if not ominous, there were plentiful opportunities of escape in popular fiction. Kipling offered an exit to the dream world of imperialism, even as its foundations were receiving their first cracking blows; Stevenson into adventure on warm seas; Anthony Hope into Ruritanian fantasy.

In this changing world Bret Harte was still able to maintain a foothold. He was entering the later years of middle age and was increasingly determined to insulate himself against new ideas; Shaw, Wilde and the others meant little to him. The younger writers aroused a minimum of interest, even less of curiosity. He met young Rudyard Kipling at a dinner party, and though Kipling confessed he owed "many things" in his own career to his reading of Bret's stories, Bret saw to it that he was seated next to Lord Roberts at table.[1] Kipling was merely another scribbler like himself while Roberts was a military hero who had dashed from one colonial war to another.

His resistance to the new modes of thought most definitely extended to Christian Science, which he abhorred; it was one subject on which he and Mark Twain agreed. When he was

[271]

visited by his wife's niece and a traveling companion, they tried to convert him with a signal lack of success. The young women argued, expounded, quoted from the works of Mary Baker Eddy until Bret was beside himself with suppressed anger. Their conversations, he wrote a friend, had been neither "flippant" nor "mildly entertaining." [2]

Self-insulated as he was against the rising stars of literature, he must have drawn some satisfaction from the respect they accorded him. He had a strong appeal for young writers; there was an enduring freshness about his work, and to a greater degree than he may have imagined, with his conception of himself as an organ-grinder playing the old tunes, he was a part of their endeavor to make literature penetrate deeper into the human condition. They regarded him as a living model.

The young John Galsworthy, unhappily articled to a solicitor at chambers in the Inner Temple, had just begun writing short stories, as he said, "in the manner of Bret Harte." His first attempt was titled "Dick Denver's Idea" and concerned an American gambler who came to the rescue of a woman married to a brutal husband by killing him in a cave. The corpse was disposed of when a geyser conveniently spouted up in the cave. Dick Denver then nobly renounced the woman for whom he had sacrificed so much. Not only the "manner" and the leading character but the unabashed manipulation of coincidence were indeed patterned after Harte. Fortunately Galsworthy soon turned inward for his inspiration. [3]

Another youthful admirer was Gilbert K. Chesterton, who considered that Bret had

discovered the intense sensibility of the primitive man . . . Bret Harte tells the truth about the wildest, the grossest, the most rapacious of all the districts of the earth — the truth that, while it is very rare indeed in the world to find a thoroughly good man, it is rarer still, rare to the point of monstrosity, to find a man who does not either desire to be one, or imagine that he is one already.[4]

In this continuing eminence among literary men it was fitting that he sit for his portrait by a member of the Royal Academy. It was painted in his fifty-fourth year by John R. Pettie, R.A., and captured him as he liked to see himself — as a man of the world, elegantly costumed, a trifle weary and blasé. The portrait emphasized his impressive profile with the aquiline nose, the darkly intelligent and skeptical eyes, the long drooping mustache and the plentiful, if graying, hair worn in bangs over his broad forehead. He was dressed in a fur-collared coat with a white scarf around his throat and one glove in hand as though on his way to the opera. That was the face, the manner he showed the world; the reality of a man hard-driven to send his wife her monthly two-hundred-fifty-dollar bank draft, almost a recluse much of his time, invisibly chained to the desk where he drained story after story out of his imagination, was not suggested. Nor was the ill-health that dogged him, which he now tried to hide from rather than hide behind; facial neuralgia, rheumatism and a chronic sore throat which warned of the more serious disorder that would kill him.

His social life grew increasingly limited and he gave up membership in most of his clubs. The club he still visited regularly was the Royal Thames Yacht Club, not because he had any interest in yachting but, as he explained, because the members "talk of nothing but their yachts." They didn't ask him questions about his work, and had little interest in a graying man who liked to sit in lonely corners for an hour or two. Perhaps Madame Van de Velde's protectiveness, her constant awareness of him as a literary genius who must be cozened and coerced into continual production, occasionally grew irksome. At any rate the yacht club was the refuge of his later years, when expatriation, in some ways became less attractive. "Time has not dulled Bret Harte's instinctive affection for the land of his birth," an English writer who knew him remarked. "He is steadfastly unchangeable in his political and patriotic beliefs." His patriotism had risen to a new crest, in fact, during a period of tension between Britain and the United States when they came close to armed conflict over Venezuela. Bret, another writer reported, "earnestly avowed his intentions of instantly returning to his own country, should hostilities break out." [5]

His countrymen may or may not have been gratified to learn of his continuing affection for them, but many were irked by slipups in physical detail contained in his later stories. Californians felt that if he must everlastingly write about them and their state he might at least return for a refresher course in geography, botany and history. He might learn, for instance, that California had largely turned from mining to agriculture; that the flumes and sluiceboxes were rotting away in the Sierra foothills; that the old shanty settlements had long ago tumbled into ruin and desolation, and that, for instance, the hills above Carquinez Strait were not wooded but grass-covered. Nothing outraged native sons more than his recollection that the poppies which emblazon the hillsides above San Francisco were scarlet. A parody titled "Plain Language to Bret Harte" in the *Overland Monthly* must, if he saw it, have annoyed him. Its last paragraph read:

> But what kills me plumb dead
> Is to see where he's writ

That our poppies is red—
Which they ain't red a bit,
But the flamingest orange and yellow—
Oh, Bret, how could you forget![6]

He looked back on the old California through a nostalgic and romantic haze; it would always be the land of his youth, which he endlessly recaptured in terms far removed from its often harsh reality. He identified himself with the cool and self-assured Jack Hamlin and John Oakhurst, those cavaliers of the faro layout and the Sacramento riverboats, rather than the frail, often timorous youth he had been. It is his pristine recollections of pre-boosterism California which make his stories as readable now — many of them — as they were in the 1890's.

In "A Protegee of Jack Hamlin's," produced in 1893, this sense of place, fogged over though it may have been in minor details, was as brilliantly recoverable as ever. The opening paragraphs demonstrated his "striking nervous compactness" * in setting the scene and delineating situation and character within the space of two hundred words:

The steamer Silveropolis was sharply and steadily cleaving the broad, placid shallows of the Sacramento River. A large wave like an eagre,† diverging from its bow, was extending to either bank, swamping the tules and threatening to submerge the lower levees. The great boat itself — a vast but delicate structure of airy stories, hanging galleries, fragile colonnades, gilded cornices, and resplendent frescoes — was throbbing throughout its whole perilous length with the pulse of high pressure and the strong monotonous beat of a powerful piston. Floods of foam pouring

* The phrase is Wallace Stegner's in his brilliantly concise introduction to New American Library's paperback collection of 1961, *The Outcasts of Poker Flat and Other Tales.*

† A bore or tidal flow.

from the high paddle boxes on either side and reunited in the wake of the boat left behind a track of dazzling whiteness, over which trailed two dense black banners flung from its lofty smokestacks.

Mr. Jack Hamlin had quietly emerged from his stateroom on deck and was looking over the guards. His hands were resting lightly on his hips over the delicate curves of his white waistcoat, and he was whistling softly, possibly some air to which he had made certain card-playing passengers dance the night before . . . He glanced lazily along the empty hurricane deck forward; he glanced lazily down to the saloon deck below him. Far out against the guards below him leaned a young girl. Mr. Hamlin knitted his brows slightly . . .

Bret's ability to take a quick, firm grasp on the reader's attention was also demonstrated in "An Ingenue of the Sierras," written the same year and likewise a story on a par with his best. In that one Bret sardonically peeled off layers of innocence to show the reality of his principals; the "ingenue" turns out to be a "lying little she-devil," in the astonished words of Yuba Bill, who was not often fooled by human nature. Again Bret grabbed the reader by the lapels in his first paragraph:

We all held our breath as the coach rushed through the semi-darkness of Galloper's Ridge. The vehicle itself was only a huge lumbering shadow; its side lights were carefully extinguished, and Yuba Bill had just politely removed from the lips of an outside passenger even the cigar with which he had been ostentatiously exhibiting his coolness. For it had been rumored that the Ramon Martinez gang of "road agents" were "laying" for us on the second grade, and would time the passage of our lights across Galloper's in order to intercept us in the "brush" beyond. If we could cross the ridge without being seen, and so get through the brush before they reached it, we were safe. If they followed, it would only be a stern chase with the odds in our favor.

Among the passengers on the stage was a pretty creature with "frank gray eyes and large laughing mouth," who was suspected of signaling to the bandit gang with her lace handkerchief. She admitted that she was eloping from her banker father with a young man who had lost his money gambling and whom Yuba Bill and the other passengers recognized as a member of the Martinez gang. Wallowing in sentiment, Yuba Bill and the others facilitate the elopement — and, in effect, the getaway. Days later they discover that the girl with the frank eyes is not the daughter of a banker and that the "clean-cut" young man they married her off to is actually the gang leader Martinez. Yuba Bill, the rude philosopher, figures he got even with the two elopers because each in time would learn what a liar the other was. "For stiddy, comf'ble kempany," Yuba Bill reflects, "give me the son of a man that was *hanged*."

The unconventional ménage at 15 Upper Hamilton Terrace was one of thousands of homes throughout the world which were stricken and bereaved by the terrible influenza epidemic of 1892. As in many other cases the flu attacked the halest and heartiest rather than those, like Bret, whose long frailty would logically have singled them out as its first victims. First Monsieur Van de Velde, then his wife and their children took to their beds violently ill; the household was filled with the traffic of doctors and nurses and the murmuring of their grave consultations. Only Bret stayed on his feet. London, as he wrote his wife, had become the "City of Dreadful Night," with the days so dark that "the streets at noon are like midnight" and the only light came from the flickering gas lamps; one could imagine what it had been like centuries before during the Great Plague. In those dark days, with friends dying all around, Bret was still the compleat writer; he was saving all *his* strength, he informed Anna, for his work. He was so out of touch with family affairs by that time that he had to ask Anna, in the same letter, whether his son Frank was in Europe or the United States.[7]

Madame Van de Velde and the children slowly recovered, but on February 7, 1892, Monsieur Van de Velde died after a six-week illness. Bret spoke feelingly of his "kindness and almost brotherly friendship." The same day Madame Van de Velde's stepfather died in Berlin. Some days later she and two of her daughters went to Berlin while Bret stayed on in the house on Upper Hamilton Terrace to look after the younger children — or rather, as he admitted, vice versa.

Reading between the lines of his letters home, it appears that Anna's hopes of a family reunion, at long last, were rising to a critical level. Surely with Monsieur Van de Velde dead there could be no thought of his lingering in that household? Surely it would hardly be respectable for a widow and a married man to be living under the same roof?

The issue was postponed, as Bret informed Anna, until his hostess of seven years moved to a new home in Lancaster Gate, near the Bayswater Road.

Meanwhile, Bret danced the old minuet of evasion and procrastination in his letters home. His dearest wish, he told Anna, was to be able to tell her to come over at once with their two daughters. However, the finances would have to be worked out first. It would cost more to maintain the four of them in a London hotel than his income permitted. In any case, he wouldn't consider having his daughters educated or living permanently in England. He thought he would look around the countryside outside London for a suitable house. Or they might tour the Continent, then settle down for a while in Switzerland or Germany. Three months after Monsieur Van de Velde died he was still vacillating behind a cloud of possibilities and speculations.[8]

That summer, still apparently undecided, he spent drifting through the Welsh highlands. The letters home were few and far between. He wrote feelingly of his duty toward the semi-orphaned Van de Velde children; a worthy sentiment which must have roused stormy emotions in Mrs. Harte. What of his own children, semi-orphaned by his absence of fifteen years? Ethel hardly remembered her father. Frank was a troubled young man. Griswold in his resentment had drifted so far from the family circle that he was rarely mentioned in his parents' correspondence; the life of a newspaperman on Park Row was often a disordered one, and his would terminate all too soon. Yet, with a curious insensitivity, Bret would harp on the theme of his responsibility to Madame Van de Velde's children.

The letter in which Bret announced to his wife that he would stay on alone in England — alone with the Van de Veldes, that is — has not been preserved. It may well have been a masterpiece. How does a man explain to his wife that it is necessary for him to live with a recently widowed woman rather than return to his own roof? No doubt he pleaded that it was cheaper that way: both he and Mrs. Harte would be able to live more comfortably in separate establishments, with most of his income going toward her support; but that meant, in effect, that he was living off Madame Van de Velde. The implications now were unavoidable, justified or not. For the next several years the Hartes broke off communication, and even after it was resumed there was no more discussion of her joining him. Bret resumed his old comfortable way of life in the new Van de Velde establishment in Lancaster Gate, its cozy atmosphere deprived now only of the late Monsieur Van de Velde's brotherly presence.

He would complain, not too seriously, that all he knew about his family's activities he read in the newspapers. Still he did make an effort to keep in touch with Jessamy, Ethel and Frank, even during the period of evident estrangement from their mother. Jessamy was showing some evidence of talent as a writer and illustrator, and he praised an article she had published on her vacation in the Adirondacks. Later he showed her drawings to his artist friends and reported back that they all praised her gracefulness of style and her eye for beauty.* [9]

His son Frank's career had taken a disappointing turn, now that he had run through the short list of theatrical managers who were personal friends of his father. Bret felt that encouraging his son's career as an actor, after first trying to quench such ambitions, had been a mistake, worse than useless in that he was now suffering from his failure to make good.

Late in 1893, without any encouragement on that score from his father, he moved to England with his wife and settled down for a time in a cottage in Weybridge. Frank made him a grandfather, and soon Bret was paying frequent visits to the home of his son and daughter-in-law. Apparently he contributed to their support, since he mentioned Frank's "quarterly allowance" in one letter to Weybridge. Bret approved heartily of his daughter-in-law, even more so of the two grandsons, Richard and Geoffrey, they eventually produced, but his relations with his son were often touchy. He was greatly irked early in 1895 when Frank announced plans to move to a London suburb — the prospective proximity of

---

* A few years later she gave up thought of a career, however, and married Henry Milford Steele.

any member of his immediate family always seemed to ring alarm bells and threaten the tranquillity of No. 109 Lancaster Gate — and urged that, instead, Frank and his family move to Germany or Switzerland where they could live more comfortably on their slender income. He bluntly wrote Frank that he had long ago given up trying to understand the reasoning, if any, behind his son's activities.[10]

A few years later his daughter Ethel decided, at a rather advanced age for such projects, to embark on a musical career and insisted that she must study in Paris. This, of course, was at her father's expense.

Family problems only spurred him to greater effort as a writer, perhaps because it was only his continued level of income that kept them at a physical distance. As he neared his sixtieth year he would have found it impossible to deal with them on a day-to-day basis. So the stories continued to flow from his pen at a regular rate, and from his room in Lancaster Gate to the Watt agency to the American, English and German publishers. Nothing he wrote seems to have been turned down. He and Watt worked so well together that each story or sketch was designed for a specific market and invariably was accepted immediately. Off the book publishers' presses came *A Sappho of Green Springs*, 1891; *Colonel Starbottle's Client and Some Other People* and *A First Family of Tassajara*, 1892; *Sally Dows and Other Stories* and *Susy, A Story of the Plains*, 1893; *In A Hollow of the Hills*, 1895, and *Barker's Luck*, 1896.

Everything was going so smoothly by the summer of 1895 that he felt able to take a vacation in Germany and Switzerland for the first time in a dozen years. By now professionalism had so firm a grip on him that he worked regularly each day even while traveling.

With Colonel Arthur Collins as his companion he journeyed down the Rhine, visited Cologne and the Rhenish cities he had known as the consul in Crefeld, and then went on to Villeneuve on Lake Geneva for a month's stay. Once again he complained of Switzerland's general inferiority to northern California. The Swiss scenery was too artificial-looking, he said, as though it had been knocked together for a ballet scene. He conceded that the composition was perfect, with every snow-peak, every chalet, every terrace exactly where they ought to be for the best pictorial effect. Hotels and pensions invaded every available crag, it seemed to him, and he began to suspect there was some truth in Daudet's witticism that "all Switzerland is a gigantic hotel company." The streets of the little mountain towns looked so much like stage sets, he said, that he was afraid to knock on a shop door because it looked like painted canvas and a slight push might topple the whole setting. He was certain that there was a whole street in Montreux which had been lifted bodily out of, or inserted into, countless operas.

One concession he was willing to make to the Swiss was the perfection of their summer climate, the unclouded days, the balmy nights, the splendor of sunsets on Alpine snow-fields. It so invigorated him, he wrote a friend, that he dreaded returning to London's dripping fogs, its dark and narrow streets, its smoke-fouled atmosphere.*

After an absence of a quarter of a century, however, he still couldn't help comparing the Sierras to his present surroundings. They grew more glorious in his imagination with every passing year. He wouldn't give a mile of the Sierras, with their fresh beauty and "magnificent uncouthness," for a hundred thousand kilometres of "the picturesque Vaud." [11]

Colonel Collins had returned to England during the final weeks of Bret's stay on the shore of Lake Geneva, and he

* The National Society for Clean Air was founded in London in 1899.

struck up amusing acquaintanceships with a retired Indian Army colonel and Baron de Blonay, who was a cousin of Madame Van de Velde's and lived in a tenth-century château decorated with Crusaders' armor and shields.

Toward the end of his stay Bret was enjoying himself so much that he had to wrench himself away from the delights of Geneva.

His homecoming in mid-October was greatly cheered by the reception given *Clarence*, a long story or short novel, which was published as a separate volume in England and the United States. He wrote his agent that he was almost as much surprised as he was gratified by the unanimous praise of critics and reviewers on both sides of the Atlantic. The background of the story was the struggle to keep California in the Union in 1861, which he had witnessed as a fairly active participant. Youthful memories, and a desire to transmit to a new American generation something more constructive than "the usual pinchbeck imitations of English society novels," as he expressed it to A. P. Watt,[12] stirred him to a new pitch of creative enthusiasm; this was not the same old tune from the organ-grinder.

The San Francisco he described in *Clarence* was tense with rumors that Southern sympathizers would seize power in the city, but one day the American flag — the old flag of the Union — appeared from one end of the city to the other and proclaimed the city's loyalty. "From every public building and hotel, from the roofs of private houses, and even the windows of lonely dwellings, flapped and waved the striped and starry banner. The steady breath of the sea carried it out from masts and yards of ships at their wharves, from the battlements of the forts, Alcatraz and Yerba Buena . . ." One of those flags, it happened, had been sewn together by Bret and his sister Margaret, who had worked all through the night to join in the display of solidarity with the Union. What pleased Bret almost equally was that reviewers in the former Confederacy, despite its partisan tone, praised *Clarence* as generously as those in the North.

During the latter months of that year Bret worked with a friend of long standing, T. E. Pemberton, a Birmingham writer, on polishing a play on which they were collaborating. Early in the year Pemberton had written him about his short story, "The Judgment of Bolinas Plain," which had just appeared in the *Pall Mall Gazette*. It seemed to Pemberton that the story would lend itself to dramatization, and he wrote Bret proposing that they collaborate on the play. Bret had suffered from so many false theatrical hopes that he was naturally doubtful. He didn't think the story had enough plot and incident to be expanded into play form, and passed along the hard-earned truism that what seemed dramatic on the printed page couldn't always — in fact, could rarely — be translated into theatrical terms. On second thought, always unable to resist even the faintest possibility of proving himself in the theater, he agreed to visit Pemberton in Birmingham and talk it over. Before the month was out he and Pemberton had discussed the latter's ideas for dramatizing the story under the title of *Sue*, and agreed it was worth trying.[13] In their collaboration Bret evidently made himself chiefly responsible for the scenario and the plotting, while Pemberton worked on the dialogue.

From then until the year's end, aside from his sojourn in Switzerland, he laid aside his regularly scheduled work every week or two to journey to Birmingham and work on the play with his collaborator. This time he and his collaborator did not quarrel over Bret's opinion of his wife's taste in interior decoration, but Bret did send a number of things — flower vases, a revolving book stand and other items — to the Pemberton home with precise instructions on where they were to be placed. With considerably more tact than he had demonstrated with Mr. and Mrs. Twain he forwarded them to Birmingham in the guise of Christmas presents. Pemberton, in any case, was more disposed to humor his friend and collaborator; after his death he wrote an entirely sympathetic biography of him, the first to appear.

One night in January 1896 he attended the theater at which Sir Charles Wyndham was appearing. Wyndham recognized him sitting in a box with a group of friends, and sent a note from backstage asking Bret to stop by his dressing room. The actor had heard that Bret was writing *Sue* and wanted to have first chance at producing it, as Bret wrote Pemberton the next day. Naturally their hopes were fired up. The play, however, did not quite measure up to what Wyndham expected. It looked as though *Sue* would be added to the considerable list of Bret's theatrical mésalliances until Pemberton, taking the initiative, sent the manuscript to the Frohman management in New York.

Much as that hope had been deferred, Bret finally experienced a qualified success in the theater. *Sue* opened on Broadway the night of September 15, 1896, and the following morning Daniel Frohman cabled them the good news: WELL RECEIVED. FINE ACTING. PRESS PRAISES.

Actually the play achieved a respectable run, and later was dispatched on a season's tour, largely because of the winsome performance of Annie Russell, an ingenue with large dark eyes and a trim figure, in the title role. Dramaturgically, *Sue* leaned heavily on coincidence and physical rather than intellectual acrobatics; the hero escaped the noose in Act III by leaping out of an upstairs window and landing in the branches of an offstage tree. At last Bret achieved a measure of success in the theater, though the proceeds were rather disappointing, particularly since they had to be divided fifty-fifty with Pemberton. A more resounding success than *Sue* was staged five years after Bret's death, an adaptation of one of his short stories.*

Without any false modesty he attributed the success of *Sue* to his collaborator. In a letter to Anna, with whom communication had been re-established some months before, he insisted that Pemberton had put in the most work on the project. Frohman, he thought, wouldn't even have read it if his name alone had appeared on the title page. Nor would any other American producer, he believed, have considered presenting it. It was all of a piece, in his opinion, with the unremitting hostility toward him in the States. Recently Max Nordau, the German novelist, critic and philosopher, had written that Bret was the "Columbus of American fiction" and that his countrymen didn't sufficiently appreciate him.

Bret hoped the literary panjandrums in America would take notice of Nordau's remarks, and was bitterly disappointed when not an echo, not even a derisory one, came back across the Atlantic. At least, he thought, his American publishers might have reprinted Nordau's statement in their advertisements.[15]

It was probably a hangover of this feeling of neglect that caused him to put forward the uncharacteristically immodest claim that he had "made the short story American." Stateside critics were quicker on the uptake on that issue and hastened to point out that Irving had made the short story American; Poe and Hawthorne had aided considerably in its development. In the same article, Bret refuted charges that such

---

* Paul Armstrong wrote the play based on Bret's "Salomy Jane." It was one of the hits of the 1907 season with Eleanor Robson, H. B. Warner and Holbrook Blinn in the leading roles.[14]

writers as George Washington Cable, Joel Chandler Harris, Mark Twain and Constance Fenimore Woolson had "imitated" him in advancing the regional and local-color novel and short story. They had not imitated him, he wrote, but "cut loose from conventional methods and sought honestly to describe the life around them." His own contribution, he said, was to "have shown that it could be done." *

As the turn of the century approached, he kept to his daily grind: there would be no resting on his laurels for the "drudge of Lancaster Gate," as he called himself. His financial obligations tended to increase, and he was almost pathetically honorable about meeting them. The man who was still considered a drunk and a deadbeat in America, unable to live down his desperate scrabbling during a few years of his last decade in his native land, prided himself above all else on giving his family everything he could in a material way. He sent Anna one hundred fifty dollars a month for her support alone, plus an allowance for his daughter Ethel studying music in Paris, plus an allowance for his son Frank, plus occasional remittances to his widowed and hard-pressed sisters. When his daughter Jessamy married in 1898, he wrote Anna that he didn't have the heart to consider how he might have made her younger years happier, but could only congratulate her on finding a husband who would take the place of Bret and his uncertain fortunes. In addition to his family obligations, he was continually running up doctors' and dentists' bills in an effort to stave off a complete collapse of his precarious health. His letters during the last years of the cen-

* The Rise of the Short Story," *Cornhill Magazine*, July, 1899. In addition to Van Wyck Brooks's contention that Harte was the legitimate patent-holder on the western story, the late Henry Seidel Canby noted that "the literary West may be said to have founded itself upon the imagination of Bret Harte."

tury were often a recital of his afflictions, his infected teeth, his chronic sore throat, facial neuralgia, rheumatism — and now the crowning indignity, painfully comic, the gout.

He had moved out of Madame Van de Velde's house — perhaps as a belated gesture to propriety, perhaps for greater privacy — but had taken rooms only a few doors away, at 74 Lancaster Gate. He and Madame Van de Velde were as close as ever, despite the change in living arrangements. Whenever Madame Van de Velde and her younger children moved to their country home — first at Arford House, Headley, in Hampshire, later at the Red House, Camberley, in Surrey — Bret generally packed up and went along with them. Often they journeyed to the country in midwinter, and Bret even became involved to a certain cautious extent in local affairs. It was deadly dull socially in the country, as he wrote his illustrator, A. S. Boyd, and that may have been his excuse for agreeing to act as chairman at a village entertainment. Bret told Boyd that he thought the chairman's duties at such a rustic festival consisted in breaking up disputes by bellowing, "'Armony, gents, 'armony!" and announcing that "Mr. So-and-So will now oblige." On the way to the scene of the frolic he joshed the organizer of the program, the Headley rector, who would devote the proceeds to something called the Clothing Club, by expressing the hope that there was nothing in the performance which called for anyone to appear in need of clothing. The "dear man," Bret recalled, almost fainted from shock.[16]

He and the Van de Veldes took shelter in Hampshire during the summer of the Diamond Jubilee against the "confusion and snobbery" of that observance, as he called it, and the influx of American tourists. Among all the peoples flocking to London that summer of 1897, he declared, the Americans were the most noisy, vulgar and objectionable. The prospect of seeing a congregation of royalty did not appeal to him. The few crowned heads he had seen close-up were hardly worth viewing singly or in ceremonial groupings. He would return to London, he announced, only after "the sawdust and orange peel" had been swept away and the tourists had departed.[17]

There would have been no danger that his swarming compatriots would have taken Bret for a fellow American. He had long ago assumed a protective coloration. With just a touch of that ostentation to which he objected to in his fellow Americans, he wore a monocle screwed into his right eye and his accent was as impeccably English as his tailoring.

FOURTEEN

Fly in Amber

TO those who saw him or met him casually around the turn of the century Bret seemed hopelessly imbedded in his past, a fly in the amber which had congealed around his youth and his briefly triumphant period of thirty years before. At best, to the skeptical and often scornful visiting American's eye, he was an elderly Anglicized dandy, a decaying fop, a Victorian relic who'd been dining out for years on the strength of ancient successes.

One such American visitor spotted him across the luncheon tables of a fashionable restaurant and maliciously noted that his elegance was rather laboriously contrived. "Was it the glint of wax on the mustache, or the hair too artfully curled, or the extra height of the collar, or the tricky cut of the coat, that no tailor would make on his own initiative?" [1]

The superficialities seemed to concern him more than the inner nourishment of his life, his clothing, his remaining contacts with fashionable society, his tasteful surroundings, his reputation as a connoisseur of wine, food and Havana cigars. If he wasn't impervious to new ideas, new thoughts, new rebellions against the restrictions of Victorian society, neither was he notably receptive. Agitation against the caste system, for women's suffrage, for freeing the colonies, against sweated labor in the mines and factories of the northern shires, for Irish freedom, for trade-unionization, for or against maintaining the balance of power against the thrusting aspirations of Imperial Germany — all causes and crusades and reformations — largely bored him, when they engaged him at all.

When Mrs. Boyd sent him a copy of Zola's latest book, he merely commented that it was "a little guide-bookish." The rather self-conscious fermentation of literary movements, the growing experimentation with form and content, had little interest for him either as a professional writer or a desultory reader.

Then as in boyhood, incredibly enough, he considered *The Count of Monte Cristo* the greatest novel ever written. This affirmation was made in an article included in a magazine series by contemporary literary figures titled *My Favorite Novelist and His Best Book*. In confessing his supreme admiration for the Dumas novel he was merely confirming his belief that life was often the rawest of melodrama and there was nothing unartistic about portraying it in melodramatic terms. He conceded that the more intellectual writers considered *Monte Cristo* an antiquated romance, but readers would always be enthralled by it. He came close to stating his credo while defending his choice of Dumas for ultimate honors as a novelist. If the readers "have been lifted temporarily out of their commonplace surroundings and limited horizon by some specious tale of heroism, endeavor, wrongs redressed, and faith rewarded, and are inclined to look a little more hopefully on Jones's chances of promotion, or to Mrs. Jones's aunt's prospective legacy — why blame them or their novelist?" [2]

This at a time when there were many writers — Crane and Norris, particularly, in America — demonstrating that the novel could be used to explain man to himself, to spur him on to improve his condition, rather than merely diverting him from it. The "specious tale of heroism," as Bret knew very well, was not the highest plateau a writer could hope to ascend. Bret would insist, partly in self-justification, that literature was a form of popular entertainment or it wasn't worth considering. The customers had to be made to laugh, cry, sit on the edge of their chairs or they might justifiably demand their money back. The new naturalism and realism were to be ignored as far as he was concerned.

Hamlin Garland, a very serious, rather priggish young Westerner who carried the banner for naturalism, came to London with letters of introduction from William Dean Howells to both Bret Harte and Mark Twain. The latter was staying at a hotel in Chelsea that season in 1899, but he and Bret never met; there was still hatred and malice on Twain's part, indifference (if nothing stronger) on Bret's.*

When Garland arrived in London, he was told by members of the American colony that Bret Harte held himself aloof, would never be found in any of the places frequented by his fellow nationals. Garland was also disturbed about other gossip he heard about Harte, he later related. Finally he came across Harte at a tea given by Joseph Hatton. Harte wore a cutaway, striped pants, fancy vest, spats, a monocle, and a haughty manner, and Garland hesitated to present his letter of introduction from Howells. With some diffidence he approached, and was not cut dead but was told he might present himself at 74 Lancaster Gate several days hence.

Garland found Harte's rooms "dainty in coloring," almost effeminate; undoubtedly they had been decorated under

* During an Australian tour in 1895 Twain, raking over the ashes of his ancient grudge, denounced Bret as "sham and shoddy" in newspaper interviews. Bret must have seen reprints, since they caused something of a stir. It had become his habit, however, to ignore Twain.

Madame Van de Velde's supervision. Harte's reserve disappeared, Garland said, and he asked eagerly for news of Howells, Aldrich, and men he had known in the San Francisco literary world.

"Sometimes," Bret said at one point, "I wish I had never come away."

His mood was deeply nostalgic, almost homesick, as Garland described it — and a strange contrast with this interview a short time later with Mark Twain, who griped endlessly about how he had been cheated by a former business partner.* Thus it turned out that, through differing vicissitudes, Harte wound up a sad old man, Twain a bitter old man; Harte's struggles had mellowed him as Twain's successes had brought only disillusion.

Garland burst out with a plea that Bret return to his homeland, seek fresh inspiration from the source of his work, perhaps find new material in the changes he would find in California since he had left three decades ago.

The suggestion, as Garland recalled many years later, brought one of the saddest looks Garland had ever seen on a man's face. He had no way of knowing whether Bret was depressed at the thought of returning to San Francisco or suffused with regret at having left it for the lure of New York and London.

Bret was so touched, at any rate, that he not only saw Garland to the door but walked out into Lancaster Gate with him. At the end of the block Garland paused and looked back: Bret was still standing in the street, his head bowed, his whole attitude suggesting that he was still thinking about what Garland had said.[3]

---

* Charles Webster, whom he accused of cheating him out of fifty thousand dollars in their publishing venture.

That was one of the few occasions on which Bret let down his guard against his professed bête noire, the visiting American.*

One visitor whom he could not, in all conscience, dodge was his wife. Thirty years of separation abruptly ended with her announcement that she was coming over to England late in 1898; Jessamy had just been married, Ethel was living in Paris, and Anna was living alone in lodgings in Plainfield, New Jersey. She would, of course, stay with their son Frank and his family. Presumably, however, she had some hopes of recalling Bret to his duties as a husband. If his association with Madame Van de Velde was so innocent, based completely on the domestic atmosphere she provided for him, there would be no reason why he shouldn't allow Anna to resume her rightful position as his helpmate and comforter. What further use would he have for the Belgian lady?

Posterity will never know what scenes took place, what blasts of wifely recrimination swept over Bret's urbane surface. Passions have not necessarily burned themselves out in persons of the Hartes' age, and Mrs. Harte must have felt herself in the position of having caught up with an absconder. The aging charmer, whose wiles had never quite worked so effectively with his wife as with other people, must have felt himself cornered, run to earth. The suggestion that Anna come to England certainly had not been forwarded by him.

Bret and Anna, at any rate, did not resume their life together. He visited her at his son's place in Caversham, but continued to live in Lancaster Gate and at Madame Van de

---

* Garland had also observed that when he and Bret were alone Bret dropped his English accent and his speech took on a distinctly Western-frontier flavor.

Velde's country place in Surrey. Mrs. Harte did not return
his visits, nor is there any indication she met Madame Van de
Velde; a confrontation between two such strong-minded,
imperious females was something devoutly to be avoided.
None of the surviving letters indicates the emotional stress
involved in Mrs. Harte's journey to England. One of the
subsidiary triumphs of Bret's life was his success in keeping
his private life mostly private. Privacy was a phobia with
him, and no major writer in literary history showed less of
himself in his writing or his public life.

Even someone as close to him as Pemberton, his friend,
collaborator and eventual biographer, got only an occasional
inkling of the domestic discord at Caversham. On that score
Pemberton wrote that Bret "bore his deep personal disap-
pointments and sorrows" with "a silence as dignified as it was
pathetic."

His visits grew infrequent as each one, it has been reported, brought violent displays of temper from Anna.[4] She
had never envisioned herself as a patient Penelope waiting for
her husband to return from the literary wars. From year to
year her hopes had been deferred until now, when they were
in their middle sixties, Bret still insisted on living apart. She
could hardly be blamed for feeling that she had been cheated
out of half her life, that she had been bilked by his constantly
affectionate and understanding correspondence, that it
would have been far kinder and juster if he had demanded a
divorce years before.

A photograph of part of the family uneasily grouped together outside Frank's house is more revealing than any of its
subjects may have intended. Mrs. Harte, seated in a wicker
chair and looking far younger than her years, stares at the
camera with narrowed, skeptical eyes and her wide firm
mouth curled at one corner in something like disdain, as

though she would be damned rather than smile compliantly for the record. Above her stands Bret looking like a prosperous retired bookmaker in his striped suit, with a watch chain heavily weighted by fobs and seals, with a curly brimmed hat sportively tilted over his white hair. He smiles with an anxious determination. Between them there is obviously a gulf as wide as the Atlantic which has separated them for thirty years.

In his conversations with Pemberton, Bret apparently referred to his domestic situation only once, and then he disguised it in a comparison of the donkey (as a symbol of the female) and the horse (as the male). "The horse," Bret said,

is always described as a noble animal. Compare him with his humble friend the donkey, and he is an idiot. He has ten times his strength, and more than ten times the strength of a man, and yet he allows himself to be saddled and harnessed, bitted and spurred, ridden and driven, lashed and exhausted, until he becomes a mere bundle of trembling, sweating nerves.

If you come to think of it, my appreciation of the donkey race is not misplaced. Are they not like the enduring yet self-willed women of our creation, while we poor harassed men are like those imbecile neurotic horses? I wonder whether you and I are "noble animals"? I wonder if the horse likes to think he's called that way? I wonder if the donkey plumes himself on the complete success of its alleged folly?" [5]

In erecting a psychological defense for himself Bret after forty years of marriage obviously saw himself as its victim. He had neurotically exhausted himself to satisfy the material wants of his wife and family. Yet his wife, "enduring" and "self-willed," had the world's sympathy for her "alleged folly" in putting up with him all these years. The facial expressions on that family portrait seem to bear him out. The "donkey," judging from photographic evidence, seems to have had the best of it.

In only one of his letters to the household at Caversham, most of them now directed to his son, with an occasional note to his wife enclosing her monthly allowance, did his impatience with his unremitting burden break through. About a year after Anna's arrival it was proposed that she and her son and his family move from Caversham to larger and more comfortable quarters. Bret put his foot down, for once, and demanded to know how they would benefit by such a move. He pointed out that the household should be maintained comfortably as it was on the income he supplied. The proposal was abandoned.[6]

The new century began without the dawning hope it conveyed to most of the world — the now seemingly forlorn hope that the twentieth century would be a cavalcade of increasing progress, peace and prosperity. Bret, for himself, could see nothing ahead but the prospect of working until he dropped. He wrote of having to spend twice as much time at his writing desk to keep up with the work his agent had contracted in advance for him.

One of the new projects was *Condensed Novels, Second Series*, a revival of the parodies he wrote early in his career which appeared first in magazines and then was published as a book in 1902. His satirical targets were mostly the popular novelists of the day, one of the more telling being "Rupert the Resembler," peopled by the jut-jawed heroes and slinking dastards and trembling ingenues of Graustark and Ruritania.

The pain of neuralgia held him in its grip from waist to ankles and his throat was so sore it seemed to be ulcerated. As a therapeutic measure he experimented with *"very* mild cigars," which he still smoked incessantly as he labored over his manuscript. But the work continued and the short-story volumes testified to his unceasing effort: *Under the Redwoods,* published in 1901, *Openings in the Old Trail* in 1902, and *Trent's Trust and Other Stories* (posthumously) in 1903. The quality of his work was undiminished by the constant misery from his ailments. "Colonel Starbottle for the Plaintiff" was marked by his return to form as a humorist and "A Ward of Colonel Starbottle's" was a skillful combination of comedy and melodrama. In the latter he demonstrated his ability to convey the essentials of character in a few paragraphs.

The colonel is found in his law office with his associate, Mr. Pyecroft, who observes that Starbottle has arrived at his desk at an unusually early hour for a man whose nights are occupied with drinking, gambling and chasing women.

"You see, sir," said the colonel, correcting him with a slow deliberation that boded no good — "you see a Southern gentleman — blank it! — who has stood at the head of his profession for thirty-five years, obliged to work like a blank nigger, sir, in the dirty squabbles of psalm-singing Yankee traders, instead of — er — attending to the affairs of — er — legislation!"

"But you manage to get pretty good fees out of it — eh, Colonel?" continued Pyecroft with a laugh.

"Fees, sir! Filthy shekels! and barely enough to satisfy a debt of honor with one hand, and wipe out a tavern score for the entertainment of — er — a few lady friends with the other!"

This allusion to his losses at poker, as well as an oyster supper given to the two principal actresses of the "North Star Troupe," then performing in the town, convinced Mr. Pyecroft that the colonel was in one of his "moods," and he changed the subject.

In addition to his parodies and short stories, during 1900 and 1901, he branched out as a lyricist and librettist for the musical stage. With Emmanuel Moor composing the music, he supplied the words for an operetta, "The Lord of Fontanelle," based on Bret's short story "The Strange Experience of Alkali Dick," which had a French setting. It was one theatrical disappointment he did not live to experience.

His letters to people he really valued, in contrast to the businesslike or dutiful correspondence with the household at Caversham, still shone with a gallant humor. One of his favorite correspondents was Mary Boyd, the wife of his illustrator. In mid-1900 he wrote her a long letter deploring the fact that he had lost a previous letter he had written her as he hurried along the Bayswater Road to post it. Such letters, he remarked, were like ghosts wandering in time with their mission unfulfilled. He then supplied Mrs. Boyd with a fanciful account of how the lost letter must have been washed down the sewers and onto the mud flats of the Thames, then into the Channel and out onto the seas, to be read eventually by some bemused sailor shipwrecked on a desert island.[7] He also wrote of plowing through the works of the immensely popular novelist Marie Corelli so he could satirize her in a "condensed novel," only to find that in her wild extravagance and her absolute lack of any sense of the ludicrous, her novels *The Gateless Barrier* and *Ziska* were parodies in themselves. *The Gateless Barrier*, he explained, had a heroine who was a ghost and materialized by degrees. Bret supposed a leg materialized one day, an arm the next, until finally the heroine presented herself in toto.

By midsummer of 1901 even the country air at Madame Van de Velde's house in Surrey failed to rally him out of his declining health. He referred to himself as a doddering old man. Death and illness among his friends also depressed him. The historian-biographer Froude, whose friendship Bret had retained for thirty-odd years, died, and Pemberton was dangerously ill with kidney disease.

He had lost his appetite to the extent that he "loathed" all food, and lived mostly on "slops." At this point his medical advisors did not seem to find anything portentous in the constant pain of his throat. They now blamed it on his teeth, and did not object when Bret maintained his steady consumption of Punch brand Havana cigars; whenever his family or friends asked him what he wanted for birthday or Christmas presents he always asked for cigars.

The more serious they became, the more he was inclined to joke about his afflictions. It was a shame, he wrote Mrs. Boyd, that he couldn't make literary capital out of his troubles with something like "Nine Months with a Dentist" or "In Surrey with a Sore Throat and an Unfinished Manuscript." [8]

On returning to London that autumn he spent as much time in consultation with his doctors and dentist as on his manuscripts. The dentist had made him a new pair of plates and tendered a bill for two hundred ten dollars, which Bret vigorously protested. He was especially outraged because the new teeth didn't fit and he still had to live on soups and jellies. His wretched body, he said, was not worth the money he was spending to keep it operating.

In the first week of December came the news that his firstborn son, Griswold, had died alone in New York. He was only in his thirty-eighth year. His name had not been mentioned for years in the family correspondence and apparently he had requested no last-minute reconciliation with his family. None of the Hartes in England went back to the States for the funeral. Wracked with pain as he was, Bret must have recognized Griswold's death, and the years of estrangement which had preceded it, as one of his signal failures as a human being. White-haired, semi-crippled, his face lined and sunken with the effects of his own grapple with death, Bret must have thought back to those hopeful and youthful days in San Francisco when he had tumbled on the floor with "Wodie" while Anna rebuked him for his lack of dignity. He may even have recalled the sentimental verse he had written about him, "On a Naughty Little Boy, Sleeping":

And then — I found him! There he lay,
Surprised by sleep, caught in the act,
The rosy vandal who had sacked
His little town and thought it play.

The shattered vase; the broken jar;
A match still smouldering on the floor;
The inkstand's purple pool of gore;
The chessmen scattered near and far.[9]

At Christmastime he sent his agent a letter-opener with an inscription he hoped Watt wouldn't consider too sentimental, adding that he believed the best hope a man had for being remembered was his talent for keeping the affection of his friends.

By mid-January of 1902 he was so ill, and his doctors so confounded, that they suggested that he seek the milder air of the seaside, and he was bundled off to the forlorn boardwalks and empty beaches of Southsea.

Anna had joined their daughter in Paris by this time, but offered to come back and nurse him. Bret gently declined, adding that he knew she would do all she could for him if the necessity arose.[10] It was the last time letters were exchanged between them — the closing out of an unfortunate marriage that both had endured, on the whole, with a remarkable dignity and an equally remarkable and laudable determination to keep their differences to themselves.

[301]

In March, his health and strength still slipping away from him, he returned to London for an operation on his throat. It was such a fascinating procedure, Bret later told Pemberton, that it "delighted even the victim." Its results, fortunately withheld, revealed not an ulcer in his throat but a deep-rooted and inoperable cancer.

The next month he spent in his rooms at 74 Lancaster Gate with Madame Van de Velde in constant attendance. Later they went to her country house in Surrey. Apparently he did not realize — or perhaps his pride would not allow him to let anyone know he realized — that he would never recover. In one of his last, all but illegible notes, addressed to Pemberton, he blamed his failure to recover on the London weather, his ancient scapegoat.[11]

On April 17 he rallied temporarily and dragged himself over to his writing desk. "I'm about to write the best story I've ever written!" he exclaimed to Madame Van de Velde. There spoke the eternal writer, urged on by a force stronger than anything but death.

At the head of a sheet of paper he wrote "A Friend of Colonel Starbottle." Several times he wrote down an opening sentence, then crumpled up the sheet and threw it away. Pain clawing at his throat, he labored for hours over these first few sentences; nothing was more important than saying what he wanted to say in precisely the way it must be said; it was worth the effort even if only one person read those words. He had finished two paragraphs before pain and debility forced him to give up the task.[12]

On May 5 he dragged himself back to that writing desk, his place in the galley in which he had slaved for almost half a century, but he had barely picked up the pen when a hemorrhage caused blood to well up from his throat. He had refused to take to his bed on returning from the hospital. Only in his last hours was he finally laid low.

Late in the afternoon he died with Madame Van de Velde at his side. In the last line of the last letter he wrote (to Mrs. Boyd) he had declared that his foot was still "in the stirrup," and that was the way he died, the man whom his American contemporaries, many of them, considered a weakling, an artful dodger, a rogue and cheat without character or principle. Not a debt of his remained to attract the world's quick scorn, though he died in possession of assets totaling only three hundred sixty pounds, six shillings and nine pence.

In England he was mourned in and out of print with eulogies given few American writers. "No writer of the present day," said the *Spectator*, "has struck so powerful and original a note as he has sounded." The *London Literary World* declared that Bret Harte was the most beloved of all writers who had died recently. Gilbert K. Chesterton wrote that Bret's humor stood alone in American writing for its sympathy, subtlety and depth. "The wild, sky-breaking humor of America has its fine qualities, but it must in the nature of things be deficient in two qualities — sympathy and reverence — and these two qualities were knit in the closest texture of Bret Harte's humor." [13]

When the news reached America the sense of loss was somewhat qualified, the note of requiem more muted. The *Bookman* rather inaccurately stated that Bret's was merely a voice from the past, the news of his passing "a rustle in the newspapers as of old love-letters and ancient flowers." [14] The London correspondent of the New York *Times* pointedly wrote that Bret had not left an enemy in the land of his adoption, and William Dean Howells observed that "if his temperament was not adapted to the harsh conditions of the elder

American world, it might well be said that is temperament was not altogether in the wrong." [15]

The *Overland Monthly*, recalling for its readership the man who had launched it and brought it a renown it never quite regained, devoted a memorial issue to Bret composed of the recollections of his surviving associates of his staff. It came out just about the time Jack London — his fate to be even more tragic than Bret's — was beginning to lay claim to the title of California's foremost writer.[16]

Many may have suspected that Bret's name would endure longer than most of his contemporaries', for all the critical cozening, the greater respectability, the evanescent flattery that adorned them and was withheld for most of his career from Bret Harte. Better than anyone except Twain he illuminated his chosen corner of place and time. If it was a narrow corner, which he never chose to widen, he at least dignified it with a tolerance rare in his contemporaries; he perceived that the problem of minorities and races would long haunt the corridors of the American dream, and his defense of the Chinese, the Indians and the Mexicans, in some measure, helped light the way to a greater understanding required for the future. His best work was characterized by a freshness and timelessness, a procession of characters lustily alive which became stereotypes only in the hands of his less talented successors in shaping the western legend, an undimmingly vivid picture of the foothill world he made his own forever, that marks a writer who outlives fashion and survives the cross-currents of literary criticism.

He was buried in Frimley Churchyard in the quiet Surrey countryside, with Madame Van de Velde firmly in charge of the arrangements. She and Mrs. Harte met, for the first and last time, as mourners silently confronting each other across the bier. Later Madame Van de Velde would remark in a magazine article that Bret had never created a "perfectly noble" woman in his stories and would pointedly ask, "Was it because such a model never offered itself to him, or because other memories clouded his perception of womanly excellence?"

With them at the graveside were Bret's son Frank and daughter Ethel, his old traveling companion Colonel Collins, and his illustrator Alexander S. Boyd. Madame Van de Velde would permit no doubts about who the chief, if unofficial, mourner was at the brief ceremonies before the expatriate was lowered into the earth of the island he had loved and honored. Her claim was recorded for posterity in the words carved into the red granite of his tombstone and, though green with the moss of that country churchyard and weathered by time and the elements, they still stand forth:

IN FAITHFUL REMEMBRANCE

M. S. VAN DE VELDE

Afterword

PRACTICALLY everything Bret Harte wrote, from his earliest sketches and poems onward, is contained in the twenty volumes of the Riverside Edition published by the Houghton Mifflin Company. Thus I have not included a formal bibliography of his works, which would be of interest only to literary scholars and specialists. Professor George R. Stewart, that most conscientious of biographers, has compiled a complete bibliography, which was published by the University of California Press in 1933. It is available at the Bancroft Library of the University of California's Berkeley campus.

Aside from the intense feeling for local color which he inherited from Washington Irving, Harte's greatest accomplishment lay in his ability to characterize vividly. His people invariably spring into life, and better yet credibility, the moment they make their entrances in his stories. His indulgent view of mankind stemmed partly from his admiration for Dickens and partly from his own tolerant nature; he was seemingly incapable of hatred, except for hatred itself. His infrequent villains are never less than human. His heroes are never priggish or self-righteous.

Here are some of the leading figures on the landscape of Bret Harte's imagination:

JUDGE BEESWINGER, an acquaintance of Yuba Bill and Colonel Starbottle, a schemer and occasional impostor who poses variously as a member of the California State Legislature and a United States Marshal. ("Mrs. Skaggs's Husbands," *Gabriel Conroy*, "Clarence," "A Ward of Colonel Starbottle's")

JUDGE BOOMPOINTER, a rather injudicious jurist who is frequently foiled or befuddled by his acquaintances. ("Brown of Calaveras," *Gabriel Conroy*, "Found at Blazing Star," "Mr. Bilson's Housekeeper," "Salomy Jane's Kiss")

CALHOUN BUNGSTARTER, a California lawyer and duelist, once a rival of Colonel Starbottle's for political honors, later his law partner. ("The Romance of Madrone Hollow," "Jinny," "The Fool of Five Forks," "Colonel Starbottle's Client")

CHEROKEE SAL, a dissolute female who dies after giving birth to the infant hero of "The Luck of Roaring Camp."

GEORGE DORNTON, a professional gambler and notorious duelist known as "Gentleman George." When the Vigilance Committee routs the gamblers from San Francisco, he reappears as a dashing stockbroker. ("A Secret of Telegraph Hill")

MAMMY AND DADDY DOWNEY, an elderly couple renowned in the mining camp of Rough and Ready for their near-saintly nature until they disappear with a large amount of money belonging to the townspeople, upon which it becomes known that Mammy is a female impersonator and Daddy, like Mammy, is an actor and swindler from Australia. ("Two Saints of the Foothills")

DR. DUCHESNE, a highly skilled and intelligent backwoods practitioner, renowned as much for his knowledge of human nature as for medicine. He saves many lives, often represents human decency in the most raffish or dangerous surroundings, and attends Jack Hamlin on his deathbed. ("M'liss," "The Man on the Beach," "The Twins of Table Mountain," "A Millionaire of Rough and Ready," "Cressy," "The Chatelaine of Burnt Ridge," "The Transformation of Buckeye Camp," "A Convert of the Mission," "In the Tules," "See Yup," "The Youngest Prospector in Calaveras," "Mr. Nilson's Housekeeper," "The Convalescence of Jack Hamlin," *Gabriel Conroy*)

Jo FOLLINSBEE, a pretty and attractive girl, the sister of the knavish Jack Follinsbee who is killed in a duel with Colonel Starbottle, who as a young man falls in love with her. ("The Iliad of Sandy Bar" and "The Romance of Madrone Hollow")

WHISKEY DICK HALL, the town drunk of Devil's Ford and the fall guy of plotters who take advantage of his inebriated condition. ("Devil's Ford," "Three Partners")

JACK HAMLIN, roving gambler, sardonic wit, a knight-errant of the foothills. He is a handsome fellow with a Grecian pallor and a languid manner. He is particularly chivalrous toward women and children; had sung tenor in a church choir, and loves to play the organ. Nothing sums up his character better than his gallantry on his deathbed, when he pretends to be re-converted to the Christian faith to ease the sorrow of his faithful old Negro servant. ("The Idyll of Red Gulch," "Brown of Calaveras," "The Iliad of Sandy Bar," "How Santa Claus Came to Simpson's Bar," "A Passage in the Life of Mr. John Oakhurst," "An Heiress of Red Dog," "The Fool of Five Forks," "Found at Blazing Star," "An Apostle of the Tules," "A Knight-Errant of the Foothills," "A Sappho of Green Springs," "A First Family of Tasajara," "The Bell-Ringer of Angel's," "A Protegee of Jack Hamlin's," "Three Partners," "Mr. Jack Hamlin's Mediation," "A Mercury of the Foot-Hills," "A Ward of Colonel Starbottle's," "The Convalescence of Jack Hamlin," *Gabriel Conroy*)

JIM HOOKER, a youth led astray by his reading of dime novels, who later acts out his boyhood fantasies as an actor in riproaring melodramas on the California stage. ("A Waif of the Plains," "Susy," "Clarence")

LIBERTY JONES, a forlorn young girl orphaned by an earthquake, who discovers a health-giving hot spring which makes her beautiful and, when the place is turned into a spa, prosperous. ("Liberty Jones's Discovery")

[309]

URANIA MANNERSLEY, a cool determined young intellectual who writes about the Indians and takes the daring step of marrying a Spaniard. ("The Devotion of Enriquez," "The Passing of Enriquez")

ELIJAH MARTIN, a shiftless and rejected citizen of Redwood Camp who, after being freakishly spared from drowning, becomes the chief of the Minyo Indians. ("A Drift from Redwood Camp")

BILL MASTERS, a young man who betrays his Harvard education by turning slovenly out West and expressing a great interest in lawlessness and barbarism and, worse yet, talks about it with his mouth filled with crackers and cheese. ("Brown of Calaveras," "The Romance of Madrone Hollow")

REVEREND JOSHUA McSNAGLEY, an uncouth, illiterate and hypocritical backwoods preacher. ("M'liss," "Roger Catron's Friend")

MIGGLES, a beautiful young woman who lives in a lonely foothill cabin and devotes her life to caring for her paralyzed lover. She refuses to marry him because then caring for him would be her duty instead of her pleasure. ("Miggles" and "A Night on the Divide")

MOTHER SHIPTON, an "abandoned" woman who sacrifices herself to save the life of an innocent girl named Piney Woods. ("The Outcasts of Poker Flat")

JOHN OAKHURST, like Jack Hamlin a handsome and chivalrous gambler, "always a notable man in ten thousand." His greatest failing seems to be falling in love with women unworthy of him. He is one of the Outcasts of Poker Flat; in that story he makes the supreme sacrifice, only to be revived in later stories. ("The Luck of Roaring Camp," "The Outcasts of Poker Flat," "The Poet of Sierra Flat," "A Passage in the Life of Mr. John Oakhurst")

JUDGE JOHN PEYTON, a wealthy easterner who has difficulty defending his lands against squatters. Kindly but hot-tempered, he adopts "a waif of the plains," who disappoints him by marrying the actor Jim Hooker. ("A Story of the Plains," "Susy," "A Waif of the Plains")

SALOMY JANE, the willful daughter of a wealthy stock-raiser who kisses a horse thief about to be hanged by the Vigilantes because he has no other friends to say goodbye. He escapes the noose and Salomy Jane elopes with him. ("Salomy Jane's Kiss")

ENRIQUEZ SALTELLO, a talkative Spanish-American whose speech is a "marvelous combination of Spanish precision and California slang." ("Chu Chu," "What Happened at the Fonda," "The Devotion of Enriquez," "The Passing of Enriquez")

SEE YUP, an ingenious Chinese laundryman who prospers through selling herbal remedies to dyspeptic miners and makes another fortune panning out the tailings of an abandoned claim. ("See Yup")

DON JOSE SEPULVEDA, a latter-day Quixote regarded as a "lunatico" by his own people, who joins his fortunes with the Americans. ("A Knight-Errant of the Foot-Hills")

MR. SMITH, the father of M'liss, whose discovery of gold at Smith's Pocket and subsequent failure to strike another vein turned him into a drunkard and M'liss into an orphan. ("M'liss")

M'LISS SMITH, daughter of "Old Bummer" Smith, a child of nature whom the local schoolmaster almost manages to civilize. ("M'liss")

COLONEL CULPEPPER STARBOTTLE, a lawyer, duelist, gentleman, who regards himself as the defender of the "full-breasted" chivalry of the Old South. His fiery elequence is sometimes enhanced, sometimes diminished by his habit of taking aboard large quantities of Kentucky dew. He is always ready — eager, in fact — to defend the "honor of a Southern gentleman." At once pompous and jaunty, and always verbose. ("Brown of Calaveras," "The Iliad of Sandy Bar," "The Romance of Madrone Hollow," "The Poet of Sierra Flat," "A Ward of Colonel Starbottle's," "An Episode of Fiddletown," "A Passage in the Life of Mr. John

Oakhurst," "Wan Lee, the Pagan," "Jinny," "The Fool of Five Forks," "Captain Jim's Friend," "Colonel Starbottle's Client," "A First Family of Tasajara," "The Bell-Ringer of Angel's," "Clarence," *Gabriel Conroy*, "An Esmeralda of Rocky Canon," "What Happened at the Fonda," "Colonel Starbottle for the Plaintiff," "Mr. MacGlowrie's Widow")

YUBA BILL, a profane and hard-drinking veteran of the California stage routes. His presence is forceful, his manner autocratic. Anyone who disputes his opinions is withered by sarcasm and scorched by profanity. Habitat ranges from the box-seat of his stage to various barrooms, where he is regarded as an undisputed authority on everything of importance to the people of the foothills. His authoritarian manner is softened only by the presence of a pretty woman. ("Miggles," "Brown of Calaveras," *Gabriel Conroy*, "M'liss," "The Poet of the Sierra," "Mrs. Skaggs's Husbands," "The Story of a Mine," "Jeff Briggs's Love Story," "In the Carquinez Woods," "Snow-Bound at Eagle's," "Captain Jim Friend," "Cressy," "An Ingenue of the Sierras," "Dick Spindler's Family Christmas," "An Esmeralda of Rocky Canon," "A Niece of Snapshot Harry's")

Notes

I. ARGONAUT

1. AN ELEVEN-YEAR-OLD POET

1. Reported by Finley Peter Dunne in his autobiography *Mr. Dooley Remembers.*
2. *The Times of Melville and Whitman.*
3. *The Autobiography of Mark Twain*, edited by Charles Neider. Except where otherwise indicated, this is the version of *Autobiography* I have used.
4. Wallace Stegner in his introduction to the Signet Classics edition of *The Outcasts of Poker Flat and Other Tales.*
5. *From a Writer's Notebook*, by Van Wyck Brooks.
6. *Time* magazine, May 15, 1964. It is a curious coincidence that both Lenin and Stalin admired the two leading chroniclers of the American gold rushes. Among Lenin's favorite reading were Jack London's tales of the Klondike.
7. Quoted in Joseph Henry Jackson's *Anybody's Gold.*
8. Oscar Lewis, *Bay Window Bohemia.*
9. Facts surrounding Bret Harte's ancestry from Henry C. Merwin, *The Life of Bret Harte*, and H. L. Davis, "Bret Harte and His Jewish Ancestor," American Jewish Historical Society *Publication* of 1931.
10. *Stories and Poems*, edited by C. M. Kozlay.
11. *Ibid.,* "My favorite Novelist and His Best Book."
12. *Golden Era*, November 4, 1860.
13. Quoted in George R. Stewart, *Bret Harte.*
14. Harte touched on his adventures on the trip from New York to San Francisco in "A Man of No Account" and "The Crusade of the Excelsior."

2. WANDERER IN THE FOOTHILLS

1. *Gold Rush Days with Mark Twain* by William R. Gillis, a hyperbolic and apparently ghost-written account.
2. Clytemnestra in *M'liss.*

3. Now the town of Melones.
4. "How I Went to the Mines."
5. *Ibid.*
6. Bret Harte Girls High School is located in Angel's Camp, which was also the scene of Twain's "The Celebrated Jumping Frog of Calaveras County."
7. From the *Etc.* department he conducted in the *Overland Monthly*, July 1868.
8. Steve Gillis, quoted in an article by Robert L. Fulton, *Overland Monthly*, August 1915.
9. Bill Gillis, *Gold Rush Days with Mark Twain*.
10. *Ibid.*
11. Fulton, *op. cit.*
12. *Ibid.*
13. Even Professor Stewart, in his *Bret Harte: Argonaut and Exile* which deals sternly with the more sensational parts of his legend, conceded that he was probably employed as a Wells Fargo guard for a short time.
14. Quoted in Merwin, *Life of Bret Harte*.
15. *The Autobiography of Mark Twain*.
16. From Stoddard's memoir, *Exits and Entrances*.
17. The town of Union is now called Arcata.
18. Murdock's recollections, from his foreword to Thomas D. Beasley, *A Tramp Through Bret Harte Country*, also an undated article by Murdock from the San Francisco *Examiner*, which is included in Murdock Scrapbook No. 1 in the possession of the California Historical Society.
19. Quoted in Charles A. Murdock, "Bret Harte in Humboldt," *Overland Monthly*, September 1902.
20. Murdock's memoir, *A Backward Glance at Eighty*.
21. T. Edgar Pemberton, *The Life of Bret Harte*.
22. *Northern Californian*, October 26, 1859.
23. *Ibid.*, April 27, 1859.
24. Quoted in Stewart, *Bret Harte*.
25. *Sheridan the Inevitable* by the author.
26. The resolution was published in the *Humboldt Times*, March 17, 1860.
27. San Francisco *Bulletin*, March 13, 1860. The account was signed "Eyewitness."
28. Murdock's *A Backward Glance at Eighty*.

3. A LESSON IN FLAG-WAVING

1. From the poem "Mad River," published by *Golden Era*, July 26, 1857.
2. Quoted in Henry W. Boynton, *Bret Harte*.
3. Quoted in Kozlay's *Stories and Poems*.
4. From "Wanted — A Printer," *Golden Era*, January 27, 1861.
5. Quoted in Boynton, *Bret Harte*.
6. *The Autobiography of Mark Twain*.
7. *Golden Era*, April 29, 1860.
8. Pemberton, *Life of Bret Harte*.

9. These were part of the *Bohemian Papers*, many of which were included in Vol. XIV of the definitive Riverside Edition of his collected works.
10. Pemberton, *Life of Bret Harte.*
11. Franklin Walker, *San Francisco's Literary Frontier*, a brilliant example of regional literary history.
12. Stewart, *Bret Harte.*
13. Harte's Civil War verse was collected in Kozlay's *Stories and Poems.*
14. Stewart, *Bret Harte.*
15. *Californian*, July 16, 1864.

4. "FILLING THE VOID"

1. Walker, *San Francisco's Literary Frontier.*
2. *The Autobiography of Mark Twain.*
3. Albert Parry's *Garrets and Pretenders.*
4. *Californian*, February 10, 1866.
5. Walker, *San Francisco's Literary Frontier.*
6. *The Autobiography of Mark Twain.*
7. *Golden Era*, December 27, 1863.
8. Lecture delivered in Chicago, December 10, 1874.
9. Parry, *Garrets and Pretenders.*
10. Quoted in Walker, *San Francisco's Literary Frontier.*
11. In an often-cited letter to Thomas Bailey Aldrich.
12. Stoddard, *Exits and Entrances.*
13. *Ibid.*
14. Walker, *San Francisco's Literary Frontier.*
15. Interesting portraits of Ina Coolbrith are to be found in Walker, *San Francisco's Literary Frontier*, and Oscar Lewis, *Bay Window Bohemia.*
16. Stewart, *Bret Harte.*
17. From Webb's column in the *Californian*, February 10, 1866.
18. Josephine Clifford McCrackin's letter to the *Overland Monthly*, September 1902.
19. In "My First Book," written in 1894.
20. *Ibid.*
21. *Californian*, December 9, 1865.
22. "My First Book."
23. *Californian*, December 23, 1865.

5. THE GOLDEN GATE TRINITY

1. Collected in Kozlay, *Stories and Poems*, published in the *Californian*, May 12, 1866.
2. From "California Madrigal," published in the *News Letter*, March 30, 1867.
3. *Californian* published its last issue February 1, 1868.
4. *San Francisco's Literary Frontier.*
5. *Mark Twain's Letters*, edited by Albert Bigelow Paine.

6. The controversy was detailed by Brooks in the *Overland Monthly*, August 1902, and in Stoddard, *Exits and Entrances*.
7. Josephine Clifford McCrackin in the *Overland Monthly*, January 1916.
8. Quoted in Merwin, *The Life of Bret Harte*.
9. Stoddard, *Exits and Entrances*.
10. Thomas Beasley, *A Tramp Through Bret Harte Country*.
11. *The Letters of Bret Harte*, edited by Geoffrey Bret Harte, his grandson. Hereafter referred to as *BH Letters*.
12. Josephine Clifford McCrackin's articles in the *Overland Monthly*, September 1902 and January 1916.
13. Roman's letter to the *Overland Monthly*, September 1902.
14. *BH Letters*.

6. *Overland Monthly* TO OVERLAND EXPRESS

1. *The Autobiography of Mark Twain*.
2. *Gold Rush Days With Mark Twain*.
3. Collected in Vol. XIV of the Riverside Edition of Harte's works.
4. New York *Globe*, January 7, 1871.
5. Collected in Kozlay, *Stories and Poems*.
6. *The Autobiography of Mark Twain*.
7. Letter to Carmany in the *Overland Monthly* correspondence, now in the possession of the University of California Library.
8. Walker, *San Francisco's Literary Frontier*.
9. Article by Brooks in the *Century Magazine*, July 1899.
10. Stoddard, *Exits and Entrances*.
11. *The Autobiography of Mark Twain*.
12. Quoted by Josephine Clifford McCrackin, *Overland Monthly*, September 1902.
13. Quoted in Merwin, *The Life of Bret Harte*.
14. Mrs. McCrackin in the *Overland Monthly*, September, 1902, and January, 1916.
15. E. S. Cummins (Mighels), *The Story of the Files*.
16. McCrackin articles, *op. cit.*

II. CELEBRITY

7. AN APPARITION IN GREEN GLOVES

1. William Dean Howells, *Literary Friends and Acquaintances*.
2. Howells, "A Belated Guest," *Harper's*, December, 1903.
3. From *The Letters of John Fiske*.
4. Lillian Aldrich, *Crowding Memories*.
5. Letter to C. H. Webb, November 26, 1867.
6. Account of Keeler luncheon from Howells's *My Mark Twain*.
7. From Kozlay's *Stories and Poems*.
8. Howells, "A Belated Guest," *op. cit.*
9. *BH Letters*.
10. London *Daily News*, March 21, 1871.

11. Lillian Aldrich, *Crowding Memories.*
12. *Ibid.*
13. Cleveland Amory, *The Last Resorts.*
14. Letter dated December 12, 1873, in *BH Letters.*
15. Lillian Aldrich, *Crowding Memories.*
16. *Harper's*, December, 1903.
17. Letter dated January 9, 1872, in *BH Letters.*
18. *Ibid.*
19. *Ibid.*
20. Letter dated May 1, 1874, in Clark Library Collection, University of California at Los Angeles.
21. *BH Letters.*

8. HAND TO MOUTH

1. Quoted in Tyler Dennett's *John Hay.*
2. From Merwin, *The Life of Bret Harte.*
3. *The Autobiography of Mark Twain.*
4. New York *Times*, May 24, 1902.
5. Thomas Wentworth Higginson, *Letters and Journals*, edited by Mary Hatcher Higginson.
6. New York *Times*, May 24, 1902.
7. *BH Letters.*
8. Quoted in Volume XIX of the Riverside Edition of Harte's works.
9. E. S. Cummins (Mighels), *The Story of the Files.*
10. *BH Letters.*
11. *The Autobiography of Mark Twain.*
12. *Ibid.*
13. *Ibid.*
14. *Ibid.*
15. *Ibid.*
16. Quoted in Margaret Duckett's *Mark Twain and Bret Harte.*
17. *Ibid.*
18. *Ibid.*
19. *The Autobiography of Mark Twain.*

9. SAVED BY AN ELECTION

1. *BH Letters.* Letter dated July 8, 1877, to Colonel Branty Mayer.
2. *Ibid.*
3. *Ibid.*
4. *The Autobiography of Mark Twain.*
5. *BH Letters.*
6. Margaret Duckett, *Mark Twain and Bret Harte.*
7. *Ibid.*
8. *Ibid.*
9. *BH Letters.*
10. *The Autobiography of Mark Twain.*

[317]

III. EXPATRIATE

10. A DISGRUNTLED WATCH ON THE RHINE

1. Quoted in *Mark Twain–Howells Letters,* edited by Henry Nash Smith and William M. Gibson with the assistance of Frederick Anderson.
2. *BH Letters.* To Anna, dated July 9, 1878.
3. Letters to Anna, July 17 and 22, 1878, in *BH Letters.*
4. *Ibid.*
5. The *Athenaeum,* June, 1878.
6. Oscar Lewis, *Bay Window Bohemia.*
7. *BH Letters.* To Anna, August 19, 1878.
8. *Ibid.*
9. *BH Letters,* dated September 6 and September 10, 1878.
10. *Ibid.,* dated November 3, 1878.
11. Quoted in Stewart's *Bret Harte.*
12. Letters to Francis and Griswold, January 18 and 21, 1879, *BH Letters.*
13. *Ibid.,* dated January 22, 1879.
14. *Ibid.,* dated February 7 and 21, 1879.
15. *Ibid.,* dated April 17, 1879.
16. From his introduction to *The Outcasts of Poker Flat and Other Tales.*
17. *BH Letters,* dated July 31, August 11, August 29, 1879.
18. *Ibid.,* dated September 13, 1879.
19. *Ibid.,* dated November 6, 1879.
20. *Ibid.,* dated January 7, 1880.

11. A NOT ALTOGETHER HAPPY GLASWEGIAN

1. *BH Letters,* dated April 1, April 15, April 17, 1880.
2. *Ibid.,* dated April 17, 1880.
3. Quoted in W. Reid's *William Black.*
4. *BH Letters,* April 22, 1881.
5. Bret quoted Hay in the above letter.
6. Bret Harte Diary (1881–1888) in the Berg Collection, New York Public Library. Entries of January 18, and January 24, 1881, and January 1, 1882.
7. *BH Letters,* dated October 11, 1882.
8. Bret Harte Diary entries June 4 and July 12, 1883.
9. Letter to Frank, dated August 4, 1883, in the Harte collection in the Clark Library, University of California at Los Angeles.
10. *The Autobiography of Mark Twain.*
11. *BH Letters,* dated December 15, 1882.
12. *Ibid.,* dated March 30, 1883.
13. *Ibid.,* dated November 8, 1883, and June 15, 1884.
14. *Ibid.,* dated March 13, 1885.
15. *Ibid.,* dated April 4, 1885.
16. From his essay on Lowell in the Kolazy-edited *Stories and Poems.*
17. *BH Letters,* dated April 4, 1885.

18. Quoted in Stewart's *Bret Harte.*
19. *BH Letters,* dated September 17, 1883.
20. *Ibid.,* dated August 3, 1885.
21. Article by Noah Brooks in the *Overland Monthly,* August, 1902.

12. A NEW RESIDENT IN GRUB STREET

1. *The Story of the Files.*
2. Letter to Millais in the Harte collection in the Pierpont Morgan Library, New York.
3. Letters to Black quoted in Wemyss Reid's *William Black.*
4. *BH Letters,* dated August 17, 1885.
5. Quoted in Boynton's biography of Harte.
6. Letter to Anna in the Clark Library collection, University of California at Los Angeles, dated April 19, 1886.
7. Stewart's *Bret Harte.*
8. Pemberton's biography of Harte.
9. *BH Letters,* dated December 28, 1885.
10. *Ibid.,* dated May 15, 1886.
11. From Reid's *William Black.*
12. *BH Letters,* dated December 20, 1887.
13. *The Autobiography of Mark Twain.*
14. *Ibid.*
15. *BH Letters,* dated February 15, 1886.
16. *Ibid.,* dated September 15, 1889.

13. THE DRUDGE OF LANCASTER GATE

1. *BH Letters.* Writing to Mrs. Boyd May 4, 1894, he told of the dinner at the Astors' and described Lord Roberts as a "dear old chap." The soldier, he said, interested him more than "our mighty intellect," Kipling. For, he added, "we are a conceited lot."
2. *Ibid.* Also a letter to Mrs. Boyd, July 15, 1895.
3. Dudley Barker, *A Man of Principle,* a biography of Galsworthy.
4. Quoted in John Erskine's *Leading American Novelists.*
5. Quoted in Merwin, *The Life of Bret Harte.*
6. From poem in the *Overland Monthly,* July 1898, by C. S. Greene.
7. *BH Letters,* to Anna, January 23, 1892.
8. *Ibid.,* April 15, 1892.
9. *BH Letters,* July 18, 1892, and Clark Library (University of California at Los Angeles) collection, January 26, 1895.
10. Letter (undated, 1895) in Clark Library collection.
11. *BH Letters,* to Mrs. Boyd, September 5, 1895.
12. *Ibid.,* October 16, 1895.
13. *Ibid.,* January 15, 1895.
14. *A Pictorial History of the American Theater* by Daniel Blum.
15. *BH Letters,* October 29, 1896.
16. *Ibid.,* February 28, 1897.
17. *Ibid.,* June 19, 1897.

14. FLY IN AMBER

1. *Christian Science Monitor,* September 30, 1919.
2. From Kozlay, *Stories and Poems.*
3. *Bookman,* July, 1930.
4. Stewart, *Bret Harte.*
5. Quoted by Pemberton in his biography of Harte.
6. Letter to Frank (undated) in Clark Library collection.
7. *BH Letters,* January 6, 1901.
8. *Ibid.,* November 3, 1901.
9. *Californian,* September 17, 1864.
10. *BH Letters,* January 17, 1902.
11. Quoted in Stewart's *Bret Harte.*
12. Merwin, *The Life of Bret Harte.*
13. *Pall Mall Gazette,* July 1902.
14. *Bookman,* July 1902.
15. *Harper's,* December 1903.
16. *Overland Monthly,* September 1902.

Acknowledgments

THE author is indebted, first of all, to that monolithic news-gathering organization, United Press International, for once having employed him in its Sacramento bureau, and thus providing him with close acquaintance with the northern California foothills and what was once known as the "southern mines district" and is now regarded, with tourism in mind, as "Bret Harte Country." I covered murders and miners' strikes in the foothill towns and the jumping-frog contest at Angel's Camp, in a countryside still bearing the scars of the gold-rushers, from wrecked sluice boxes to washed-away hillsides.

For assistance in research I am especially indebted to Mrs. Edna C. Davis, reference librarian of the William Andrews Clark Memorial Library of the University of California at Los Angeles, which has the largest number of unpublished Harte letters; to Mr. Herbert Cahoon, curator of autograph manuscripts at the Pierpont Morgan Library in New York; to Robert Woodward, head of the Bangor Public Library; to Miss A. J. Lewis of the Department of Manuscripts at the British Museum; to James de T. Abajian of the California Historical Society; to Mary Isabel Fry of the Huntington Library at San Marino, California; and to the staff of the Berg Collection at the New York Public Library.

I am also indebted, less personally but none the less deeply, to Professor George R. Stewart of the University of California for having written his splendid and compassionate *Bret Harte: Argonaut and Exile* (1931) and Margaret Duckett, associate professor of English at the University of Washington, for her more recent *Mark Twain and Bret Harte* (1964), an exhaustive study of the personal and professional relations of the two men.

Selected Bibliography

Adams, Henry, *The Education of Henry Adams,* New York, 1931.
Aldrich, Lillian (Mrs. Thomas Bailey), *Crowding Memories,* Boston, 1920.
Barker, Dudley, *A Man of Principle,* London, 1963.
Beasley, Thomas D., *A Tramp Through Bret Harte Country,* San Francisco, 1914.
Blum, Daniel, *A Pictorial History of the American Theater,* Philadelphia, 1960.
Boynton, Henry W., *Bret Harte,* New York, 1903.
Brooks, Van Wyck, *From a Writer's Notebook,* New York, 1958.
——, *The Ordeal of Mark Twain,* New York, 1920.
——, *The Times of Melville and Whitman,* New York, 1947.
Cummins, Ella Sterling (Mighels), *The Story of the Files,* San Francisco, 1893.
DeVoto, Bernard (editor), *Mark Twain in Eruption,* New York, 1940.
Duckett, Margaret, *Mark Twain and Bret Harte,* Norman, Okla., 1964.
Dunne, Finley Peter, *Mr. Dooley Remembers,* Boston, 1964.
Erskine, John, *Leading American Novelists,* New York, 1910.
Farwell, Byron, *Burton: A Biography of Sir Richard Francis Burton,* New York, 1964.
Frémont, Jessie Benton, *Souvenirs of My Time,* Boston, 1887.
Gaer, Joseph, *Bret Harte: Bibliography and Biographical Data,* mimeographed, 1935.
Gillis, William R., *Gold Rush Days with Mark Twain,* New York, 1930.
Harte, Bret, *The Writings of Bret Harte,* 20 volumes (Riverside Edition), Boston, 1896-1914.
Harte, Geoffrey, editor, *The Letters of Bret Harte,* Boston, 1926.
Higginson, Thomas Wentworth, *The Letters and Journals of Thomas Wentworth Higginson,* Boston, 1921.
Howell, John, *Sketches of the Sixties,* San Francisco, 1926.
Howells, William Dean, Literary Friends and Acquaintances, New York, 1901.
——, *My Mark Twain,* New York, 1910.
Jackson, Joseph Henry, *Anybody's Gold,* New York, 1941.

Kirk, Clara M. and Rudolf, *William Dean Howells*, New York, 1962.
Kozlay, Charles M., editor, *Stories and Poems and Other Uncollected Writings by Bret Harte*, Boston, 1914.
Lewis, Oscar, *Bay Window Bohemia*, New York, 1956.
Marberry, M. M., *Splendid Poseur: Joaquin Miller — American Poet*, New York, 1953.
Merwin, Henry Childs, *The Life of Bret Harte*, Boston, 1911.
Murdock, Charles A., *A Backward Glance at Eighty*, San Francisco, 1921.
Neider, Charles, editor, *The Autobiography of Mark Twain*, New York, 1956.
Nevins, Allan, *Frémont*, New York, 1926.
Paine, Albert Bigelow, *Mark Twain: A Biography*, New York, 1912.
——, editor, *Mark Twain's Autobiography*, New York, 1924.
Parry, Albert, *Garrets and Pretenders*, New York, 1933.
Pemberton, T. Edgar, *Bret Harte, A Treatise and a Tribute*, New York, 1903.
Quinn, Arthur, *American Fiction*, New York, 1936.
Reid, Wemyss, *William Black, Novelist*, New York, 1902.
Stewart, George R., *Bret Harte: Argonaut and Exile*, Boston, 1931.
Stoddard, Charles Warren, *Exits and Entrances*, Boston, 1903.
Thayer, William Roscoe, *The Life and Letters of John Hay*, Boston, 1908.
Van de Velde, M. S., editor, *Bret Harte's Birthday Book*, London, 1892.
Walker, Franklin, *San Francisco's Literary Frontier*, New York, 1934.
Wingfield-Stratford, Esmé, *The Victorian Sunset*, New York, 1932.

Index